MW00609217

A *Black* *History* READER

101 Questions You Never Thought to Ask

Dr. Claud Anderson

PowerNomics
CORPORATION of AMERICA ™

PowerNomics® Corporation of America, Inc.
P.O. Box 30536
Bethesda, Maryland 20824
Phone: (301) 564-6075 | Fax: (301) 564-1997
Email: powernomics@aol.com
www.powernomics.com **Exclusive location for purchase.**

This book contains information gathered from many sources. It is published for reference and not as a substitute for independent verification by users when circumstances warrant. It is sold with the understanding that neither the author nor the publisher is engaged in rendering any legal, psychological, accounting or business advice. The author and the publisher disclaim any personal liability, either directly or indirectly, for any advice or information presented within. Although the author and publisher have used care and diligence in the preparation of this book in an effort to ensure the accuracy and completeness of information contained herein, we assume no responsibility for errors, inaccuracies, omissions or any inconsistency herein. Any slights of persons, places, institutions, publishers, books or organizations are unintentional.

Every effort has been made to trace copyright for all photos and drawings in this book. If omissions have been made, please notify the publisher.

Book cover and interior design: Jessica Tilles of TWA Solutions.com

PowerNomics is a trademark of PowerNomics® Corporation of America, Inc.

U.S. Library of Congress Card Number:
1. African-American history 2. American history 3. Slavery 4. Blacks, economic empowerment of 5. Race relations, economic aspects of 6. Race relations, political aspects of

ISBN: 978-0-9661702-7-6

Other Books and Educational Materials by Dr. Claud Anderson

Published and produced by
PowerNomics® Corporation of America, Inc.

To purchase Dr. Anderson's books and DVDs,
go to www.powernomics.com.

Books

PowerNomics: The National Plan to Empower Black America
Black Labor, White Wealth: The Search for Power and Economic Justice
Dirty Little Secrets about Black History, Its Heroes and other Troublemakers
More Dirty Little Secrets about Black History, Its Heroes and other Troublemakers

DVDs

Exceptionalism: The Path to Black Empowerment
Vision Beyond the Dream
Inappropriate Behavior: A Roadblock to Empowerment
1866 Indian Treaties: Benefits Due Black Americans
Wake Up America
The Power of Blackness: Reclaiming the Gifts of God
Reparations
On the Firing Line with Questions and Answers

Courses, Videos and other Lectures

www.powernomics.tv
www.vimeo.com

New

Dr. Anderson's VIDEO VAULT
www.powernomics.com

Dedication

I dedicate this book to my granddaughters, Elena and Claire, who are my inspiration for life and justice.

Acknowledgements

I owe a debt of gratitude to those whose contributions enhanced this work. I thank my wife Joann Anderson, Ph.D, my son Brant Anderson, and Ed Sergeant for their insights, suggestions and editing and Jessica Tilles for her editing, cover design and layout. For photographs, I thank the U.S. Library of Congress, and Gwen and Joe Ragsdale who loaned photos from their Lest We Forget Slavery Museum in Philadelphia, Pennsylvania. Other photos came from my own personal collection. I thank Dr. Rosie Milligan for her moral encouragement, professional input and friendship, Dr. Angela Finley Molette, spokesperson for Black Indians United Legal Defense and Education Fund and William Warrior for their continuous support and inspiration.

TABLE CONTENTS

I. FOUNDATION CONCEPTS

II. CURRENT ISSUES

III. Rethinking Social Integration

IV. The Dark Side of the Constitution

V. HISTORICAL IRONIES

VI. POLITICS OF RACE

VII. Profiling Presidents and Authorities

VIII. Immigration and Naturalization

IX. Sites and Signs of the Times

X. BLACK ECONOMIC EMPOWERMENT

XI. FORGOTTEN CHAMPIONS AND DEFENDERS

XII. BLACKS AND RELIGION

XIII. BLACK REPARATIONS AND AFFIRMATIVE ACTION

XIV. SCIENCE AND MEDICAL EXPERIMENTS

XV. BIRTH OF NEW CLASSES

XVI. A POWERNOMICS® AGENDA: ETHNO-AGGREGATION

NOTES TO THE READER

▶ Because of the Q & A format of this book, readers may choose to read it cover to cover or to select questions of particular interest. Each question must stand alone, so the reader will notice some repetition and re-use of foundation facts when it is necessary to discuss points based on concepts that are also addressed in other sections of the book.

▶ I use an editorial style with which the reader may be unfamiliar. I capitalize Black and White out of respect for both races. It would be inappropriate to capitalize Asian, Hispanic and the names of other groups and not capitalize White and Black.

▶ I sometimes refer to the descendants of slaves in America as native Blacks. Generally, I use the term Black or Blacks. I do not capitalize native in that instance because it is not an official Census designation. I do capitalize Native Indians because it is an official Census designation.

▶ I frequently use the term *overclass*, which is meant to include elected officials, civil rights leaders, ministers and sometimes celebrities, individuals who have great influence and power over the masses.

▶ In this book, I have purposely provided detailed legal components of reparations strategies developed from my personal research. My intention is to share the strategies I have unearthed in enough detail to provide a substantial legal basis for challenges that could result in reparations for Blacks. I ask that credit be given to my intellectual efforts.

INTRODUCTION
A Black History Reader

Within a nation that perceives itself as the world's greatest superpower, worldwide police force and a home for all immigrants seeking the so-called *American Dream*, Black Americans are a forgotten people who remain an impoverished out-group and an abandoned labor class. After nearly 500 years of institutionalized slavery, Jim Crow semi-slavery, public policies of Benign Neglect and political correctness, Blacks are consigned to the lowest level of this nation's ranking order of social acceptability. In this book, I try to answer the question, *Why?*

In coming to an understanding of the fixed position of Black America at the bottom of the well, we must first come to terms with what has changed and what has not changed in race matters, especially in urban areas, immigration, economics and other aspects of policy in the United States. The internal strength of the country is connected to the fate of Blacks, a significant population group within the country. There are mutual benefits for mainstream society and Black Americans to fully understand the nature of the Black dilemma. Although race is an uncomfortable and almost taboo topic, for those who truly want Black people to be a self-sufficient group within American society, race must be examined, but any examination must be based on an understanding of history and facts. In all my books, my goal has been to clarify the issue of race *for the purpose of corrective action*. That is also the case in this book, *A Black History Reader*.

The purpose of *A Black History Reader* is threefold:

- The first purpose is to present to the reader the nation's Constitution-based social construct that historically established and fixed the racial relationship between

Blacks and Whites. The Constitution was the nation's first Affirmative Action plan. It assured the mal-distribution of nearly 100 percent of the nation's wealth and resources into the hands of Whites, who subsequently bequeathed their unearned wealth, power, rights, privileges and resources into the hands of succeeding generations of Whites. Contrarily, the descendants of slaves were left impoverished and powerless. This Constitution-based disparity between Blacks and Whites was kept intact by the U.S. Supreme Court, the chief guardian of racism, and other courts, educational institutions, conservative ideology and extra-legal activities of groups such as the Ku Klux Klan, the White Citizens Council and the modern-day Freedom Party.

- The second purpose of the book is to declare the exceptionality of the descendants of slaves in America, their unique and substantive contributions to the development of this country and their maltreatment by all segments of the society. Their exceptionality distinguishes them from any other group in America

- The third purpose of the book is to highlight the acute need in Black America for long-overdue reparations based on the exceptionality of the way their group has been viewed and treated. In our journey forward, native Black Americans must be recognized, compensated and put into a protected class like Native Americans.

It is my hope that this book and *PowerNomics®: The National Plan to Empower Black America* will inspire new thinking from which will grow a more conscious class of Black leadership that will design and assert a new, transformative social construct, including a new Black Code of

Conduct that puts the interests of Blacks foremost. A new social construct will require society to unlearn prevailing myths, lies, assumptions and distortions about Blacks, Whites, racism and political correctness. This shift will not come easily. It will be met with pushback by mainstream society and many in the Black overclass which is made up of Black civil rights leaders, ministers and elected officials.

Newly trained thinkers who understand PowerNomics® principles and strategies will design a new social construct on race that will replace social integration and civil rights. From these new thinkers should arise new Black leadership who will produce a new legal infrastructure in which Blacks are included as system beneficiaries; guide the Black masses to build functioning Black economic communities; set-up Black independent political parties; and assert the value of Black lives.

A Black History Reader explains how racism became imbedded into our national culture and offers a new direction. It explains how the overt racism that was expressed in slavery, progressed through Jim Crow segregation then became submerged and replaced by Benign Neglect and political correctness policies that continue to demonstrate hateful indifference toward Black people. The purpose and net effect of these two policies rendered Blacks invisible and irrelevant.

The Black Civil Rights Movement, though well-intentioned, sought integration based on the assumption that all people were equal. Equality of the races was not intended under the Constitution. Blacks were designated specifically as a laboring class of property to be controlled by the dominant White society. Consequently, Blacks have never been able to acquire more than one-half of one percent of the nation's wealth or anything of value. Even after Blacks acquired voting rights, without wealth or political influence, their votes were easily rendered null and void. National immigration policies kept Blacks as the only permanent minority within a society where the *majority wins and the minority loses*.

Blacks are now a permanent minority in every respect. For example, in two important sectors, politics and business ownership, Blacks represent less than one-half of one percent of the nation's elected officials and are less than one-half of one percent of the nation's business owners. These historical conditions are not accidental. They reflect the enduring quality of the design of the founding social construct on race that was codified in the Constitution. These Constitution-based race disparaties allowed Whites to dominate and control Blacks in all respects throughout the centuries. Although Blacks were intended to be at the bottom, that status can be changed if Blacks and our society truthfully assess the circumstances created and have the courage and fortitude to take the necessary steps prescribed in this and my other works.

The goal of my collective work is for Black America to become self-sufficient and competitive as a group. In *A Black History Reader*, I offer Black Americans, and others who seek true racial justice, a way to build a future in which the unique history and socioeconomic needs of Black Americans are considered. I invite you to join me in that quest. Begin reading now then do the right things!

PART I
Foundation Concepts

Question 1. What is a social construct and how was it used in the making of America?

A social construct is a *purposely created* idea developed by one group with authority that defines another group with lesser or no authority. A social construct frames the perception of, and the relationship between the groups. It becomes part of the culture, infused into the social norms and practices of every part of society including legal, educational, financial, political and interpersonal relationships.

The most important social construct in America is *Race*. The Founding Fathers purposely constructed the societal position of Blacks and Whites. Blacks were to *be* property that served Whites, and Whites were to be the only beneficiaries of the new country that they created.

"The Planning Committee for the U.S. Constitution."
Source: The Library of Congress.

Christopher Columbus *discovered* the new land that was to be America in the same timeframe that the Pope declared that Blacks from Africa should be made slaves. It was the promise of free land and free labor that fueled the rush of Europeans to settle the new land. To implement their plan for the free labor, Europeans designed the relationship between Blacks and Whites.

The social construct on race was formally stated in the Articles of the Confederation and restated in the Constitution of the United States as well as the first immigration laws. (I will discuss these documents in detail later in this book.) The social construct on race is the thread that weaves through Black enslavement, U.S. Supreme Court rulings, laws, institutions, conservative and liberal ideologies, extra-legal (e.g., Ku Klux Klan) activities and all aspects of the nation's culture. It is fundamental to the founding of our country that Blacks would always be pressed to the bottom and that Whites would always retain superiority over Blacks. That relationship endures to this day.

The social construct on race was deliberate and permanent. It is so fundamental to the issue of race that the topic cannot be considered in any serious way without understanding it. It is therefore, the first question in this book.

PART II

Current Issues

Question 2. Are Black Americans an official, socioeconomic underclass?

Whether Black Americans are this nation's official underclass depends on the criteria used to define the term. In the broadest sense, an *underclass* is that segment of the population that occupies the lowest possible position in a ranking order of social acceptability. The enactment of the nation's Constitution in 1789 and the first Naturalization Law of 1790 established a rank order that placed Whites at the top and entitled to all of society's benefits, and consigned Blacks to the bottom rank with no entitlements, not even to life itself. The Naturalization Law declared America to be a *White nation*, with Blacks acceptable only as slaves. In subsequent years of Jim Crow semi-slavery, and political correctness, a deliberate and carefully interlinked set of laws and public policies assured Black presence as a subordinated labor and consumer class. Consequently, Black people became the designated, official underclass and it has yet to be repudiated or changed. Until that happens, Blacks are restricted to conditions that placed them outside and beneath mainstream society.

Governmental agencies and scholars have broadened and modernized the definition of an underclass as any group in America that lives as if they were in a poverty-stricken country. This immigration-based, politically correct public policy is designed to shift the nation's focus from Blacks to Hispanics, Asians and other immigrating ethnicities. However, this gesture changes nothing in the original underclass designation, because immigrant groups have always ranked above Blacks in the order of social and political acceptability. Immigrant groups are credentialed by federal authorities and are granted access to benefits. As soon as the next generation loses its accent, even those with some color, are accepted as White and move into the middle- and upper-classes. Blacks, as a caste, have never had the class mobility granted to immigrants.

The U.S. Census chart below, "Real Median Household Income by Race and Hispanic Origin of Householder: 1967 to 2014[1]," shows how Blacks stay fixed in an underclass income status. It depicts the racial hierarchy in our society and presents the reality that Blacks are fixed at the lowest income level.

Real Median Household Income by Race and Hispanic Origin of Householder: 1967 to 2014

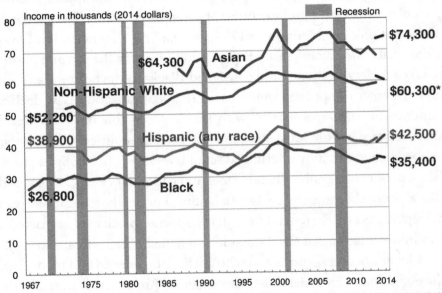

*The difference between the 2013 and 2014 median household incomes is statistically significant. Note: The 2013 data reflect the implementation of the redesigned income question. See Appendix D of the P60 report, "Income and Poverty in the United States: 2014," for more information. Income rounded to nearest $100.
Source: U.S. Census Bureau, Current Population Survey, 1968 to 2015 Annual Social and Economic Supplements.

United States Census Bureau | U.S. Department of Commerce
Economics and Statistics Administration
U.S. CENSUS BUREAU
census.gov

---

[1]"Real Median Household Income by Race and Hispanic Origin of Householder: 1967 to 2014, U.S. Census Report, United States Department of Cencus Commerce, Washington, D.C.

The Census Chart on page 4 shows that at the peak of the 1967 Black Civil Rights Movement, White median Household Income was $52,200, double the $26,800 median household income of Blacks. The chart also depicts the changed immigration policies that, in response to the 1965 civil rights laws, opened the doors for immigrants based upon ethnicity and family ancestry. The newly arriving immigrants were classified as minorities and made eligible for benefits and opportunities that Blacks had been historically denied. The massive influx of Hispanic immigrants began in 1970, and the U.S. Census Chart indicates that at the outset, their incomes began at $38,900, well above the income of Blacks, and by 2014, Hispanic income had reached $42,500, $7,000 higher than Blacks even though 90 percent of all Hispanics in America in 2014 had been in the country less than 45 years. Similarly, in the late 1980s, Asians, who had been combined in classification with Arabs, began to enter the country. Their median household income was $64,000 and by 2014, their median income was $74,300, double that of Black Americans. It is noteworthy that the U.S. Census chart indicates not only that all groups entered with higher incomes than Blacks, but by 2014, the median household income for all groups was up while the income for native Black Americans was headed downward. The downward trend for Blacks, further indicates that, as a group, they are the nation's official, underclass.

A report by The Urban Institute, *The Color of Wealth in the Nation's Capital*, the subject of an article in *The Washington Post*[2] on November 2, 2016. The grim statistics in this article on Black wealth reinforce the Census Chart and are further evidence that Blacks, as a group, are the nation's official underclass. The Urban Institute Report pointed out that in the District of Columbia Region, the net worth of White households was 81 times that of Black households. Whites had a net worth of $284,000 and the net worth of Blacks was only $3,500. This disparity was even more stark because within the region, Prince Georges County, Maryland

---

[2]"The Color of Wealth in the Nation's Capital," *The Washington Post*, November 2, 2016.

has the highest concentration of wealthy and educated Blacks in America, yet Hispanic immigrants in the D.C. region have acquired four times the net worth of Blacks, even though, as a group, 90 percent have been in America and the D.C. region barely 40 years.

The same bottom rung status applies to Blacks in business ownership, wealth accumulation and in the hiring process. A group becomes a *permanent underclass*, when regardless of individual exceptions that exist, the group remains fixed at the lowest levels, century after century, regardless of whether the mainstream economy is experiencing boom or bust times. An underclass, the Black race and its members are routinely blamed for their own socioeconomic dilemma. Conservatives argue that Black underclass status results from failure to take advantage of the limitless social, political and economic opportunities that this nation offers to all groups. They further postulate that Blacks are handicapped by their attitudes, values, culture and work ethic, which differ from that of mainstream White society. Blacks did not become a permanent underclass on their own.

It is critically important that Black Americans understand the disadvantages of an underclass status. By the very nature of its socioeconomic conditions, an underclass is predestined to live at the lowest level of the system as beggars or criminals. Neither civil rights nor social integration can effectively help them to escape from their underclass status. America's ranking order of social acceptability is tightly woven into the nation's psyche. Some group *has* to be at the bottom. It is not possible for every group to be equal in socioeconomic status. The question is can Blacks muster the mental focus, resources and determination to break out and escape after so many years of being frozen at the bottom? If someone steals your car, you want your car back or something of equal value to replace it. Blacks must find a way to recapture what was lost or stolen from them and to use it to escape their constitutionally-designated underclass status.

Question 3. How has social integration failed Black America?

Social integration was posited to eradicate institutional racism and remedy the negative socioeconomic impact of centuries of slavery and Jim Crow segregation, but it failed. As a result, Black Americans remain burdened by the economic, social and pathological impacts that resulted from their historical maltreatment. In his book, *The Tragic Failure of Integration*[3], liberal author Tom Wicker concludes that Rev. Dr. Martin Luther King, Jr.'s *dream* had turned into a Black *nightmare*, and that the successes of the movement failed to translate into full integration or first class citizenship for most Blacks. Nearly 60 years after the Black Civil Rights Movement was hijacked by newly-created or fabricated minorities, a growing number of Black Americans are reaching the same conclusion: that they are still an out-group in American society. They are learning the lesson that Jewish people in Europe learned in the 1500s when they tried to integrate into mainstream society. Jews were a hated out-group. They quickly learned that to protect their group, it was better to circle the wagons than divide and scatter themselves into the larger population making them weaker and more vulnerable. This is a lesson yet to be learned by Black Americans.

After 50 years of marching and singing, "We shall overcome some day," they are still fixed at the bottom of American society, buried beneath an unrelenting flow of immigrants, and more economically dependent than they were in the 1960s when social integration began. The integration process made Blacks unwanted guests in what Whites and their sub-ethnic groups owned and controlled. Blacks still own and control less than one percent of anything of value, but bear six-to-eight times of everything that is bad or negative. A few Blacks have become visible as public officials, athletes, entertainers and media personalities, but there is little connection between their elevated public images and

---

[3]Wicker, Tom. *The Tragic Failure of Integration*. William Morrow and Company, Inc., New York, 1996, pgs. ix-xii.

the low socioeconomic status of the Black masses. Younger Blacks are just beginning to grasp the weight of the losses of Black communities, schools, businesses, culture, history, leaders, sports teams, music and exceptionality in mainstream society. They have never had the positive experiences of living in a Black community. It is increasingly difficult for Blacks to become a functional part of American society without physical communities or a broad sense of community.

The years between 1960 and 2014 could have produced a more self-sufficient Black race if the civil rights movement had worked to address and correct the mal-distribution of wealth, income and resources that occurred because of 500 years of slavery and Jim Crow semi-slavery. While Blacks were chasing the illusive social integration dream, the horrors inflicted on Blacks receded from the consciousness of society and Blacks lost their moral and political leverage. Blacks were displaced in the nation's conscious by immigrants in general, and Hispanics in particular, who publicly boast of their successful efforts to totally displace Blacks in every aspect of American society. In his book, *Presumed Alliance: The Unspoken Conflict Between Blacks and Latinos and What It Means for America*[4], the author, Nicolas C. Vaca, disdained a rainbow coalition and *presumed alliances* with Black Americans. He said that Hispanics were no longer interested in being classified as White, that they wanted to be viewed as a minority, who could then compete with Blacks for political and economic power. Even though Hispanics from the Caribbean Islands and the Americas were the descendants of slaveholders and had never been enslaved or Jim Crowed, they felt that by the mere fact that they were more socially acceptable than Blacks in American society, they could gain socioeconomic benefits and become the nation's majority-minority population. Their goal, according to Vaca, was to displace Blacks in every way possible.

---

[4]Vaca, Nicolas C. *Presumed Alliance: The Unspoken Conflict Between Blacks and Latinos and What It Means for America*. HarperCollins Publishers, New York, 2004, pgs. x-xiii, 194-196.

As an official out-group and primary target of conservative hate groups, there are neither rewards nor incentives for immigrants, women, LGBTs or poor Whites to identify publicly with Black Americans. This nation's policy of political correctness allows all of these groups to rank higher than Blacks in the nation's order of social acceptability. The majority of immigrants are classified as White. They get double benefits when they are also classified as *aggrieved minorities* and compete against Blacks for public recognition and financial resources.

Integration did not produce racial or economic equality for Blacks because it was a sentiment. It was not a doctrinal commitment by White society. The dream of Dr. King and liberals of a color-blind society took the nation's focus off Blacks and gave the illusion of integration and equality. It destroyed the Black unity that was forced on them by segregation. By the 1960s, convinced to believe in social integration, Blacks gave up their communities, their businesses, the jobs those businesses created, their sports teams, schools, professionals and culture. By the 1970s, the immigrant groups pouring into the country created cohesive ethnic communities, often in the same physical locations that Blacks were beginning to vacate. Integration was a failure for native Black Americans, because they did not fully understand or appreciate the value of the communities they so eagerly abandoned.

Question 4. What is the history of today's diversity policies?

The word *diversity* was not selected at random. It has a purpose. The purpose of the policy of diversity was to divert resources, attention, opportunities and population power away from Black Americans[5]. Today's

---

[5]Adams, Francis D. and Sanders, Berry. *Alienable Rights: The Exclusion of African Americans in a White Man's Land*, 1619-2000, HarperCollins Publishers, New York, 2003, p. 135.

diversity policies are simply the old anti-Black policies wearing a new set of clothes. The primary goal of the diversity policy, after redirecting resources from Blacks, is to obliterate the unique role Blacks played in the development of this nation, and to give a mythological impression that all groups contributed equally to the development of this nation. Nothing could be further from the truth. The diversity concept is designed to keep Blacks powerless and impoverished, obscure the social construct that socioeconomically cripples Blacks, and then give rights, resources and protections earned by Blacks to newly-fabricated and cobbled-together minority groups.

The concept of diversity was first introduced into American society centuries ago in the Slave Codes of 1705. The diversity provision in the Slave Codes[6] was a method to maintain racial balance in numbers and to monitor Blacks when they aggregated. Diversity procedures regulated the number of Blacks who could gather at one time, and kept them under surveillance so that Whites could be alerted to and avert any efforts which might ignite insurrections.

To effectively manage large Black populations in the South, the Diversity Act mandated that a slaveholder must have at least one White person to control and monitor every four Black slaves brought into the colonies. The slave-to-White ratio was difficult to keep in the mid-1700s, because England, the chief slave-trading nation, wanted to have as many slaves as possible in the colonies in order to produce as much commercial product for England as possible. To prevent or reduce the possibility of Blacks and Native Indians forming a coalition to drive Whites back to Europe, when the Black slave population reached nearly 40 percent in 1750, White colonial planters requested the British government do two things: 1) reduce the number of slaves being shipped into the Southern colonies and 2) send more Europeans to be in the management class in

---

[6]Jordan, Withrop D. *White over Black: American Attitudes Toward the Negro, 1550-1812,* W W Norton & Co., Inc., March 1977, pgs. 77, 106, 109, 111, 123.

the South, but in the North, to do the reverse; to import four Whites for every Black so the nation's majority population would remain White.

Colonists in the South wanted to prevent slaves from escaping to nearby Florida, which was Spanish territory and where the slaves would be free Spanish citizens upon arrival. The colonists, therefore established a new colony—Georgia—as a buffer between South Carolina and the Spanish territory of Florida. A primary purpose of the Georgia buffer zone was to impede Black slave runaways from escaping South Carolina plantations and migrating to slave sanctuaries in Spanish Florida. To secure the buffer colony and to maintain the required ratio of Blacks to Whites, more White bodies were needed. To meet that demand, colonial powers convinced the British government to empty its prisons, poorhouses and insane asylums and ship large numbers of White immigrants to settle in the newly established colony of Georgia. Meanwhile, the Spanish government and the Catholic Church continued to encourage slaves to come to Florida. Hundreds of slaves successfully escaped into Spanish Florida, where they were granted land and became settlers and free citizens. The Catholic Church, the official church of Spain and the power source behind the Spanish Crown, typically assisted the escaped slaves to establish themselves in the new country.

The 1705 Diversity Act included a provision that *required* White males to be members of the local militia, to bear arms and to perform slave-monitoring duties. All communities had to have plantation police or paddy rollers to monitor the movement of slaves and to patrol for runaway slaves. The diversity provision that required Whites to be the dominant population and possess arms to control and monitor slaves was the foundation for the 2nd Amendment to the U.S. Constitution, and a tool to establish and maintain a country for a *Free White* population that controlled everything. White population domination was the stated national goal, but the reality was quite different. The North had limited use for slaves. In the South, plantation owners needed Black slaves for labor and Blacks were the dominant population in many of the colonies.

When the diversity policy was first initiated in 1705, the slave population was nearly 40 percent nationally, and over 50 percent in the Southern states and was continuing to grow. The North saw expansion of the Black population as a threat. Southern plantation owners could not achieve a majority White population, because cheap White labor could not compete with free Black labor and White immigrants did not want to migrate into the South and Southern culture. As a practical matter, the plantation owners accepted large Black populations, but devised cruel physical and psychological control measures that were so horrific and brutal that the slaves endured intense fear, pain, anxiety and continuous terror. They were not permitted to be human. Some died from their experiences, but most gave in to the conditioning and did not revolt. The slave owners took these measures to protect themselves and to control the majority. By the time the Civil War began in 1861, states like South Carolina, Mississippi, Alabama, Louisiana and Georgia had Black populations that were approaching the 50 percent mark.

The Diversity Act that required White men to carry weapons and to monitor slaves, led to the 2nd Amendment that was included as a requirement in the U.S. Constitution. Today, 160 years after the American Civil War ended, the diversity concept in race matters has again reared its head. Just like in previous centuries, present day diversity policies devalue Blacks and equate every newly-fabricated minority to the historical struggles of Black Americans. In 1978, the U.S. Supreme Court's decision in favor of Allan Bakke accelerated the shift from Black to diversity. Bakke was a White medical student who claimed that preferences given to Blacks were the underlying cause of his rejection from medical school and that those preferences amounted to discrimination against him. A minority opinion stated there was no constitutional justification for preferential treatment for any group other than Black Americans, but the majority sided with Bakke. Public and private policy makers responded. They adopted the language of civil rights, but applied it to diversity, which only nominally included Blacks, and in reality benefited groups more acceptable to the public, groups that did not conjure up uncomfortable images of slavery, segregation or Black Power. White policy makers knew that the shift away from corrective preferential treatment for Blacks to generalized diversity would be detrimental to Blacks. The policy shift of unearned entitlement to groupings of diverse people was made behind closed doors, deemed politically-correct then announced to the public.

Liberals felt that growing opposition from Whites would impede any corrective actions for Blacks so liberals switched gears and eagerly embraced diversity for any certified new *minorities* as the new national civil rights goal. Black civil rights leaders who sensed they were politically powerless and had gone as far as they could go, followed liberals by embracing diversity and political correctness that made Blacks invisible. Having knowingly sold out their people, the civil rights establishment kept silent and promoted the newly-fabricated minority classes with the hope that some Blacks might inadvertently benefit through diversity inclusion programs and political correctness attitudes, which were popular in mainstream society.

Both government and the private sector accepted the legal diversity rationale with the clear understanding that Blacks would be nearly excluded from preferential treatment and public resources diverted to the newly-fabricated minorities[7]. The federal government's failure to enforce the nation's immigration laws, enabled a massive influx of legal and illegal Hispanics immigrants to enter the United States. They soon surpassed the native Black population, and became the majority-minority and the nation's *preferred minority* in terms of receiving benefits and privileges. By the year 2000, such large numbers of Hispanics had entered the country that they displaced Blacks in population and from the nation's consciousness. Blacks moved down from second-class to third-class citizens. The reduction of Blacks to third-class citizens gave

---

[7]Steinberg, Stephen. *The Ethnic Myth: Race, Ethnicity, and Class in America*, Beacon Press; 3rd ed. edition, January 16, 2001, pgs. 201-206.

Hispanics greater political leverage than Blacks in voting potential, business development and the public consciousness. The preferential immigration policies that sparked the growth of Hispanics were in response to the gains Blacks made during the civil rights era. By 2014, there were 55 million Hispanics in the U.S., making up more than 17 percent of the population. Ninety-three percent of Hispanics had been in the country less than 40 years. Since the year 2000, Hispanic organizations, authors and media personalities publicly boast that they have made Blacks obsolete, replaced them as the majority-majority and made them instead the minority-minority. Adhering to a trickle-down belief, Hispanics argue that Blacks have had their day.

The diversity concept, as a public policy, offers a menu of preferred gender or ethnic groups from which the White overclass can choose to direct resources and opportunities. Diversity is a broad and ambiguous concept, which hides from public view who actually receives the targeted benefits. Traditional politicians and policy makers embraced diversity and put a screeching halt to the efforts that were just beginning to be put in place to correct some of the governmental actions that had excluded Blacks from the economics of the U.S. for 360 years. Diversity policies became a façade for covering up the abuse inflicted on Blacks by the U.S. government. Each class group that receives gratuitous special treatment further dilutes and redirects resources away from Blacks. It is a continuous assault. An example of the way groups are gratuitously added to diversity without connection to American history is the proposal by President Barack Obama in October 2016, his final year in office, to add Middle Eastern people as a new racial category for the census and public policy. This would be the biggest realignment of federal definitions of race in decades and would further lock native Blacks into the lowest level of the nation's rank order of social acceptability.

Amazingly, 50 years after the massive influx of immigrants began to displace native Black Americans, Black-elected officials and civil rights leaders remain committed to open-door immigration and diversity even though those policies are injurious to members of their own race. Liberals argue altruistically that diversity and recognition of gender, language and ethnic groups is good for the nation. Liberals found practically no resistance when they abandoned Black Americans, whose suffering was out of vogue, and eagerly jumped on the bandwagon of diversity. After decades of refocusing the nation's attention away from Blacks to preferential treatment and Affirmative Action for diversity, the nation can easily point to the accomplishments achieved by women, Hispanics, Asians, LGBTs, Arabs and the handicapped in the corporate boardrooms, contract offices, college classrooms and government jobs. The gains of Blacks in those categories however are miniscule. They are on the bottom and over the past 50 years, those gains have mostly evaporated. Black people, replaced by diversity, remain excluded, abandoned and quiet. President Donald Trump was unique among presidential candidates in that he acknowledged the needs of Black people specifically and promised to address them, but Blacks have not yet made an effort to hold him to those promises.

Question 5. Did Reverend Dr. Martin Luther King, Jr.'s color-blind dream take the focus off Black rights?

Rev. Dr. Martin Luther King, Jr.'s principle of color-blindness diverted Blacks from prioritizing their own group self-interest, and guided them backwards to being altruistic, thinking first of others. His shift from Black to color-blindness reversed the long fight of Black leaders to draw a singular focus to their own group. In that respect, Dr. King's altruism took Blacks back to the way they had to think when they were slaves. When the Civil War and slavery ended in the 1860s, Black ex-slaves had an opportunity for something they had long prayed for: a chance to place their own group self-interest first. For centuries, they were denied the right to have personal or Black group self-interest. The sole focus of a slave's life was to care for the master, his interests and to view the world through his master's eyes only. During slavery, some Blacks did fight for Black rights. The strength of their advocacy varied from the extremely aggressive efforts of Nat Turner, Gabriel Prosser and Denmark Vesey, to milder advocates like Frederick Douglass, Harriet Tubman and Booker T. Washington. After slavery ended, Black activists hoped they would be able to direct their energies and resources to benefit their own people.

However, that was not to be. The Civil War ended in 1865. Reconstruction lasted about 10 years, ending about 1875. As that period ended, the dominant White society issued laws and public policies that socioeconomically bridled Black group self-interest. They were limited in the kinds of businesses and schools they could operate. Black candidates for public office were instructed to speak in generalities. They could not speak out in the interest of Blacks or hold Whites accountable for past injustices. Around 1915, a pro-Blackness period finally did emerge and lasted for a full generation. W.E.B. Du Bois began advocating Black-based politics, Marcus Garvey advocated Black economics, Carter G. Woodson emphasized Black education, Elijah Muhammad organized the Black Muslims and Black entertainers and artists pushed Blackness through the Harlem Renaissance.

The increased focus on Blackness resulted in the rise of Black leaders, who in 1928 petitioned the federal government to codify Black self-interest by passing a *Negro Bill of Rights*. Their intent was to recognize and focus public attention to relieving the historical legacies that kept Blacks fixed at the lowest rung of society's social hierarchy. In the late 1950s, Rev. Dr. Martin Luther King, Jr., a 28-year-old Black preacher, burst into the nation's conscience and became the leader of the civil rights movement, which was focused singularly on Black issues at the time. As time went on, however, the movement lost focus. Dr. King was the first Black leader to convert Black problems into a broad category of *minority issues*, which included gender, ethnicity, language, religion, handicapped status and poverty classes.

Thomas E. Woods, Jr., in his book *33 Questions about American History*[8], pointed out and discussed how Dr. King proposed that the nation institute a *Bill of Rights for the Disadvantaged*, not a Bill of Rights for Black Americans. The term disadvantaged became synonymous with *minority* and equated government-instituted slavery to contemporary issues, such as poverty, gender and immigration. Instead of framing the focus of his work to long-suffering Black Americans, Dr. King's euphemism of *disadvantaged* opened the door to a myriad of ambiguous groups that made the case that they, too, had suffered institutional mistreatment, deprivation and exploitation. Dr. King's actions started Black America down the slippery slope of competition with fabricated minority issues in 1960 when he said, "We're going to take this movement and reach out to the poor people in all directions in this country, into the Southeast after the Native Indians, into the West after the Chicanos, into Appalachia for poor Whites, and into the ghettos after the Negroes and Puerto Ricans. And, we are going to bring them together and enlarge this campaign into something bigger than just a civil rights movement for Negroes."

When Dr. King folded poverty, class, gender, ethnicity and language groupings into the Black Civil Rights Movement, he effectively destroyed the movement for Blacks. It took away the issues of their exceptionality in society, issues which had never been fully addressed nor remedied. The unique historical experiences of Black Americans became synonymous with minorities, multiculturalism, diversity, people of color and poor people. These off-course issues confused racial issues with class issues.

Dr. King's redirection of the nation's attention to poor people and other oppressed people of the world put Black Americans on the back seat of the bus and voluntarily reversed the course of Black self-interest to the days when they were denied the right to even have a group self-

---

[8]Woods, Jr., Thomas E. *33 Questions About American History*, Crown Forum, New York, 2007, pgs. 11-16.

interest. He and the movement became broadly focused on *everyone, all* people and everything except Black rights. Dr. King's actions absolved Whites of any need to fulfill the requirement of the 13th Amendment to the U.S. Constitution to "lift the burdens and incidences of slavery from the shoulders of Black people."

The nation's attention continues to shift more comfortably toward class and gender groups, leaving the legacies of slavery and Jim Crow segregation proportionately unchanged between Whites and Blacks. The concept of color-blindness did indeed take the focus off Black rights. Whether that is a positive or a negative depends upon the perch on which you sit.

Question 6. Are Black Americans more vulnerable to terrorism than other Americans?

Black Americans are most definitely more vulnerable to terrorism than other Americans. Terrorism is rooted in human psychological pathology that seeks to intimidate, injure and control other humans based upon the religious, political or racist ideologies of the terrorists. Five centuries of institutionalized enslavement, Jim Crow segregation and Benign Neglect have made Black Americans a favorite target of conservative terrorists, hate mongers and religious zealots. Blacks are the most identifiable and vulnerable population group in America because they are totally dependent upon non-Black racial and ethnic groups for their safety and daily needs. Just as they are unprepared to protect themselves in the case of civil unrest or natural disasters, it will be even more difficult for Black Americans to protect themselves from institutional-based, cultural-driven terrorism, because they live in culture-less, porous, dysfunctional neighborhoods instead of close-knit functional Black communities. Blacks lack a defensive code of conduct.

The definition of a functional community is a physical community that has a culture and code that supports an alternate and semi-independent economy that produces services, goods, jobs and has a tax base for its residents. In a functional community, people are familiar with each other and have common needs and interests. It is where they store and secure their wealth, power, businesses, heritage, jobs, products and other resources. A functional community has an identity and an operational network of obligations between its members and socioeconomic enterprises. To successfully protect its members, a community must have a physical location and infrastructure that can be marked and closed, if necessary, against outsiders who might pose danger. Members who live outside the physical community, can still identify with it by having a broad sense of community and sharing the common history, needs, interests and goals, and the responsibility to protect and support the physical community and its members.

The bane of the vulnerability of Blacks to modern terrorism results from their not having functional communities. Blacks were complicit in White society's destruction of the Black communities that did exist until the 1960s. Now Blacks have surrendered their community resources, sense of community and collective ability to protect themselves from outside, competitive and hostile groups that can and have historically terrorized them. In most instances, Black neighborhoods lack organizational institutions, local communications systems, surplus food, water, energy and medical systems. The integration process diluted or removed experienced Black leadership from Black neighborhoods, leaving those left behind unprepared to deal with terrorists or other life-threatening crises.

Just like the Ku Klux Klan symbols and marches, the primary goal of terrorism is to create fear and confusion horrendous enough to disrupt socioeconomic systems, paralyze citizens and inhibit the flow of needed daily resources. Terrorists are unlike a classic standing army. They do not wear uniforms or bear standardized flags. They are advantaged by being unknown and invisible. They pledge their total allegiance and lives to a political ideology or religion, and most importantly, they do not actually exist until after they have committed a terrorist act. If they are successful in committing an act of terror, the media becomes complicit by promoting the successful act, which publicizes the cause of the terrorists and demonstrates their ability to achieve their objectives. They are not interested in how they are labeled or what consequences befall them. Terrorism functions best in open societies, where people have many freedoms and their movements and activities are not under suspicion. Terrorists thrive on publicity and seek the notoriety of public identification. Although episodes of terrorism are newsworthy events, extensive media coverage sets the stage for even more terrorist acts of violence.

"Klan Members Parade Down Pennsylvania Avenue in Washington, D.C. in 1925." Source: U.S. Library of Congress.

Again, just like Blacks have been impotent against the Ku Klux Klan and other forms of White terrorsim, the United States of America itself is totally ill-prepared to fight, let alone win, a holy war or a terrorist waged virtual war. Our government leaders promote the belief that America is the world's superpower, a world police force that has politically obligated itself to be the moral conscience of the world. Our response to terrorism as a nation is anemic, illogical and ignores what is known about the true nature of international terrorism. Black America is even more defenseless and vulnerable than the larger society that has organized institutions and resources. There is no interest, nor any incentives for other ethnic or class groups to take care of the needs of Black people.

There is also no visible evidence that Blacks have made preparations to protect themselves. The electrical blackout of 2003, which impacted the entire Northeast region of the U.S., sent messages to Blacks that other groups felt no obligation to share their resources with Blacks during a major crisis. In the Detroit area, for example, many White and ethnic suburban communities did not permit Blacks from the city to enter for food, gas or other essentials.

Blacks must have their own back-up resources. Whether in a dependent Black neighborhood or socially-scattered guests in White communities, they must have protection and the daily necessities of life in emergencies. When terrorism, man-made or natural disasters strike, it will be very difficult, if not too late, for Blacks to gain access to vital resources, such as doctors, hospitals and grocery stores. Black elected officials, civil rights organizations, churches and educational centers should take major responsibility to alert, organize and prepare Black communities to deal with terrorism in any form, because Black Americans are a vulnerable out-group.

Question 7. Where are the Black leaders?

The term *Black leader* is an oxymoron. Based upon the definition of *leader*, one has little choice but to conclude that Blacks do not have leaders. A leader is a guiding or directing head of a group, one who leads toward a new direction after critical analysis of the social, economic and political condition of the group, the leader would then develop a plan with strategies to take them to a better place. Moses in the Bible was such a leader. Clearly, the civil rights movement of the 1960s[9] began with the intent to lead Blacks in a new direction, but the movement had no national plan, no destination or group-centered, measurable goals. The main issues were desegregation, voting rights and discrimination and did not target equal distribution of resources, a measurable goal that had the potential to change the social construct on race for the group. Because the goals did not challenge the foundation problem of Blacks, and the movement became dependent upon government and corporate support, it was easily controlled, marginalized and consumed into the policies of Benign Neglect and political correctness. Once engulfed, Black leaders were easily controlled and marginalized. On Black matters, they became invisible. Black leadership today has become symbolic and ceremonious. Old civil rights personalities, entertainers and public officials have no objective basis or purposeful destination to lead Blacks to, or away from the conditions in which Blacks are already mired. In most instances, those Blacks who want to be leaders have not studied or examined the economic and political conditions of the Black dilemma nor have they crafted a corrective plan to improve the quality of life for the group. Their words lack academic discipline and the solutions they propose are most often without direction or purpose.

In other words, most visible Blacks do not equate to Black leaders[10]. They are *double agents* who intentionally represent everyone—all races, ethnicities, cultures, religions, genders and classes. They skillfully identify *Black* issues, but propose *minority* solutions to address them. They do not even purport to represent Black interests. However, Whites, the media and those seeking to influence Blacks accept their symbolic leadership. Most visible Blacks are wedded to playing party politics, toeing the line as politically correct individuals and identifying with mainstream issues. They demonstrate more self-interest than group interest and deliver no

---

[9]Anderson, Claud. *Black Labor, White Wealth: The Search for Power and Economic Justice*, PowerNomics® Corporation of America, Inc., Maryland, 1994, pgs. 24-27.

[10]Smith, Robert C. *We Have No Leaders: African Americans in the Post-Civil Rights Era*, State University of New York Press, New York, 1996, pgs. 220, 278-279, 366.

tangible nor measurable benefits specifically to their own race. Whether they pretend to be color-blind or simply do not recognize the suffering of their own people, they seem to relish engagement in symbolic activities that are meaningless.

Symbolic leaders ignore the exceptionalism of Blacks and proclaim inaccurately that *all* groups have contributed equally to the development of this nation. When they accepted the myth that Blacks were not treated any differently than any other ethnic or population group, it became easy to neutralize or obscure Blacks and their historical exceptionality. As the loose purpose of the civil rights movement expanded and became more diffused, Black leaders and would-be-leaders found more comfort and safety in advocating for realization of the dream of a color-blind society than fighting for a more self-sufficient and competitive Black America. They are now so color-blind they cannot even see their own Black color. As a result, Black America increasingly views symbolic leadership as irrelevant and harmful to the Black struggle for survival.

The years between the 1870s and 2017 have been a transition period for Black leadership. It has gone from practically no leadership during slavery, to symbolic leadership in what is incorrectly labeled by some a post-racist society. In the early 1800s, Black ministers provided monitored leadership for free and non-free Blacks. These leaders were appointed by the White power structure which also instructed the ministers in what they could and could not say. After the Civil War, a few elected officials, community activists and businessmen joined ministers in the leadership ranks and began shaping a Black overclass. In the 1960s, Black leaders were community activists, ministers and civil rights organizers, who collectively pushed Congress to enact new voting rights laws. Those laws resulted in a large number of Black-elected officials who became the new overclass and began the shift to symbolic leadership from the previous Black-focused community activists, ministers and civil rights organizations.

What happened to Black leaders in a socio-political context is so critically important that it demands further elaboration, even at the risk of being repetitious. In the 1970s, government made aggressive efforts to shift focus from Blacks to fabricated classes. Civil rights activists acquiesced and new social movements filled the vacuum, sparked by the simultaneous social impact of a massive inflow of immigrants from developing nations and the growing momentum of the women's liberation movement. The public policy of political correctness also took hold, cemented the refocus of official attention from Blacks to women and newly-created minority groups. President Richard Nixon's public policy of Benign Neglect was successful and caused the public and private sectors to lessen their interest in Blacks and to shift to women, minorities and immigrant groups. Black leaders and their respective organizations were successfully persuaded to abandon their own people and to take up the cause of broad and ambiguous groupings under the façades of diversity, multicultural, minorities and people of color. Never before has any religious, gender, ethnic or language group been required to shift their attention away from their own people. Once Black leadership was marginalized and incorporated into the system of political correctness, there was little that they could do to address the needs of Black Americans. Apparently, they did not suspect that once inside they would become irrelevant. Since they were politically separated from their own people, they had no means to pressure the power structure.

No other group—European Whites, Jews, Asians, Arabs or American Indians—was expected to divorce itself intentionally from its culture and primary group. In politics, the detachment of Black-elected officials gives them the latitude to promise nothing and deliver nothing to the Black electorate which continually votes for them as a bloc. Electing Blacks to public office therefore has made no *measurable difference* in the quality of life for Black Americans or the status quo in racial disparities. The Black electorate receives no direct relationship, tangible or measurable benefits, from electing a Black person to a public office. In the 30-year time period between 1960 and 1990, the number of Black-elected officials increased from 103 to over 9,000, which constitutes a 9,000 percent increase in the total number of Black-elected officials across America. Yet, when comparing the social discomfort indicators in 1960 with the indicators in 1990, after a 9,000 percent increase in the number of Black-elected officials, the conditions of Black Americans did not improve, but worsened. Those parallels are apparent today, in 2017, which suggests that there is no direct connection between Blacks electing a political candidate into public office and receiving tangible benefits for their vote, such as: 1) increased employment, 2) business ownership, 3) improved housing, 4) functional schools, 5) safe streets, 6) medical services, 7) wealth, 8) income, 9) social acceptance or 10) political power. These observations seem to hold true even when assessing the legacy of President Barack Obama, known as the nation's first African American president. At the end of his presidency, Black people were in the same state they were in before he was elected to the highest office in the land.

In summary, the White overclass response to the civil rights movement was typically slow and most often symbolic. They rejected nearly everything that required a substantive change in the racial status quo. The old-line civil rights organizations have failed to address the historical legacies and dilemmas of Black America. Most Blacks recognized by the general public as leaders are simply tools that the White overclass uses to keep the Black masses placated and Black neighborhoods under control— non-competitive and powerless. Symbolic Black leadership has become largely irrelevant in the struggle for Black survival and socioeconomic competitiveness. They will continue to routinely appear in print and electronic media to support or discuss non-Black issues. They will boast about *racial progress* and minority political alliances to justify their appeal to White society for financial support. Sadly, at the same time, the Black masses will sink further into a permanent underclass status.

Question 8. Can Blacks be a competitive group without group self-interest?

It would be very difficult for Black Americans to become a competitive group if they cannot shake the unique social conditioning imposed on them during five centuries of slavery and Jim Crow semi-slavery.

Normally, a group that has been systematically oppressed for a prolonged period develops a heightened sense of group consciousness, self-interest and closes its ranks against outside threats. Blacks appear to be different. The twenty-first generation of Black America remains bound by lessons learned in slavery that stripped them of a group self-interest. They remain altruistic, dedicated to the welfare of others before themselves. They love everybody, are forgiving, long-suffering, hardworking, self-sacrificing dedicated to taking care of others first and look for a reward in heaven after death. Today, that mindset has resulted in Blacks who believe that because of their long status as sufferers, they ought to be the moral conscience of the nation and the world. Few Black ministers tell their congregations that it is actually against Bible instructions to sacrifice themselves, abandon their homes, families and race to save others, regardless as to whether they are immigrants, ethnics, homeless, impoverished, gay or any other fabricated minorities. Blacks carry the moral and civil rights banner for *all* people, while most people look out for themselves and ignore the needs of the Black masses.

In a race-based society, every group is competing to win in their own group self-interest. As a group, by not having self-interest and being altruistic, Blacks lose by default[11]. They are poor and powerless. Their labor and culture have enriched nearly every group on earth except their own. With a sense of self-interest, a group can recognize competitive advantages, opportunities and ways to protect and build on what it has that is valuable. Success will come only when they can unify and compete in the best interest of the group.

---

[11]Montagu, Ashley. *Man's Most Dangerous Myth: The Fallacy of Race*, 6th Ed., The World Publishing Company, New York, 1964, pgs. 273-274.

Question 9. What is the difference between a Black American and an African American?

The terms *Black American* and *African American* are not equivalent or interchangeable, although they are generally, but erroneously considered as such by Whites and some native Blacks. Black Americans are born in America and are descendants of slaves. African American is a term most accurately applied to a person born in Africa that has relocated or migrated to America. In reality, each term is derived from totally different cultural, language, political, religious and racial experiences[12].

Any group is a sum total of its unique experiences, which dictate the way group members see themselves in this world. Ninety-nine percent of all the Black people in America are descendants of slaves who were born in America. Their only connections to Africa are the oral stories told to them by their parents and grandparents, which faded with each generation. They have no personal connection to Africa and not one country on the African continent ever sent a single vessel to this country to rescue any of the millions of Blacks who were kidnapped, enslaved, killed and psychologically crippled. Enslaved Blacks in America were de-cultured and forced to devise their own survival skills and attitudes. These enslaved persons and their off-spring were stripped of everything and forced to adapt and survive under the most inhumane conditions for over 360 years. During that period of time, they developed a blended culture and emerged as Black Americans, no longer Africans.

Black Americans are totally unlike any other humans on this earth. They are a combination of cultures and uncommon experiences, therefore, the group is special, an exception. Some avoid the term Black because they do not want to identify with the negative and evil historically associated with the word by Whites and other groups. Some Blacks shun self-identification by color because it means being less than a full human,

---

[12]Lind, Michael. *Next American Nation: The New Nationalism and the Fourth American Revolution*. Simon & Schuster Books, New York, 1995, p. 125.

stripped of all honor, and subjected to all forms of White rule and power. They have allowed others to frame their thinking of the label or the word Black[13]. Those who avoid Blackness, in effect, have surrendered their greatest strength and badge of identity. Black Americans are unique. The enslavement process stripped Blacks of their African-ness and forced them to forge together their own unique culture. It is so unique that it is copied, mimicked and appropriated by non-Blacks all over the world.

Many Blacks, non-Blacks and especially conservatives prefer the term African American. It is a term that removes race from a race-based dilemma and redirects focus to culture. African American is a less specific term than Black, just as substituting terms like *minority, people of color* and *poor people* is less threatening than the term *Black*. The term *African American* obfuscates, dilutes and erases the unique history of Blacks in this country. Blacks should never be equated to African Americans or other groups within minority classes. Using the term African American is an example of changing Black problems to a minority solution. Since all life began in Africa, in the broadest sense, the label African American can be applied to any human from any place on the earth that migrates to America. Once they establish residence in America, they can legitimately claim to be African American.

Black exceptionality is a fundamental key to unlock the doors leading to group self-empowerment, recognition, respect and appreciation for their contributions to the socioeconomic development of this nation to which they are entitled as *special people*. They must distinguish themselves by claiming their exceptionality as *Black Americans*, just as Europeans in the 1680s distinguished themselves by officially labeling themselves *White Americans* instead of Pilgrims or Puritans. The label White distinguished them thereafter. Due to the fact that the masses of Blacks in America are totally ignorant of Africa, they identify with the *African American*

---

[13]Robinson, Randall. *The Debt: What America Owes to Blacks*, Penguin Random House, New York, 2001, pgs. 7-10.

label only out of love and respect for the Black people residing on the African continent. In physical and genetic makeup, they are as far from being African Blacks as they are from being European Whites. There are enormous differences in the experiences of a Black person born and raised in America versus an African born and raised on the African continent. Native Blacks in America were stripped of their African-ness centuries ago when their ancestors were transported to the Americas. It was at that point that their differences began. Blacks were forced to create and fabricate a culture that blended the various African tribal backgrounds with the American culture they found here. Being enslaved in America was a very different experience than being colonized on the African continent. African Blacks were not stripped of their culture, languages, families, relatives, homeland, communities, religion, and sense of people-hood. Where, on the other hand, Black Americans were stripped in all respects, reduced to the level of field animals and treated as disposable property.

Consequently, African Blacks who visit or migrate to the United States sense they are different from native Blacks, and tend to express a degree of superiority over the descendants of slaves. They *are* different. They came here voluntarily, have homelands and relatives in Africa with whom they identify and communicate, and they have a place to return whenever they so choose. Americans recognize the difference, also, and accord greater respect to African visitors and dignitaries than to native Blacks. In fact, it was not unusual, prior to the civil rights movement of the 1960s, for some Black Americans to dress in African garb and pretend to be African visitors or dignitaries just to garner greater respect from White Americans.

Using unspecific terms like African American obscures the unique history of Blacks in America and can have harmful effects similar to what happens when the terms *minority, people of color* or *poor people* are used instead of Black. A lawsuit filed by a Pakistani, who applied for the African American Banneker Scholarship at the University of Maryland in the 1990s, demonstrates the folly of imprecise language. The university denied him a scholarship because recipients had to be African American. The Pakistani student filed a lawsuit charging the university with discrimination. The student's case was based on a very simple, but reasonable, explanation. The Pakistani student said he had lived in Africa before migrating to the United States and considered himself African. Now that he lives in America, he is an African American. The Maryland Supreme Court agreed and ruled in the student's favor, awarding him $150,000.

The message to native Blacks is a caution. In circumstances where a race label is necessary, do not permit the use of broad and ambiguous terms to define you. The school did not meet its goal of providing scholarships for the specific purpose of attracting Black students. The school's needs were specific, but the term African American was not. It expanded the target group in an imprecise way. Had the school used the term Black, the Banneker Scholarship fund would have had an additional $150,000 to distribute toward worthy Black applicants.

The distinction between Black and African America is important. Blacks came here as Africans, but what they experienced in this county made them different. They were stripped of everything—their culture, language, religion, the right to benefit from their own labor. They were not acknowledged as human and were denied the expression of natural human longings. They could not love, protect or plan for their families. Blacks endured these experiences, all the while their labor drove the economic engine that built this nation. Withstanding and surviving these experiences became the badge of courage that distinguishes native Blacks from any other group in America. Those experiences signify this country's indebtedness to them. There may be a difference in the terms and historical experiences, but the two groups are genetically linked. It is imperative, therefore, that native Black Americans, support and recognize Africa, the birthplace of mankind, and strive to protect its people and material resources from further abuse and exploitation by foreign entities.

Question 10. What is racism and can a Black person be a racist?

Racism is a group based power and economic control phenomenon in which one racial group owns and controls so much wealth and resource power that it can enslave, subordinate, exploit, exclude or render another group non-competitive. The dominant racial group can make life and death decisions for potential competitor groups. It can predetermine what the lesser powered group can own, control, its wealth and the extent to which it will be allowed to compete.

Racism is one of the most contentious and dangerous terms in the English lexicon and is overused and misapplied by laymen and scholars alike. In a society in which the policy of Benign Neglect is still operative against Blacks, there has been an effort to equate and replace racism with classism. Class is defined by economic status, educational level and employment status and professional accomplishment. Class is fluid. Racism against Blacks is fixed. Classism and racism are not the same. Blacks, as a group, cannot cross the color or race line. Religious, gender, ethnic or cultural groups, are not the victims of racism, but of classism. The power and economic control phenomenon of racism is non-applicable to them because classes are subcategories of the larger society, and generally, they participated in the economic enrichment from Black enslavement. Further, classes are open and fluid and promote the right to compete for equality.

Racism came into existence on the eve of the Civil War after all the resources had been distributed to European Whites. The practice of racism was originally designed to deny Blacks the right to compete, to be equal and to become a class. While racism is group based, class discrimination is individualized and arises from prevailing societal issues. For instance, when Arabs are profiled and connected to terrorism, it is discrimination, but it is not racism. When Hispanics are profiled and associated with illegal immigration, it is not racism but discrimination arising out of contemporary social concerns. In neither of the recited instances, is the purpose of the class discrimination to exploit, enslave or segregate all members of the classes. It is inaccurate to equate class *minorities* to Blacks and racism.

History reveals that the concept of racism has undergone a metamorphosis in both meaning and application through the centuries. To understand racism and deal with it effectively, it is important to understand the historical origin and purpose of racism, to know what it is and what it is not. Racism, as a word and concept did not just pop-up out of the blue. It evolved from a confluence of events and circumstances. The practice of equating individualized gender, ethnic, cultural and religious discrimination to institutionalized racism against Black people provides justification for continuing the racial status quo.

In the late 1400s, two essential factors came together from which racism evolved—the possibility of free land in the Americas and free labor from African Blacks. At that time, the entire continent of Europe was dysfunctional, ravaged by famine, crime, poverty and disease. European countries were looking for lands to conquer to infuse their nations with new energy and wealth. The Catholic Church was the leading invader and controller of world expansionism. During that period, the Vatican was given 16 Black slaves as a gift. A short time later, Pope Innocence issued a special edict and declared that Blacks *should* be used as free labor, thereby establishing a new kind of slavery. Until that time, a person could be enslaved for only three reasons, religious persecution, personal indebtedness or for being a prisoner of war. When, Columbus returned to Europe with news that he had *discovered* a new, *uninhabited* land, a vision took hold; to merge available *free* Black labor with new *free* land. At that precise point, racism replaced tribalism, the social structure of Europe at the time.

Nine European nations went into competition. A politico-economic race commenced to see which country could best exploit free Black labor and use it to capture land, resources and wealth to enrich their countries. That economic race, using free Black labor, lasted until the eve of the 1861 Civil War in the U.S. The race between the European nations ended at this point because the resources and wealth of the Americas had been distributed and nearly 100 percent of everything was now in the hands of White Europeans. At the same time, European slaveholders denied enslaved Blacks the right, not only to enjoy the fruits of their labor, but also the right to acquire land, wealth and political power. These exclusions were instituted as law and Blacks were defined as powerless property. The Founding Fathers rigged the race. They crafted a social construct that locked Blacks into a constitutional underclass status and White society as a group, remains opposed to corrective redistribution of wealth, power or resources to Black Americans.

After all the resources had been distributed to Whites by the 1860s, the concept of racism morphed from an economic issue to one of biology with Charles Darwin's theory of Natural Selection presented in his 1859 book, *Origin of the Species*. In this book, he ranked living organisms and classified Blacks at the bottom of human species. Out of Darwin's biological theories, grew the requirement that all persons be identified by racial designations on birth certificates, driver licenses and other public documents. Race remained a biological issue until a century later with the advent of the Black Civil Rights Movement when racism morphed again. The concept of racism expanded and took on a more colloquial and casual meaning that signified not power but personal feelings about liking or disliking individuals. This misdirection and misapplication of the term racism allowed the original objective of racism, to maintain the inequality between Whites and Blacks, to continue unabated.

Racism grew out of the competitive race between groups to control wealth and power. As early as 1516 in North America, Whites have been the winners and Blacks the losers, allowed only to react to White racism. Blacks do not have power or wealth. It is, therefore, not possible for them to be racists.

PART III
Rethinking Social Integration

Question 11. Has education been the great racial equalizer for Blacks?

Education is a class issue bound by race, and has no magical powers to equalize social and economic conditions between Blacks and Whites. Generations of Black children were indoctrinated to believe the pathway to success and racial equality was education, just as it appeared to be for White children. Schools have consistently presented a paradox for Blacks. First, if fortunate enough to get an education—a tool—they were limited as to where they could use their tool. There were few places within the Black community to apply their acquired educational tools, and if they ventured outside, Whites would determine if they were wanted and the value of their Black labor. This paradox placed Blacks not too far from where they had been in slavery. It was still hard for Blacks to earn enough to support their families.

Education, generally considered the mechanism for upward class mobility, has been an issue for Blacks since the founding of this nation. First, it was against the law and public policies to teach a slave to read or write. Any person caught teaching a slave to read and write would suffer 39 lashes with a whip and a fine of $100. Following the Civil War, after nearly 360 years of slavery and being denied an education, approximately five million penniless, landless, jobless, uneducated, unclothed, homeless and unprotected Blacks were set free to wander the countryside. They could neither read nor write. Some public and private schools were set up by sympathetic churches, abolitionists and individuals to teach Blacks manual skills and to be subservient. Congress established the Freedmen's Bureau, a government agency to aid the transition of former slaves to a life of freedom. Before it became dysfunctional, the Bureau funded what are known today as Historically Black Colleges. Those schools started as elementary-type schools, grew and progressed to high schools, teachers' colleges and finally to full colleges and universities. Although 96 percent of Blacks in America were suffering from planned ignorance after the Civil War, they believed in the possibilities of an education. They believed if they acquired education—reading, writing and deciphering—they could overcome imposed ignorance and become a self-sufficient and competitive group. Blacks diligently pursued education in the new schools. Parents went all out to make their children attend whatever school was available, whether public, private or religious missionary schools.

During the 30-year time period between 1866 and 1896, former slaves set an educational achievement record that has yet to be broken by any racial or ethnic group. When slavery ended in 1865, approximately 98 percent of Black Americans were illiterate. By 1896, Blacks had reduced their illiteracy rate by more than half, from 98 percent to 45 percent. They educated themselves faster than the 26 million Europeans who entered the country during the same 30-year time period with nearly the same illiteracy rate as ex-slaves. Never in recorded history, has an enslaved race or ethnic group reduced their illiteracy rate by 50 percent within a 30-year time period. But, education was not an equalizer. While Blacks were achieving educationally, the expected benefits were not accruing to them. The 26 million immigrants were being installed over them as a management and ownership class. With a lower educational achievement rate than Blacks, newly-arriving Europeans outdistanced Blacks in employment, business, politics and income. Unfortunately, higher class status and monetary benefits that typically follow academic achievement did not follow Black educational achievement. The European Whites became business owners, managers, administrators and prominent public servants. Blacks, with greater educational achievement, simply became low-level workers and domestic servants.

By 1920, Blacks again reduced their illiteracy rate, this time by 20 percent, which was equal to that of Jewish and Asian immigrants entering the country. By the 1950s, the national illiteracy rate for Black Americans was down to sixteen percent. Yet, when the Black Civil Rights Movement began in the 1960s, Blacks with a college education did not earn as much as White high school dropouts. Black Americans, in general, earned only $0.56 for every dollar earned by Whites. In the 10-year period, between 1966 and 1976, the earnings ratio of Blacks moved up to $0.66 for every dollar earned by Whites. The nation entered the 21st century with Black Americans attaining even greater educational achievements. However, their income had reverted to $0.56 for every dollar earned by a White person. David O. Sears, author of *Racialized Politics: The Debate about Racism in America*[14], argues that Whites' accusation that Blacks need more education provides a façade for hiding White racism. It misdirects Blacks to search for power in education to propel them into upward mobility rather than searching for power in economics.

Education power is illusionary because socioeconomic benefits did not fully track academic and achievement gains[15]. By the 1950s, a Black person with a college degree could not earn the salary of a White high school dropout. Black teachers earned less than half of what White teachers earned. Blacks with one or two college degrees worked part time as domestic servants in White homes or in low-paying jobs in White businesses. In 2017, young Black college graduates are often unemployed or underemployed. Many grew up believing the myth that racism was a thing of the past, that all they needed was a good education to succeed in life. The reality that racism still exists is a shock to the young people who are trained to be chemists, engineers, writers, physicists, computer programmers and biologists. Their skin color continues to be a handicap for them in the 21st century.

---

[14]Sears, David O., Sidanius, James, and Bobo, Lawrence. *Racialized Politics: The Debate about Racism in America*, University Of Chicago Press; 1st edition, February 2000.

[15]Hacker, Andrew. *Money: Who Has, How Much, and Why*, Scribner Books, New York, 1997, pgs. 24, 151-153, 156-157.

Education can only be a *potential* for upward mobility. The benefits are bound by race, which entraps Blacks. Those who manage to get an education generally move up some, but do not achieve the same degree of socioeconomic mobility as Whites. Blacks do not have a competitive alternative economy or any place in which to use their skills and training to better themselves or their own group. Blacks need their own communities where they can own businesses and be employed so they can practice group-based competitive economics in a capitalistic society, and use their education to 1) benefit themselves individually and 2) benefit their race.

Question 12. What was Meritorious Manumission and does it still apply to Blacks?

Meritorious Manumission was the legal act of freeing a slave for good deeds, as defined by the national public policy. The term meritorious means *something earned*. Manumission means *becoming free or freedom*[16]. During slavery, a slaveholder could grant freedom to a slave who distinguished himself by saving the life of a White person, inventing or designing something that enriched a White person, or snitched on other members of his race, especially, those Blacks who were resisting and contemplating a revolt. Meritorious Manumission policies[17] were not intended to unify slaves or make them more self-supportive humans. Instead, the policies were designed to keep Blacks non-threatening and under control. Meritorious Manumission became a public policy in the early 1700s and was introduced into the Virginia legislature as a law in

---

[16]Anderson, Claud. *Black Labor, White Wealth*, PowerNomics® Corporation of America, Inc., Maryland, 1987, pgs. 166-167.

[17]Quarles, Benjamin. *The Negro in the Making of America*, 3rd ed., Touchstone, 1987, pgs. 102-103.

1710. Incorporated into every aspect of the slavery system, it remained an active carrot and incentive through the social integration process and it is still an operating principle at this present time. Meritorious Manumission recognized and rewarded Blacks who accepted their assigned position, but for personal gain would thwart, openly or nefariously, the efforts by other Blacks to alter the racial status quo. The first person known to have received Meritorious Manumission set the baseline for benefits. Peter M. Bergman, in his book, *The Chronological History of the Negro*[18], said, "The first person to receive [Meritorious Manumission] was a Negro named Will, who was recognized for having impeded *a slave revolt* in the South Carolina colony. He was awarded his freedom for performing a public service. Will's freedom papers provided that he enjoy and have all the liberties, privileges and immunities of or to be a free Negro." Once the public policy was in place, an endless number of slaves became sensitive to freedom opportunities that they could earn. In the 150 years between 1710 and 1860, Black slaves reportedly revealed the plans for over 300 possible slave revolts or insurrections. Slaves warned slaveholders or the general public of the pending revolts in hopes of receiving Meritorious Manumission in the forms of personal recognition and material benefits.

Another notable example of a Black person seeking Meritorious Manumission occurred on the eve of the Civil War. In 1859, abolitionist John Brown and his raiding party traveled to Harpers Ferry, Virginia, to capture weapons from a U.S. Marine Corps armory to use to free Black slaves. When John Brown and his party entered the town, a Black man, who had already won Meritorious Manumission, was sitting on the porch of the railroad station and recognized Brown and his party. The Black man, Hayward Shepherd, ran to alert the town that Brown was in town to free the slaves. Brown's raiders shot Shepherd down in the street. He was free to sit on the porch that evening because he was no longer a slave. In gratitude for Hayward Shepherd's outstanding behavior of placing

---

[18]Bergman, Peter M. *The Chronological History of the Negro in America*, Harper and Row Publisher, New York, 1969, p. 25.

White society's political economic interest above the freedom and needs of members of his own race, the town erected a monument honoring him. The Hayward Shepherd statue was stored beside the city's major museum and covered with a wooden box in the 1960s. The inscription on the statue that the town of Harpers Ferry erected to honor Hayward Shepherd read:

"Hayward Shepherd Statue in Harpers Ferry, West Virginia." Source: Author's Personal Collection.

On the night of October 16, Hayward Shepherd, an industrious respected colored freeman, was mortally wounded by John Brown's raiders, in pursuance of his duty as an employee of the Baltimore and Ohio Railroad Company. He became the first victim of this attempted insurrection. This boulder is erected by the United Daughters of the Confederacy and the Sons of Confederate Veterans as a memorial to Hayward Shepherd, exemplifying the character and faithfulness of thousands of Negroes who, under many temptations throughout subsequent years of war, so conducted themselves that no stain was left upon a record which is the peculiar heritage of the American people, and an everlasting tribute to the best in both races[19].

---

[19]Anderson, Claud. *Dirty Little Secrets About Black History, Its Heroes, and other Troublemakers*, PowerNomics® Corporation of America, Inc., Maryland, 1997, pgs. 102-103.

Meritorious Manumission behavior is often observed, especially in the ranks of Black-elected officials, ministers, civil rights leaders, athletes and entertainment personalities. These visible people, anointed by others as leading Blacks, are sometimes aloof and disconnected from their own race. They are often required to disavow and abandon their own people in exchange for public attention, financial resources and personal comfort. Once co-opted by the power structure, they are effective tools to be used against or to control the Black masses. The divide-and-conquer scheme makes a Black minority even weaker and more exploitable. Blacks seeking Meritorious Manumission, for instance, will endorse political candidates knowing they will deliver nothing to Black people. They will support integration with any group before seeking to strengthen their own people. Worst of all, those seeking modern-day Meritorious Manumission believe that the advancement of their own race is wholly dependent on the advancement of the White race and all the other peoples of the world.

Meritorious Manumission opportunities today are typically presented as symbols and incentives for satisfying race relations, such as being asked to support public policies that subordinate the interest of native Black Americans to the interest of women, LGBT, immigrants and other fabricated minorities. Most Black civil rights leaders and elected officials that allow these groups to be equated to and ranked over Blacks, are seeking their Meritorious Manumission. So, keep your eyes on FOX, CNN or NBC television news channels and see if you can identify Blacks seeking and getting Meritorious Manumission rewards and recognition.

Question 13. Does the social integration policy have a hidden racial quota?

The U.S. Supreme Court's 1954 *Brown v. Board of Education* decision mandated social integration by nullifying state and local segregation laws. But, real school integration never occurred. White society pushed back in numerous ways that made the social integration process a rhetorical and symbolic exercise rather than a physical and racial reality. White society viewed social integration as a threat to their long-standing social privilege, skin color preferences and economic advantages. After centuries of being a majority and mistreating the nation's Black minority, Whites fear becoming a minority within any majority-win setting. They view being a minority as being a loser. Worse, they wonder if Blacks would seek revenge against them. Therefore, they pushed back and made it clear that they would accept social integration only on the most minimal of terms that would allow them to continue being the majority in nearly every situation. So, to structure integration rules they went back to the old Diversity Act, which had a racial quota that required a White majority over a small Black minority in all social and physical situations.

The Supreme Court's 1960 ruling on *Brown v. Board of Education* may have signaled the end of legal segregation but, skin color remained a factor in immigration policies and still determines who and how many immigrants from a given country are admitted. Considered superior, those with White skin have full entitlement to advantages, privileges, respect and acceptance in mainstream society, while those with Black skin receive something less. Immigrants whose skin color allows them to blend in with this nation's White majority are accepted and given access to the nation's resources, opportunities and political power. In addition to allocating resources according to skin color, Whites try to live in communities that have some kind of physical barrier between the races, like a river, bridge, park, shopping mall or railroad tracks.

If, by chance, Blacks and Whites live in the same neighborhood, Whites are reasonably comfortable with Black neighbors so long as the percentage of Blacks does not exceed five percent. Once the percentage of Blacks exceeds five percent, a mental alarm sounds, signaling a threat to the community's racial balance. Whites become sensitive and on guard to the possibility of a Black minority challenging a White population for dominance and majority status. When the Black population exceeds six or seven percent, White flight commences. Whites sell their homes, resign from organizations, withdraw their children from public schools and re-register them in private schools, segregated academies or religious schools. They move to all-White communities and partake in all-White activities. The same alarms do not go off when the population moving in is Hispanic, Asian or any other group on probation to become White.

Andrew Hacker, in his book, *Two Nations: Black and White, Separate, Hostile, Unequal*[20], was more generous with his figures. Hacker felt the trigger quota for White flight could be as high as 10 to 20 percent. Either way, Whites are adamantly opposed to giving up their historical superior and advantaged positions in society that allow them to own and control nearly 99 percent of the nation's wealth and political power. Unfortunately, too many Black Americans mistakenly presume that, as a result of the surge of non-European immigration that began in 1965, the incoming immigrants would ally with America's Black underclass and make the collective group a majority. However, that did not happen. There are no incentives for any immigrant ethnic group to give up its preferred status in mainstream society and align with a powerless Black underclass. The dominant White population would also never allow that to happen. Immigrants coming to America from any place other than Africa or the Caribbean Islands will, as necessary, be classified as *White*, ensuring that a White majority will continue to maintain numerical dominance over and rule the Black minority population.

Question 14. Why do Blacks need communities instead of neighborhoods?

Physical communities and a strong sense of a community are essentials for surviving and prospering in a competitive, group-based society. Today, across America, Blacks have neighborhoods instead of communities. A

---

[20]Hacker, Andrew. *Two Nations: Black and White, Separate, Hostile, Unequal*, Charles Scribner's Sons, New York, 1992, pgs. 36-38.

community is where a group lives, works, learns, competes and thrives. It is where they store their valuables, history, culture, businesses, jobs and functional schools. Black neighborhoods are like buckets with holes in them. They are porous and do not hold in things of value. A neighborhood is dysfunctional, crime-ridden, impoverished and transitory in nature.

As world societies become increasingly more competitive and nationalistic, for the survival of Black America as a group it must also become competitive by building functional communities. When the first European immigrants entered this country one of the first things they did was build their respective ethnic communities within which they lived, worked, learned, competed and thrived. As the integration movement of the 1950s emerged, White ethnics became fearful that Blacks would move into their small, ethnic communities and overwhelm them. So, they rallied around their strength, their greatest commonality, which was not ethnicity. It was their skin color. They sought to strengthen themselves against Blacks and social integration by abandoning their separate ethnic communities and assimilating into a larger group, the national community of oneness and Whiteness. Then, as a national community, they were able to protect themselves from Black Americans' march toward social integration and a color-blind society.

Just like European Whites surrendered their ethnicity, came together and built a national White community, Black Americans could come together for group strength as a national Black community and cease pursuing social integration. However, to convert neighborhoods into communities and bring back Blacks who no longer live in Black neighborhoods, the targeted areas must have certain things.

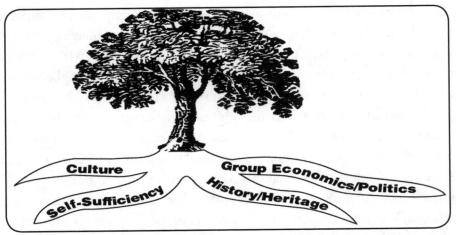

"Community Tree of Life." Source: PowerNomics Corporation of America, Inc. Like a tree, a community must have healthy roots to survive, compete and prosper.

The following are the key elements that a community must have:

1) Support of those who do not live there but identify with and support the physical community;

2) An alternative, wholly independent business district that produces goods, services, wealth, jobs and business opportunities for its own residents and supporters;

3) A unifying code of conduct that conditions residents to protect, respect, care for, buy from and support members of their own community;

4) A form of governance with public officials or community representatives who advocate for and defend the collective interests of the community once it is established; and most importantly;

5) A functional Black community must be marked and identified with distinctive signs to denote that it as valuable and closed

to destructive activities, such as drugs, prostitution and garbage dumping. Marking a community occurs when towns, buildings, street signs, expressways, airports, parks and public statues are named to reflect the community residents and their culture.

Before the integration process began in the 1950s, Blacks had notable towns and quasi-communities, which, if nurtured instead of destroyed, could have become functional communities. There was Harlem in New York, Black Bottom in Detroit, Watts in Los Angeles, Sweet Auburn in Atlanta and many more throughout the country. Within those communities Blacks operated businesses, schools, churches and social organizations. They stored wealth, culture artifacts, jobs, history, political capital, business opportunities, spiritual values, middle-class values and produced Black leaders. Blacks patronized, cared for and worked with their own people.

Jim Crow segregation had a positive side for Blacks. It provided a nurturing place for their quasi-communities and the businesses, culture and other institutions stored inside. They were not perfect, but these quasi-communities were valuable and were at a midway point in development. De jure laws forced Blacks to have a sense of oneness and an internal cohesiveness. It was during segregation that Black businesses and industries bloomed across this nation. One hundred years ago, during Jim Crow segregation, Blacks reportedly owned 10 times more businesses than they own today. Social integration stripped Black communities and removed the physical places where all classes of Blacks could live and work together, whether they were doctors, teachers, bus drivers, business owners, lawyers or janitors. Today, Blacks do not have the role models next door, business ownership, the jobs those businesses produced for their own people, and they are no longer in control of their culture, because they no longer have communities or a sense of community. In such a state, it is difficult, if not impossible for Black Americans to communicate, organize and compete as a team. Racism is a team sport and competing in a race-based society must be a team effort built around a group's strong self-interest and need for self-preservation.

Unlike Black Americans, non-White ethnic immigrants see the value of coming together as a group and do not pursue the scattering integration process. They know there is strength and camaraderie in numbers. Instead, newly-arriving immigrants aggressively seek out their compatriots, old friends and families to form social and commercial networks. Their ethnic enclaves become culturally-protected markets from which they draw business financing, a skills bank and a consumer support group. An ethnic enclave or physical community gives a group a primary area in which to aggregate their businesses, cultural products and employment opportunities.

As an example, when Vietnamese refugees arrived in the U.S., the federal government, in an effort to encourage social integration, physically scattered the Vietnamese immigrants in settlements throughout the country. It was difficult for the Vietnamese to adjust and assimilate as a new minority in a majority White society. According to Richard T. Schaefer's book, *Racial and Ethnic Groups*, the U.S. government's attempt to socially integrate the Vietnamese refugees failed because the refugees sought out their compatriots and reunited, built their own communities, and once again established the sense of community they had in their home country. Where individual Vietnamese lived outside of a Vietnamese physical community, their *sense of community* energized them to commute long distances to support and purchase products from Vietnamese-owned businesses and maintain social and religious connections. Their communities gave them a place to grow and gain strength. The second and third generations may assimilate into Whiteness, but they gain strength from and remain connected to their group.

Residential areas in which Blacks are the majority population ought to model their communities using ethnic immigrant enclaves as models. Without communities or a sense of community, Black businesses will have no primary consumer market for their products and services. Unlike neighborhoods left opened and abandoned, Black communities should be marked, closed and monitored. Just like Beverly Hills, Chinatown, Korea

Town or Little Mexico, marking and closing a community signifies not only a sense of pride and security, but also connotes that it is valuable turf. Once closed, ethnic enclaves are culturally marked. For instance, ethnics may mark their turf by changing the names of buildings, erecting statues, or displaying signs and symbols that reflect their culture. In urban centers, in which Blacks have been the dominant population for centuries, major streets and buildings are still named after prominent slaveholders. Blacks rarely mark or close their territory, allowing access to interlopers who are able to disrespect and exploit the area.

Before Blacks were able to move into White neighborhoods, they enjoyed some of the benefits of Black cohesiveness. They built and operated their own community-based business districts across the nation. Though Black business districts may have been smaller than White business districts, they provided a number of jobs, products, services, pride and safe sanctuaries for Blacks. When the integration process began, many Blacks did not see the value of staying together as a group, pooling their resources and buying from their own businesses. Nor did they see the greater political and economic importance of having their own communities and business districts. So, they allowed those valuable foundations to be destroyed in the name of social integration and political correctness. They jumped on the bandwagon with White liberals who convinced them it was better to be in close, physical proximity to Whites than to each other. They chose to be politically correct and voluntarily destroyed the positive foundation of the Black communities that they had worked so hard to build for themselves after slavery.

Today, it is amazing to see the opinion makers again pushing a politically correct view that proclaims that all classes of people are equal to Black Americans and there is nothing special about how Blacks have been historically treated in this country. The reality of the matter is that, as a group, Blacks are locked onto the bottom rung of the social and economic ladder, they are scattered and they are not like any other group. Blacks are a special people with an exceptional history. Black Americans need functional residential communities and business districts in which to gain and store wealth and political power. Strategies for community building are discussed in my book, *PowerNomics®: The National Plan to Empower Black America.*

Question 15. Should Black Americans practice socioeconomics as a team?

Group-based socioeconomics is essential for success within our race-based competitive society, in which Blacks are over-burdened by poverty and powerlessness. Wealth and power follow numerical dominance and in our society the majority wins. Therefore, Blacks must Ethno-aggregate, or pool as great a number of resources as they can, whatever the category—consumer dollars, votes, economics—and work together as a team. Remember, racism is the power of one group, Whites, to control the lives and opportunities of another group, Blacks. The word racism came from the economics of slavery. The economic and social injustices racism imposed on Blacks because of their skin color are now institutionalized. Blacks must work together as a socioeconomic team.

Although the historical social construct consigned Blacks to the lowest levels in society, they have a chance to win if they organize into a functioning socioeconomic team totally committed to gaining group political and wealth power just as Whites and other groups have done for centuries. But there are obstacles. Contrary to the socioeconomic practices of other groups, many members of the Black race don't want to play as a team. Too many prefer to support others teams rather than their own team. They are adverse to their own skin-color uniform. There are also some Blacks who take pride in denigrating and sabotaging efforts of conscious Blacks who struggle to socioeconomically elevate the Black race. Such inappropriate behaviors impede Blacks from winning a team-based competition or even getting scores on the socioeconomic score-board. In a race-based society, team playing is essential and the groups with the best chances of winning will be those that keep the most control over their own fate and fulfill their self-interest first.

From this country's very founding, Whites have prospered militarily, politically, economically, educationally and racially because their team spirit empowered them. Whiteness is a unifying concept defined by the social construct as the race that holds group-based power that can be used over out-groups like native Blacks and Native Americans. The central purpose of the social construct on race was to enrich only members of the White team with wealth and power. The White team members were classified as first-class citizens. Blacks were classified first as property, later as second-class citizens and lastly as a group that refuses to play as a team. Although Whites have historically operated as a skin-color team, they have had an underlying foreboding that one day Blacks might wake up and also begin playing as a race-based team.

The racial social construct *required* that Whites operate as a team for mutual tangible and intangible benefits. Whites as a team established the slave trade, crafted the nation's founding documents, maintained Black subordination and Jim Crow segregation. Whites denied and controlled Black education and kept Blacks illiterate for centuries by design, over-saw the legal and extra-legal organizations that abused and criminalized Blacks, regulated the political system, Wall Street stock markets, nearly all major businesses, the media, real-estate, and international affairs as the White team. The White code of conduct was so powerful that Blacks could never be any more nor any less than what the White society needed or wanted Blacks to be. Consequently, Whites play as a team with an accountability code of conduct. To the contrary, Blacks play as individuals, with uneven team spirit and no code of conduct. As a result, Blacks have yet to win a game whether they compete against gender, ethnic, or simply poor White groups who play as teams.

Knowing that power and wealth tends to follow the numbers, Whites generally prefer to interact with Blacks by keeping them as a non-threatening non-competitive minority. As an example, when the prospects of the integration of professional sports arose, Whites were fearful of integrating existing professional Black baseball, basketball and football teams into the existing White professional leagues. The social integration process meant Black sports teams were required to disappear, to disband and to release hundreds of the best players in the sports world so that White players could dominate and their teams could hire one or two Black players.

Politics offers another example. White fear of Blacks as a team permeated major political decisions. According to a national poll, on the eve of the Civil War, 98 percent of Whites were fearful of and opposed freeing Black slaves. After the Civil War, Whites in the North did not want ex-slaves to migrate North. A century later, 75 percent of White Americans were still opposed to, and felt Blacks were moving too quickly into social integration. Recently, in 2010, national opinion and public attitude polls indicated that 63 percent of Whites and other groups had negative feelings about Blacks and they did not like and did not want to be around Blacks. While there are Black/White friendships on an individual basis, the majority of Whites oppose and are fearful of advances by Blacks as a group.

Liberals generally conceive of progress in race relations as the one-to-one assimilation of deserving Black individuals. However, in a race-based, society, wealth and power align with the numbers and follow the social construct on race. While Whites venerate individualism, they play as a team. Their individual accomplishments contribute to the power and influence of the White team. Blacks on the other hand, do not play as a team. Individualism does not work for them in the same way it does for Whites and other groups. The social construct on race is historically restrictive. It allows Blacks to benefit, only individually and as an exception. It will not allow individual Black accomplishments to lift the group out of its bottom status. Blacks were enslaved, impoverished and made powerless as a group. Therefore, individual Black accomplishments, while important, do not make it easier for the group to compete in the market place, the political arena or any other place in which group solidarity is strength. Individual Black accomplishments tend to stay just that. The benefits do not accrue to the group.

Now is an opportune time for Blacks to change the social construct on race and to choose a new path in order to achieve a new outcome, one of prosperity and unity. They must acknowledge their history and make their own sustained effort to chart a new reality for themselves and their children. That was the intent of *PowerNomics®: The National Plan to Empower Black America*[21], to offer a guide to purposeful change based on group-based strengths and competitive advantages. Immigrant groups such as Asians, Hispanics and Arabs are out-groups for a short time. They demonstrate socioeconomic teamwork in the way they link their businesses to their physical communities and to a sense of community. It is beneficial for Blacks who wish to build a strong competitive team to study the success of immigrant groups who practice nationalism and cooperative economics and model a number of useful practices that Blacks could use to create a new social construct and build a socioeconomic team.

To build a socioeconomic team, the following strategies could be useful to Blacks:

1. Think of your group as a nation within a nation in America;

2. Reduce consumption of goods and services produced and sold by competing groups and increase spending with Black-owned businesses;

3. Build businesses and industries around competitive advantages of the group, for example, Blacks are the only source of Black hair, therefore, their team should control the entire Black hair care industry from manufacturing to salon and other retail sales. Similarly, Blacks should have vertical control of all music they create from production, distribution to the music halls of fame.

---

[21]Anderson, Claud. *PowerNomics®: The National Plan to Empower Black America*, PowerNomics® Corporation of America, Inc., Maryland, 2001, pgs. 190-192.

4. Increase individual savings and create group saving mechanisms such as investment clubs or susus (money pools or informal loan clubs common in the Caribbean and Asian countries).

Pooling resources and dominating in business wherever you dominate in population or consumer spending patterns are PowerNomics® principles that can guide Black America to success as a socioeconomic team. It is the only way that Black America can work within the realities of racism and transform the historical economic disadvantages of being Black into advantages.

Question 16. How are demographics changing in majority Black urban cities?

In the 21st century, the majority White population is in the midst of recapturing urban cities through a combination of gentrification, privatization and immigration, initiatives used in urban cities to displace Blacks, to push them out and to push those who remain, into minority status with no power. Major political and economic efforts across the nation are systematically redeveloping those cities into comfortable havens for affluent Whites and ethnic immigrants who are taking over the assets of urban cities.

Since the early 1980s, city planners took the lead from social conservatives and initiated specific projects to attract Whites, under the guise of attracting new money to major urban centers, which had become majority Black during the 1960s and 1970s civil rights movement. The key strategies of gentrification and privatization offer returning Whites incentives such as cheap residential and commercial property and ownership and control of public-owned assets—bridges, museums, school buildings, airports, bridges, golf courses, parks, waterfront property and anything that could be used to generate capital. The Black elected officials, business leaders, ministers, civil rights leaders and celebrities often cooperate with and encourage these asset transfers from Black control to White control.

From Washington, D.C. to Chicago and in Black-dominated cities across the nation, it is easily observed that social and economic conditions have caused life to regress to a jungle like existence. Many hold the disquieting belief that Black Americans squandered their chances to build, maintain and manage urban cities, but there is more to the story than the contemporary snapshot. After riots, racial disturbances and as the integration movement took hold, about 50 years ago, Whites began to flee urban areas and to cede control. They moved their families to the suburbs and took with them everything they owned. Blacks began to gain limited control over those cities but White flight had drained the essential resources. By the time Blacks took control, the cities were weakened and poor. Although abandoned by Whites, urban cities are situated in desirable locations with many natural assets such as rivers, ports and other amenities, which led to their selection as major population centers in the first place. Whites eventually wanted to regain control and that process is in full swing.

The first generation of Black urban politicians that had control of cities came in the mid 1960s and for the most part were determined, pro-Black personalities, but they did not have the resources to manage and maintain the cities. The following generation of Black elected officials tended to have color-blind attitudes and began to work along with Whites who wanted to regain the cities that they had given up. The most successful strategy to recapture control of the cities was to ignore Black city dwellers and to elect Black or White officials with color-blind attitudes about race. Invoking concepts such as minority, diversity, color-blind and people of color makes any form of Blackness invisible. Blacks do not seem to notice that when politicians use the color-blind strategy, Blacks are not even mentioned; they are ignored and, for all practical purposes, disappear, except for photo-ops. When Blacks disappear, then politicians and development can literally be color-blind. The sleight of hand trick is performed in full view of Blacks who are watching, but do not seem to notice that they no longer exist.

When Black elected officials inherited control of the urban cities amid White flight to the suburbs, the urban centers began to deteriorate because of scorched earth policies. Fleeing Whites took everything they owned and controlled out of cities. Black mayors inherited the cities but not the financial resources. All but the first generation of Black mayors also lacked the vision to use the opportunity to build those cities into strong Black competitive economies. In addition to Whites leaving the city, related social phenomena began to weave into the pattern. The Highway Transportation Act of 1956 routed and built expressways right through Black business districts and Black communities, destroying them. A few years later, urban renewal, more popularly called Black removal, finished off the Black businesses and the Black middle-class communities in the cities. As Whites moved, Blacks became the majority population and elected Black mayors and city councils. Black mayors did not destroy the urban centers. The White response to integration did the trick.

The immigration onslaught stared at about the same time. After the 1965 Immigration Act, immigrants from Mexico, South America, Asia and the Pacific Islands flooded into the cities and further displaced Blacks in what had been their communities. The Black middle-class had many pressures. With their businesses and homes demolished, they made the choice to abandon their own cities, their own people, the land they controlled in the city and the potential for building competitive Black businesses, industries and functional communities capable of practicing capitalism. They followed the White middle-class into the suburbs that surrounded major urban cities. The exodus of the Black middle-class left the Black masses leaderless, divided and incapable of competing with an endless influx of ethnic immigrants.

These social forces will make Black Americans a minority underclass in what were once majority Black urban centers. It is unlikely that a second chance for control will ever happen again. As Whites return to revitalized urban areas, they will flush Blacks out and force them to the aging suburbs, which will become the new Black ghettos. The combined effects of gentrification and privatization in urban centers will fix Blacks in the ranking order at nearly the same level they were in 100 years earlier. Whites and other ethnics, who receive approximately 98 percent of Black Americans' annual disposable income, take comfort in the non-competitiveness of Black Americans and are reassured that racism and the nation's social construct is working as designed.

PART IV

The Dark Side of the Constitution

Question 17. Why did the Founding Fathers use ambiguous terms to refer to Blacks in the U.S. Constitution?

Thomas Jefferson and James Madison, the primary drafters of the U.S. Constitution and Bill of Rights, had no intentions of providing freedom and the blessings of liberty to Black people. They sanctioned, codified and institutionalized Black slavery into this nation's founding documents. Jefferson, Madison and other drafters of the Constitution carefully avoided using the words *slaves, Negroes* or *Blacks.* They intentionally used broad and ambiguous terms to disguise and minimize debate about the caste system they were creating. Moreover, they wanted to avoid leaving fingerprints in those documents that specifically identified the human beings who would be enslaved, dehumanized, exploited, crippled and killed[22]. So, they agreed to use broad euphemisms to distinguish White Europeans immigrants who would be granted rights and opportunities from the millions of Blacks who were being imported into lifetime enslavement and suffering.

The dictionary definition of euphemism is *substitution of a mild indirect or vague expression for one thought to be offensive, harsh or blunt.* When writing about Black slaves or aspects of slavery, the founders used euphemisms such as *those who are bound, those who are indebted, those in servitude, those who are bonded, such persons, all other persons, that unhappy lot* and *that species of property.* When a particular constitutional provision applied to Blacks only, sometimes the founders used another obfuscating

---

[22]Davis, Kenneth. *Don't Know Much About History*, HarperCollins Publisher, New York, 2003, p. 114.

technique. Instead of saying the provision applied to Blacks, they listed all of the groups to whom the provision did *not* apply. When referring to European Whites, the Founders used broad but different terms such as, *we the people, all the people, free person, immigrants* and *American citizens.*

Jefferson, Madison and the other framers spent the first week of the Philadelphia Convention discussing the necessity of the caste system they were putting in place legally, and the importance of choosing langauge to offuscate their intentions. The framers also wanted Blacks and slavery obscured to avoid looking like hypocrites while preaching freedom, democracy and equal justice to the rest of the world. But they were convinced that this nation could only develop and prosper with free Black labor, which would be the heart and soul of the evolving nation. Therefore, the nation's most sacred documents—the U.S. Constitution and the Declaration of Independence—were inspired and shaped by the most notoriously inhumane institution in world history. To the authors of this nation's founding documents, Black slaves were an absolute necessity and also represented personal wealth and the country's greatest natural resource, though never acknowledged in public documents.

The attending delegates swore an oath of secrecy and James Madison even refused to allow his notes of the meetings to become public until after his death. The founders did not want Madison's notes to reveal that slavery had dominated the internal discussions or the nature of those discussions. The conflict was whether to state specifically that Blacks were not included in the benefit of this new country, or to define the rights and privileges they were institutionalizing, as specific to and applicable to Whites only. They finally concluded that they could resolve the issues by simply using broad and ambiguous terms in the document to identify which groups were included and which were excluded from constitutional benefits and protections. The founders wanted to protect Whites as well as their own reputations and the drafting of the U.S. Constitution. They did not want to be judged as duplicitous or the Constitution they drafted as hypocritical, proclaiming freedom and democracy for Whites while at the same time establishing a *peculiar institution* for Blacks.

The record does not indicate that even one delegate demanded that Blacks have the same rights as Whites to pursue life, liberty and *property* (later changed to happiness) in the developing nation. The debates were heated and divisive. However, Jefferson and Madison prevailed, arguing that, "It would be better not to stain the Constitution with the word *slaves*." Instead, they decided to make a low key approach in identifying the victims. Nearly a century later, conservatives of the U.S. Congress employed that same tactic in writing the 13th, 14th and 15th Amendments to the Constitution. In the 1960s, again conservative policy makers persuaded Congress to use broad, ambiguous terms to avoid specifying the benefits and rights targeted to Black Americans. The pattern of using euphemisms to obscure intent is entrenched in the nation's polity.

Historical patterns can only be recognized if you know history. Again, during the 1960s Black Civil Rights Movement, conservatives and liberals alike used euphemisms to misdirect Black leaders into accepting the designation of Blacks into broad and ambiguous categories such as diversity, minorities, multicultural and people of color. How ironic it is that Black civil rights leaders, elected officials, ministers or liberals seldom seem to recognize the euphemism tactic, perfected centuries earlier, that specifically rendered Black people invisible. Conservatives instituted the use of broad and ambiguous terms to halt the Black Power movement in the early 1970s and were totally surprised that neither Black leadership or White liberals objected. Instead, Blacks leading the movement adopted and supported the transition in public policies from Black to broad euphemisms. The Black leaders quietly gave in to political correctness and Benign Neglect policies and presided over the shift from Black to broad groupings which displaced and rendered Black Americans null and void. Those who were leading may have grown tired, frustrated and even afraid, but they bear responsibility for misdirecting and not speaking up for Blacks in public policy formulations. The obfuscation technique introduced by the Founding Fathers in drafting the first U.S. Constitution has been successfully employed in the legal aspect of race matters through the present day.

Question 18. Why were Black slaves classified as three-fifths of a human?

Blacks were classified as three-fifths of a human to settle a battle between Northern and Southern legislators over the rights of states and the status of slaves as property[23]. In 1820, slaveholders wanted to bring Missouri into the union as a slaveholding state. Northern legislators feared that if Missouri entered as a slaveholding state, with a significantly large number of slaves, the Southern states could outnumber the Northern states in congressional representation and taxation based on property wealth. The Southern states had the lion's share of the nation's slave population, which was legally classified as personal property equal to field animals. Southern slaveholders opposed paying assets and property taxes on Black slaves. However, when it came to counting state voting populations to determine a state's number of representatives in the Congressional and Electoral College, slaveholders demanded that their slaves be counted as human voters even though they were not permitted to vote. The Missouri Compromise of 1820 consummated between Southern and Northern states, granted several advantages to the South. The South would pay no property taxes on Black slaves and could count them as three-fifths of a human being for voting and congressional representation. This three-fifths solution was a compromise so favorable to the South, and granted the region so much political power, that it dominated and controlled the U.S. Congress for nearly two centuries.

Modern day Black Americans remain highly sensitive to the fact that their ancestors were classified as only three-fifths of a human being. For Black Americans, the three-fifths of a person provision added insult to the injuries that 360 years of enslavement as field animals had inflicted on them. The actual language of the Missouri Compromise, found in Section 2 of the U.S. Constitution says, "Representatives and direct taxes

---

[23]Foner, Eric. *The Story of American Freedom*, W.W. Norton & Company, New York, 1994, pgs. 35-36.

shall be apportioned among the several states which may be included within this Union, according to their respective numbers, which shall be determined by adding to the whole number of free persons, including those bound to service for a term of years, excluding Native Indians not taxed, three-fifths of all other persons."

This section of the Constitution is also an example of the skill of the Founding Fathers in framing slavery and its rules without even a mention of the word. The South also used the leverage from their non-voting Black population to elect White politicians to public office, then used the Black body count against them by electing and sending to Congress representatives who would use their office to maintain White superiority and control in the South. It is noted that the three-fifths provision applied only to Blacks. It did not apply to indentured servants, White women, children, Native Indians, Asians, Hispanics or any group included in today's fabricated classes of minorities.

In general, the Missouri Compromise of 1820[24] injured Black Americans in at least three different ways. The Compromise allowed Missouri to: 1) enter the Union as a slave holding Southern state; 2) allow Black slaves to be counted as part of the total population; and 3) establish an Electoral College system that reduced the power of the popular vote in national elections. Since the 1820s, Southern states had been able to out-number the North in electoral votes and could wield enough regional political power to win most presidential elections and control the U.S. Congress. When the Founding Fathers were debating the Missouri Compromise, James Madison, a slaveholder, described the crux of the dilemma when he said that unifying the states, without Blacks being counted as three-fifths of a human presented, "difficulty... of a serious nature." As part of the compromise, Madison proposed a prototype Electoral College system, which is the very same system we have today, the system that proclaimed Donald Trump and four

---

[24]Goldstone, Lawrence. *Dark Bargain: Slavery, Profits, and the Struggle for the Constitution*, Walker & Company, 2005, pgs. 194, 195.

previous presidential candidates, President of the United States, even though they lost the nation's popular votes. While slavery was supposedly abolished in the 1860s, and Black ex-slaves were granted voting rights, the Electoral College system remains intact and linked to red Southern and conservative states, which continue to count on Black bodies to win elected offices, but avoid representing Black interests in race matters and seldom provide Blacks with tangible benefits to improve their quality of life. With the increasing influence of conservatives, there is a chance that the entire United States of America just may again become all Southern as it did when the Civil War ended in the 1860s.

Question 19. Is the 13th Amendment legal according to the U.S. Constitution and did it end slavery?

The approval of the 13th Amendment did not occur in accordance with the constitutionally mandated process and consequently, many legal scholars question the amendment's legitimacy. The amendment was approved by a Civil War Congress, but before it could be included into the U.S. Constitution, ratification was required by three-fourths of the duly elected state legislatures. Therein lays the problem. That step was never completed. When the Civil War ended in 1865, the U.S. consisted of 35 states—24 were Union and 11 were formerly a part of the old Southern Confederacy. Congress therefore needed 27 states to ratify the 13th Amendment. Since two Union states—Kentucky and Delaware— rejected the 13th Amendment, Congress needed the remaining 22 Union states, plus five Confederate states. At that time, the 11 Confederate states were in total political disarray in the aftermath of the Civil War. The Southern states had no *duly elected* federal or state representatives in office, and even if those officials had been in place, they would have refused to ratify the 13th Amendment which was crafted to officially end slavery and free nearly five million Blacks.

How did the Northern Union respond to the disarray in the Southern states and secure the mandated number of elected state officials? The U.S. Congress used its legislative power to install Union military commanders in the needed eight Southern states to function as judiciaries in the absence of duly elected state legislators. Congress authorized the Union military commanders to cast the needed *yes votes*. The military troops pulled out a few years later. Their yes votes on the 13th Amendment were generally accepted, but it appears that they were never recalculated and ratification by duly elected legislators in those Southern states.

The second concern about legitimacy emanates from a parenthetical clause in the 13th Amendment. When the Civil War ended, plantations and farmlands were returned to the previous White owners who again needed unpaid or cheap labor to work the land. White European immigrants were unwilling to migrate to the South and compete with Black labor for low wage jobs. The 13th Amendment provided a partial answer for the South's renewed need for unpaid or new forms of slave labor. It contained a claw-back provision, that allowed White society to re-enslave Blacks. The 13th Amendment reads, "Neither slavery nor involuntary servitude, *except as a punishment for crime whereof the party shall have been duly convicted*, shall exist within the United States." Beginning in the 1860s, following emancipation, every Southern state enacted an array of interlocking laws intended to criminalize people with Black skin, in general, and Black men, in particular, and to legalize Black re-enslavement. It was totally understood that the new Jim Crow segregation laws and Black code provisions were targeting Blacks and would rarely, if ever be enforced on Whites. The parenthetical clause in the 13th Amendment was used to return Whites to total political control and Blacks to their former low-level position in society.

Whites, as symbols of authority, could criminalize Blacks by merely charging that a Black violated the White code of etiquette. The whole code of etiquette was informal and included requirements that made it criminal for Blacks to dispute a White person, count change in front of them, look down on them or look a White person in the eye, speak to a White person with your hat on, step off of the sidewalk to let a White person pass, own a more valuable house, land or automobile than a White person, call a White person a liar, be in the presence of a White woman in the absence of a White male or to express familiarity with a White woman. The list of what was considered a criminal act if violated, was endless. Perceived violations of the Southern code of etiquette could easily cost a Black person his freedom or life. There were hundreds of thousands of instances, in which a Black person, charged with having committed a crime or violating a code of etiquette was beaten, run out of town or lynched. If a public authority simply said a Black person was guilty of a crime, whether the crime was fabricated or not, that person would be imprisoned and used as free labor. Taking advantage of that impactful parenthetical clause, the Southern states, and their local communities enacted the Black Codes and Black peonage laws that instituted the system of Jim Crow segregation and subjected Blacks to another 100 years of semi-slavery. Like codes of etiquette, the Black Codes criminalized Blacks, making it a crime to be homeless, unemployed, not to have on their person a written contract to work for a White person, especially during planting and harvest times. Peonage laws allowed a person to be held in servitude or partial slavery so they could work off a debt or serve a penal sentence. A common charge was the failure to pay a debt to a White person or to be caught carrying a firearm or weapon.

Once arrested and charged, the court system would typically follow up an arrest with no more than a kangaroo trial. In many instances, trials were denied altogether, but the end result was always the same. Blacks, especially men, were sentenced to long prison terms, sometimes for their entire lives. Incarcerated Black persons were assigned into public road gangs. It was not unusual for prisons to loan out Blacks to local businesses, farmers and White households. The practice of creating a free pool of labor by incarcerating Blacks for breaking frivolous laws continued from Reconstruction well into the 1960s. In the 21st century, private prisons are common and constitute a lucrative business in which thousands of corporations and businesses profit by using prisoners to replace paid employees. So, was the 13th Amendment to the U.S.

Constitution legitimate? Ask those Black men who were re-enslaved and their families, and the scholars who will always wonder to what extent they should draw attention to the improper ratification process of the U.S. Constitution.

Question 20. What nuclear option did the 14th Amendment grant Black voters?

Believe it or not, Black Americans are the only citizens for whom the U.S. Congress enacted specific laws that assured Black citizens could vote, and imposed punishments on states if those voting rights were interfered with or abridged. The 14th Amendment provided safeguards to Black voting rights. Section 2 of the 14th Amendment to the U.S. Constitution says,

> "*When the right to vote at any election for the choice of electors for President or Vice President of the United States, Representatives in Congress, the executive and judicial officers of a state or the members of the legislature thereof, is denied to any of the [Black] male inhabitants of such state, being 21 years of age, and citizens of the United States, or in any way are abridged…the basis of representation therein shall be reduced in the proportion which the number of such male citizens shall bear to the whole number of male citizens 21 years of age in such state*[25]*.*"

This provision means that a state in which there were efforts to suppress the Black vote would lose elected representation in national, state and local elections. Black voters have been intimidated, harassed,

---

[25]Lazare, Daniel. *The Frozen Republic: How the Constitution is Paralyzing Democracy*, Houghton Mifflin Harcourt, 1 ed., January 1996, pgs. 329-330.

denied the right and even killed to prevent them from voting. They have marched, protested and filed lawsuits, but in over a century, this provision has never been used and no state has ever suffered any consequences. I call this provision of the 14th Amendment a *nuclear option* because while it would require a complex mathematical formula to implement, it would provide such a powerful punishment tool that once used, voter suppression would stop.

Blacks are this nation's only *planned* minority. Whites outnumber Black voters nine to one. No other population group has been continuously harassed and denied voting rights. Free White male citizens over 21 years of age have always had the right to vote. So have White female property owners. Even White females who did not own property were allowed to vote with enactment of the 19th Amendment in 1919, which by the way, did not grant the same unfettered voting rights to Black female voters. Section 2 of the 14th Amendment should have been a tool to prevent the actions of White conservatives or extra-legal groups such as the Ku Klux Klan, who sought to deny the Black vote, regardless of gender.

The haunting question then is, why hasn't this option ever been used? Did Blacks not know about this provision? Did they know about it, yet chose not to invoke it because they feared repercussions from Whites? Do conservative Whites know about this provision? If so, why would they risk the consequences of losing elected representation?[26] For 150 years, conservative Whites have employed intense efforts to suppress Black votes. When Blacks are a planned minority and make up only 12 percent of the population, why do Whites continue their efforts? If every Black man, woman and child could vote, which is not even possible, the maximum voting impact of the group could not exceed 12 percent. Do conservative political forces engage in various superficial voter suppression schemes simply to deflect the attention of Blacks away

---

[26]Black, Eric. *Our Constitution: The Myth that Binds Us*, Westview Press, Boulder, Colorado, 1988, pgs. 90-91.

from substantive issues such as the Constitution's social construct on race or the historical mal-distribution of nearly 100 percent of this nation's resources away from Blacks? Blacks have put aggressive effort into voting activities—registration, getting out the vote, enthusiastically supporting candidates who promise them nothing—but they have never exercised the nuclear option of the 14th Amendment to secure their right to vote.

Black voters should replace marching, praying and begging for the right to vote with understanding, planning and using Section 2 of the 14th Amendment. If Blacks could get the nation's attention by using the nuclear option, they could then redirect their own focus from voting to the more fundamental issues of economics and demand corrections. Those demands could include reform to immigration policies to reduce the harm it causes to native Blacks, industrialization of Black urban areas, building functional schools for Blacks, enforcing the 1866 Indian Treaties and providing reparations in some form. The nuclear option in voting could be used as leverage to correct other structural issues as well.

Question 21. Does the U.S. Supreme Court have the constitutional power to overrule Congress in Black civil rights issues?

The U.S. Supreme Court does not actually have the right to override actions by the U.S. Congress in Black civil rights matters or other provisions intended by Congress to protect vulnerable and impoverished Black ex-slaves. The U.S. Constitution defines the task of the U.S. Supreme Court[27] as threefold: 1) to decide appeals from trials held in lower courts; 2) to get involved in the appointment of ambassadors and finally; 3) to rule in cases in which a federal official failed to carry out his duties. Nowhere does the U.S. Constitution authorize the Supreme

---

[27]Black, Eric. *Our Constitution: The Myth that Binds Us*, Westview Press, Boulder, Colorado, 1988, pgs. 65-68.

Court to overrule or second-guess Congress or to act as a third level of government. Congress passed laws regarding slavery, the former slaves and race. However, the U.S. Supreme Court has been rendering decisions on race, mostly anti-Black, for centuries. The Court invented its authority to overrule the U.S. Congress over 200 years ago. Surprisingly, there have not been any legal challenges to the Court's assumed authority in race matters.

The first time the Court assumed authority to rule on acts of Congress was in the year 1803 in *Marbury v. Madison*. In this landmark case, the U.S. Supreme Court overruled a law passed by Congress and declared it unconstitutional. Since then, the Court has bolstered its power by promoting itself as the supreme law of the land. In the democracy of the U.S., the Supreme Court was allowed to become an unelected third branch of government, a body of life-tenured biased individuals who made no pretense of neutrality in race or political matters.

A few prominent personalities of that day did take issue with and questioned the Court's right to assume overriding authority, but the effort eventually waned. The Court and its authority came under scrutiny 54 years later when Chief Justice Roger Taney and his fellow jurists, all White, wealthy, slaveholders and supporters of slavery, issued their infamous 1857 Dred Scott decision, just three years before the beginning of the American Civil War. The legal issue was over Dred Scott, a slave who claimed that he was free because he had traveled to a free state. The U.S. Supreme Court slaveholders ruled, "A Black man has no rights that a White man is bound to respect." Further, the Court restated the sentiment of the Constitution, that Black people were property, equal to field animals, and as property, the owner of the property held the rights, not the Black man. Even though the Court professed to be objective, fair and honorable, how could slaveholding jurists make a just decision? Although the conflict of interest of the justices was clear and their decision not neutral, the Supreme Court was within the parameters of the law because at that time nothing within the Constitution gave rights to Black people. The Dred Scott decision had far-reaching effects and it has never been overturned. The sentiment of that decision, that a Black man has no rights a White man is bound to respect is infused in the culture. It is on display today in many ways, including the numerous conflicts between law enforcement and the Black community.

Following the Civil War of the 1860s, a number of Radical Republicans (the liberals of the day) attempted to reverse the Supreme Court's Dred Scott decision by enacting the 13th, 14th and 15th Amendments to the Constitution and passing civil rights laws specifically to aid and protect the newly-freed Black slaves[28]. On the floor of Congress, Senator Charles Sumner proclaimed slavery to be an economic issue and said there were only two things that Blacks could ever be in America. They could be slaves or they could be free. But, they were released from slavery with nothing, therefore to be free, at a minimum, they had to have 40 acres of land, a mule and $100. The land, the mule and the money were the essential tools necessary to make the economic transition from slavery to independent living. Without all three, the slaves would always be in some form of enslavement. The Radical Republicans enacted the 1865 and 1866 Civil Rights Laws to assure Blacks a minimum level of economic assets. President Andrew Johnson, who replaced Abraham Lincoln after his death, vetoed both bills, but was over-ridden by Congress on the 1866 Civil Rights Law. To ensure Black civil rights, their ability to be economically competitive with Whites and to protect Blacks from being re-enslaved, Radical Republicans enacted the 14th Amendment to the U.S. Constitution. The 14th Amendment confirmed the citizenship of former Black slaves and forbade anyone to deprive them of their rights to be treated in a manner that Whites would be treated under similar circumstances. This is the equal protection and due process provision that was specifically enacted for newly-freed Black people. These provisions were not designed to benefit immigrants or fabricated *minority* classes.

---

[28]Fireside, Harvey. *Separate and Unequal: Homer Plessy and the Supreme Court Decision that Legalized Racism*, Hatchett Book Group, New York, 2009, pgs. 21-22.

Whites and other groups were granted their rights under the 5th Amendment of the U.S. Constitution.

The Supreme Court, as the self-appointed guardian of the racial status quo and champion of White superiority, went on the offense and crossed over the line[29]. Before the Civil War, the Constitution gave no rights to Blacks and the Court did not have authority to overrule Congress in issues related to the Black race. However, in the mid-1860s, following the Civil War, Radical Republicans had sufficient political power to enact three constitutional amendments and civil rights laws to give Blacks rights and to reverse the Dred Scott decision. At this point, Radical Republicans were too strong for the Supreme Court. However, a decade later, in the mid-1870s, the Court assumed authority and ended the Reconstruction Period by ruling that all the civil rights laws that Congress enacted for Blacks in the 1870s were unconstitutional. The U.S. Supreme Court ended Civil War Reconstruction and laid the foundation for the re-enslavement of Black people. With the Southern states needing Blacks in peonage and semi-slavery and the North not wanting Black ex-slaves to migrate into the North, there was no resistance to the Court fully establishing itself as a co-equal branch of the federal government along with the Executive and Congressional branches.

The Supreme Court continued expanding and exercising powers in race matters in the first reconstruction period of the 1870s. The Court's members have been guardians of White superiority, appointed to maintain the social and economic privileges of the White race. Supreme Court jurists for the first 100 years were slaveholders. For the second 100 years, with very few exceptions, they were White males who protected the White race.

The Supreme Court's declaration that the federal government had no enforcement powers for equal treatment of Blacks opened the floodgates to a torrent of racial exploitation and abuse. Two hundred years ago, the

---

[29]Conant, Michael. *The Constitution and the Economy*, University of Oklahoma Press, Oklahoma, 1991, p. 252.

actions of the Supreme Court may not have been authorized, but they dug a deep hole from which Black Americans will always have to fight to escape.

Question 22. What is the connection between Blacks, gun control and the U.S. Constitution's 2nd Amendment rights?

The U.S. Constitution curiously binds Blacks, gun control and the 2nd Amendment together. When the Constitution was crafted, the *we* in "We the people have a right to bear arms" did not include Black people, who were classified as slaves, three-fifths of a human being and equal to a field animal. The 2nd Amendment was enacted to enable Whites to protect themselves in the event of slave revolts and to maintain the system of slavery. Blacks were forbidden to possess weapons to protect their person or to defend their lives, homes or families. Unarmed free Blacks were vulnerable and marginally more secure than enslaved Blacks. Free or enslaved, Blacks were dependent upon Whites for whatever protection they were willing to offer.

Gun control laws and Black slaves entered the American colonies about the same time, even before the U.S. Constitution was written. The first gun control laws, enacted in 1643 by most colonies, permitted all people, including Native Indians, to carry weapons for hunting and recreation, with one exception—Black people. They would be needed as an enslaved labor class and slavery was just beginning to take hold in the colonies. Blacks from Africa were being shaped into a non-competitive, non-threatening non-paid labor class. The colonial societies knew an armed Black population would not willingly allow itself to be enslaved and denied their human rights. White slave owners so feared what Blacks would do if they had weapons, that even during the early days of the Indian wars, colonial law forbade weapons being issued to Blacks to help fight off raiding Native Indians. A few years later, in 1667, *The Act to Regulate Negroes on British Plantations* was enacted. It forbade Blacks to carry or have access to weapons within any of the colonies[30]. While forbidding Blacks to carry weapons, the colonial gun laws mandated that White males carry weapons, chase down, capture and return runaway Black slaves to their White masters.

"Armed Militiamen Monitoring Black Slaves to Ensure the Safety of Whites and Property During Slavery." Source: U.S. Library of Congress.

Like the colonial laws, the language in the U.S. Constitution, ratified in 1789, made it perfectly clear that Blacks would not have rights to bear arms or weapons of any sort. In a nation that was being founded on a racial caste system, White people would be the management and wealth-enriched class. Black people from Africa would be the enslaved labor class. The White management overclass needed public gun and weapon laws in place to keep Blacks defenseless, vulnerable, non-threatening and under control at all times. The right to bear arms or weapons was institutionalized into the 2nd Amendment to the U.S. Constitution and

---

[30]Lind, Michael. *Up From Conservatism: Why the Right is Wrong for America*, The Free Press, New York, 1996, pgs. 220-222.

other laws[31]. The laws regulated even the carrying of clubs, knives as well as firearms. Slaves could not even raise their hands to strike a White person or defend themselves. Native Indians were exempt from most of these weapon regulations because the colonial powers needed their help in maintaining slavery and did not have control over them. Moreover, the colonies feared slave revolts more than Indian attacks, because slaves had access to the slave owners' homes and families.

According to the *Congressional Globe, 39th Congress, 1st Session, 1065, 1090-91,* on the eve of the Civil War in 1860 some members of Congress criticized White Southerners for, "denying all Blacks the right to keep and bear arms." Congressional debate changed nothing, because the North was not seriously committed to Black people. When the Civil War did break out, slavery was not the primary issue as is usually taught in history books. The Civil War broke out, not over slavery, but over the concentration of slave-based wealth, political power and industrial power in the South. Ending slavery was a secondary issue. Both the North and the Southern Confederacy had serious concerns about arming Blacks. The South feared Blacks would use the weapons against them. When the Civil War ended, the Northern states abandoned all pretense of interest in the newly-freed slaves. Northern states sought White European immigrants to migrate in and aid the North in rebuilding its businesses and a management class. The North did not want the newly-freed Black slaves to come in their direction, so the Northern states cut a deal with the old Southern Confederate states. The North gave the former Southern Confederate states the right to put Black ex-slaves into semi-slavery by using them and treating them in any manner Whites chose. The North turned their heads when the South enacted the Black Codes and labor peonage.

---

[31]Cornell, Saul and DeDino, Nathan. "Historical Perspectives: A Well Regulated Right: The Early American Origin of Gun Control," *Fordham Law Review*, 73 Fordham Law Archive of Scholarship, vol. 731, Issue 2, Article 3, 2004.

The Black Codes were fashioned around the language of the 13th Amendment, which said that slavery and involuntary servitude were abolished, "…except as punishment for crime whereof the party has been duly convicted…" The Black Codes proceeded to make nearly every ordinary life function a crime and kept Blacks under control and in a subservient socioeconomic condition, very much like that of slavery, for another 100 years. White Southerners were faced with the fact that Blacks were still the dominant population in the South and would surely resist re-enslavement. So, the Southern leadership retained the provisions of the U.S. Constitution's 2nd Amendment, which mandated White militias and required every White man to carry a gun. Just like during slavery, Southern states permitted extra-legal terrorist organizations, such as the Ku Klux Klan and Knights of the White Camellia, to monitor and control Blacks. The Black Codes continued to deny Black people the right to bear arms to protect their homes, families, property and communities, even after slavery ended. During the days of Jim Crow segregation, disarming Blacks gave Whites a monopoly ownership of weapons. This set the stage for White authority and terrorist organizations to ravage Blacks at will.

Today, after 100 years of Jim Crow semi-slavery in the South and racial separation, a sobering reality of our race-based society is that the White majority society entered the 21st century armed to the teeth. In June 2013, the Pew Research Center estimated that there were over 300 million guns in the United States, which was one firearm for every man, woman and child. Whites own over 98 percent of all the firearms.

It is puzzling that the last five presidents of the United States, along with gun control advocates, continuously conducted campaigns in urban cities admonishing Black citizens to turn in their guns. Blacks own less than one half of one percent of the nation's guns. Few, if any, Blacks are owners of gun shops, gun ranges or firearms-manufacturing companies. If the concern was to reduce the number of available guns, would it not make more sense to conduct turn-in-your weapons campaigns in suburbs and rural communities in which Whites are the majority owners and producers of firearms?

PART V
Historical Ironies

Question 23. Who were the first humans on earth and in the Americas?

After years of studying archeological artifacts, DNA links and genes in populations around the world, a large body of scientists has repeatedly concluded that the first humans originated in eastern Africa. However, there are also scientists who have produced opposing research, proclaiming that the first humans originated in Europe, China or Australia instead of Africa. Their arguments are puzzling and perplexing since biologists and geneticists recognize that all colors are contained only in melinated or dark cells. Anthony T. Brower, in his book, *From the Browder Files[32]*, stated a basic biological fact when he wrote that the Black race can produce a race of brown, yellow and White people, but it is impossible for a race of Black people to be produced from White, yellow or brown people. In 1871, Charles Darwin, who became known earlier for his theories on the origin of the species, publicly credited Black Africa as the cradle of all mankind.

As would be expected, in response to the insatiable curiosity of people regarding where humans came from, theories about the origin of mankind usually track whatever attitude is considered politically correct at the time. People expect and prefer that any origin of mankind theories align with the population group that is dominant and most preferred. Since Black people hold such a low socioeconomic status in world societies, it is only natural that many people find it offensive for science to imply that their

---

[32]Browder, Anthony T. *From the Browder File: 22 Essays on the African American Experience*, 10th ed., Institute of Karmic Guidance, Washington, D.C., 1989, p. 5.

"Migration Patterns of the First Human Migrating from Africa into North and South America."

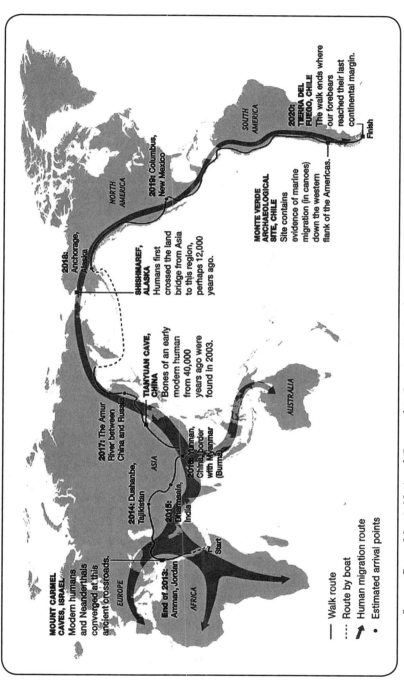

Source: Ryan, Morris National Geographic Creative, National Geographic Magazine, "To Walk the World," December 2013, Volume 224, Number 6, pgs. 31-47.

ancestors were Black or that they have Black blood surging through their veins. They prefer to bury their African lineage and identify instead with a political state, language or the culture of their country of origin. For Whites, Asians and other non-Blacks to have feelings of superiority, they need positive images of themselves over Blacks. For centuries, ethnic and religious groups have propagandized negative images of Africa while they exploited the continent of its material resources.

It is the rare non-Black person who chooses to accept their linkage to African or Blackness. The word *Africa* was originally defined as the land of the Blacks. Just like in America, other countries have established a ranking order of social acceptability for populations within their borders. In almost every country, the people have been indoctrinated to assign Black people or those persons of African descent to the lowest level of acceptability. For nearly two centuries, inquiring minds have studied everything from the single-cell amoeba to buried bones and fossilized footprints to determine the cradle of mankind. *National Geographic Magazine* published a migration pattern (see page 75) that tracked Black people as they moved from Africa, across the Bering Straits, into the North American continent and became the original Native Americans.

Similarly, in early 2000 the Discovery Channel aired, *The Real Eve,* a documentary on the origin of humankind. Archeologists used secular records, archeological artifacts and other tools to establish that the birthplace of Eve, the female from whom all life descended, was African. They then used genetic material and other scientific evidence to track humans from their original birthplace in Africa and their migration patterns around the world. The timeline presentation showed how human traits mutated according to their migration patterns and in response to changing climatic conditions.

The color black is powerful. It is the base of and contains the essence of all colors. It is physically impossible for Asians, Whites, Latinos, Chinese or Australians to be the first humankind on earth. Recognition as the first people of the earth makes Black people very special and unique. As amazing as that fact is, Blacks as a race, have not yet demanded the respect that should accompany that scientific finding. They have not proclaimed the work of those scientists that identified Blacks as the world's first humans and the labor engine that drove economic development around the world. The first humans were Black and their Black descendents should claim them in the name of Black exceptionalism, which is the key to Black people's survival and empowerment.

Question 24. Why is there such hatred toward Black people?

Undoubtedly, every Black person and many other people in this country and around the world have pondered the question of why there is such hatred toward Black people. Inquiring minds search for satisfying answers. Black people are puzzled, especially after considering what they have done to benefit Whites over the centuries, without reciprocity. After 460 years of formal slavery and Jim Crow semi-slavery, Blacks remain outside and beneath the mainstream society and benefit only incidentally when the general public benefits. Twenty-two generations of Black Americans spent and devoted their entire lives to provide enrichment and comfort to White Americans. Black unpaid labor built government buildings and universities, businesses and factories, roads and bridges and canals. Black maids and servants cleaned their homes, cooked and served their food and raised White people's children. Though most Blacks were humble and loyal to this nation, they were still lynched, robbed, raped and castrated by Whites who burned down Black towns like Wilmington, North Carolina (1899); Statesboro, Georgia (1905); Springfield, Illinois (1908);Tulsa, Oklahoma (1921); and Rosewood, Florida (1923). In the summer of 1919, known as the *Red Summer of Hate*, Whites rioted in 25 cities across the nation, and burned, looted and killed thousands of Black persons who were simply seeking access to jobs, housing, educational opportunities and the basic necessities of life. Until the 1960s Black Civil

Rights Movement, Whites initiated nearly 100 percent of the race riots that occurred in this nation.

A contradictory behavior pattern has always existed between the way Whites and Blacks have treated and cared for each other, but what is at the root of White behavior toward Blacks? Winthrop Jordan, author of *White Over Black: American Attitudes Toward the Negro, 1550 -1812*[33], states that the first European immigrants coming to the Americas had preconceived, negative and hateful attitudes about Black people that were formed by their European traditions, religion and culture. The fear and loathing they felt toward Blacks were a part of European culture passed down through the centuries and across the continent into Asia and other countries. Jordan says that Europeans associated blackness with evil, badness, filth, the devil and damnation, while associating their own white skin color with goodness, innocence, cleanliness, purity and an angel-like quality. In 1638, the European colonists institutionalized their hatred of Blacks into a public edict in the Maryland colony. That edict of 1638 established a baseline relationship between Blacks and Whites. The first European colonialists had brought a few Blacks with them to America as servants. The edict stipulated that neither those Blacks, nor their offspring, would be permitted to enjoy the fruits of White society. In 1663, the Maryland Legislature confirmed the public edict with a law stipulating, "All Negroes shall serve as slaves for life." That legal expression of hatred toward Blacks carried over into the Articles of the Confederation, the U.S. Constitution and was the foundation for the creation of racial slavery in the U.S.

Moving along the timeline of history, other writers hypothesize that White hatred of Blacks relates to the American Civil War and the destruction of the Southern genteel culture and lifestyle. These writers speculate that Southerners hold Blacks responsible for the South losing the Civil War.

---

[33]Jordan, Winthrop D. *White Over Black: American Attitudes Toward the Negrom 1550-1812*, W.W. Norton & Company, New York, 1968, pgs. 110-113.

In his book, *Honor and Slavery*[34], Kenneth S. Greenberg explains White hatred of Blacks. Greenberg postulates that it stems from two things. The first reason was the belief of Southern Whites that there is no honor in being a slave. Southern Whites had come from European countries where honor was of paramount importance and many men had died in duels defending their honor. According to their cultural mores, no honor was due a group of people that allowed itself to be enslaved. Such a group was not entitled to sympathy, pity, respect or honor. Secondly, according to Greenberg, Southern Whites in particular and Whites in general view Black people as a docile, submissive, compromising, forgiving, weak people who lack manhood, therefore deserve to be feminized through symbolic or physical castrations. In summary, Greenberg presents the position that some Whites hold that Blacks would have been better off fighting and dying rather than allowing themselves to become the lowest and most subservient individuals in society. Greenberg links the dueling-to-the-death-for-honor attitude of Europeans and Southern gentlemen to the way Whites feel about Blacks having been slaves. If there is truth to Greenberg's work, then the non-violent passive resistance, compromising and acquiescing attitudes taught by Black ministers, Black civil rights leaders and Black elected officials only reinforce the lack of respect and hatred of those who hold those opinions.

While these theories are a window into the thinking of some, it is not possible to determine the precise etiology of the negative attitudes held by Whites toward Blacks. It is a long-standing complex subject.

---

[34]Greenberg, Kenneth S. *Honor and Slavery*, Princeton University Press, Princeton, New Jersey, 1996, pgs. 33-37.

Question 25. What is the Doctrine of Unequal Exchange and is it still being applied to the Black race?

The Doctrine of Unequal Exchange is the practice of unbalanced socioeconomic trade in which weaker parties foolishly trade, or are tricked into trading, their valuable goods, services or properties for money or items of far less value than what the weaker party is trading. Frequently the weaker exploited parties receive diminished monetary value or only intangible or symbolic benefits. The exploiting party receives excessive value, thereby creating a balance of trade in favor of the exploiting party.

The lack of reciprocity or equality of trade creates unbalanced socioeconomic outcomes between the exploiter and the exploited. The concept of unequal exchange as an economic strategy was evolving as the entire European continent was suffering catastrophic conditions. Europe had been in a prolonged period of suffering from famine, diseases, crime and dire poverty. Traders and explorers were in search of resources in new world markets. They maximized their economic advantage when they engaged classical African societies.

The untapped Black human gold in Africa and an abundance of free land with minerals in the Americas became high priorities in resuscitating the European nations with wealth and power. European slave traders could purchase Black human beings in Africa for trinkets, but made huge profits, typically 1,500 percent, when they resold them as slaves in America. The slave trade and the Doctrine of Unequal Exchange created a balance of trade in favor of European countries, the exploiting parties. It infused capital into European nations and gave them massive wealth. The African continent, with its various tribes, had not yet been divided into different nations by European powers. The entire African continent became an exploited party in an exchange in which human and mineral resources were being traded for cheap trinkets, colored cloth, Bibles and valueless symbols. The historical consequence of the practice of the Doctrine of Unequal Exchange left the African continent and its

Black population exploited, impoverished and powerless even today, in the 21st century.

After Columbus' so-called discovery of the Americas, European nations began to realize that their socioeconomic salvation could be the commercial enslavement of African Blacks. They could see that not only were there enormous profits to be reaped from the slave trade itself, but huge profits could also be realized from owning and processing the slave-made material goods. Europe was poised for slavery to become the cornerstone for worldwide socioeconomic development. A massive number of trading companies emerged with the intent of trading with African native chiefs who would sell members of their own tribes. African chiefs or tribal potentates who unwittingly engaged in providing the human capital for slave trading were ignorant of the long-range consequences of their acts. They did not foresee the system of physical and psychological exploitation that the European countries were creating around a sense of White communal solidarity and systematic debasement of Black people. Black slavery became indispensable and was incorporated into all facets of emerging economies around the world. Religious organizations conjured up theological justification for slavery. Slave traders loaded their boats with Bibles, religious artifacts, cheap consumer goods and old guns and traded them to Africans for slaves, natural resources and mineral assets. Records indicate that the worth of one African slave far exceeded the useless items slave traders were dumping into African and other international markets.

Trade expeditions started out looking for strong Black slaves, called Black Gold, but soon expanded to include natural and mineral resources. The massive displacement of human capital and natural resources weakened the ability of Black Africans to become self-sufficient and to profit from the economic development of their own African continent. In 1886, the European nations met in Germany, put a map of the African continent on the table and divided it up, with each European nation selecting a region of Africa to colonize and take control of the people and natural resources. This gang rape of the world's richest continent further divided and crippled the Black population. They were forced to accept European cultures and languages imposed upon them by the conquerors. With each unequal exchange transaction, the countries of Africa grew weaker and more dependent.

"White Traders and Slave Hunters Exploiting African Blacks."
Source: U.S. Library of Congress

In the 1960s, as the world watched the televised Black Civil Rights Movement in America, the European nations ceremoniously officially released their rule over African colonies. However, they installed local African Blacks in high public offices to be political figure heads. While cutting the colonial ties gave the appearance that all power and independence had been turned over to Africans, European Whites retained ownership of and exploited the continent's massive natural and mineral wealth from behind the scenes. As Asian countries grew stronger economically, they aggressively joined in the rush to control some part of the African wealth. The destruction from the unequal exchange has been cumulative. Once the pattern became entrenched, that Black African nations accepted symbolic payment for their valuable human and natural resources, it was not possible to reverse the effects. Impoverished Black African nations are still forced to surrender their massive natural resources to the world, and in return are granted welfare loans from the World Bank and International Monetary Fund, which they are unable to repay. Clearly, the continuous pattern of unequal exchange has had permanent consequences on Africa.

The Doctrine of Unequal Exchange effectively invigorated Europe and engorged its nations with wealth. European nations then introduced the Doctrine of Unequal Exchange into America. In order for the incoming population of poor Whites to settle and control this new nation, two elements were readily needed: free land and free labor. The Native Indians possessed all the land and Black slaves were the free labor. European Whites had no intentions of paying for either. With Native Indians, Europeans simply replicated the same techniques and trading model the slave traders had successfully used in Africa. Whites colonizing America met with various Native Indian Chiefs and offered friendship, Christianity, Bibles, trinkets, clothing and housing in exchange for the right to take title to one billion acres of land, with its valuable minerals and natural resources. The unequal exchange left Native Indians nearly depopulated and poverty-stricken with no land to support themselves. The negative effects of the unequal exchange were cumulative also for the Native Indians. White immigrants became wealthy from the land and resources they gained from the Native Indians, who became weak and dependent. While Native Indians never totally recovered the loss of their physical country, they were put into a protected class and the tribes have been able to reclaim some of their economic losses and to restore some independence, because they were allowed sovereignty.

After emancipation, the unequal exchange continued to define the operational relationship between Blacks and Whites into the 21st century. It has become an accepted relationship that is rarely questioned and is practiced openly; Whites take what is valuable from Blacks in exchange for symbolism or trinkets. Blacks have never been able to break free from the resultant weakness, and Whites expect that the uninterrupted practice of unequal exchange gives them permission to continue it. After 360 years of this practice, Blacks in America have been successfully marginalized. They have remained an economically non-competitive people through the centuries. The practice is so embedded, it is rarely recognized, however the following are descriptive of the phenomenon:

- Blacks give nearly 100 percent of their vote to the Democratic Party, they are promised nothing, receive only photo-ops, yet have remained loyal party voters, no matter what happens to them;

- Blacks created towns in which to live to escape terrorism. Whites either took the property or paid very little for it and built luxurious resorts or developments, most often that excluded Blacks;

- Blacks produce a continuous flow of music and dance forms for the world. Whites learn how to sing it, claim it and enrich themselves by copying, covering and commercializing what Blacks produce;

- Blacks put their scarce dollars into the Freedman's Banks for safe keeping. Whites misappropriated all of the funds and Black depositors received no compensation;

- Blacks owned thousands of acres of land in Spanish Florida that was stolen by Southern plantation owners from Black settlers without having to pay the Black owners;

- The cervical cancer in the body of Henrietta Lacks, a poor Black woman, who produced cells that were immortal, changed medical research, produced a new medical industry that generated great wealth for the entrepreneurs, but not for her family. (See Question 91.)

Blacks own and control only one-half of one percent of anything of value in the society. The Doctrine of Unequal Exchange has continuously kept them drained of wealth-generating resources, disposable income, culture, leadership and material resources. Blacks frequently wonder out loud how Whites are able to live in such opulence across America, own industries, businesses, skyscraper buildings, magnificent homes and mansions, with manicured lawns and luxurious automobiles parked in the driveways.

The answer is simple. Whites acquired the base assets—free land and free labor—through the Doctrine of Unequal Exchange, and then practiced group economics to keep 100 percent of their disposable annual income and wealth within their own race. They also draw in 98 percent of the disposable income from the pockets of Black Americans.

Practicing PowerNomics® principles is the only way Blacks can hope to correct the trade imbalances that have been fostered by unequal exchange. The most important of these PowerNomics principles is that Blacks must never support anyone, any organization, political party or business that does not support the Black race. The second PowerNomics principle is the practice of group-based economics, which means making money bounce 8 to 12 times within their own community before letting it exit into non-Black hands and businesses. Black Americans are nearly 100 percent consumers and nearly zero percent producers. When they do not practice group-based economics, they are contributing to the negative balance of trade that allows the outflow of money from their group to other groups make other groups wealthy, without requiring even a promise to patronize Black-owned businesses.

Blacks must renegotiate their relationship with individuals, political parties and businesses that profit from them, and stop the practice of unequal exchange. If a business is located in a Black neighborhood, require something from them. Demand that in exchange for the wealth the business extracts, the business must purchase items from a list of Black-produced products, as well as provide jobs, support efforts to improve the neighborhood and otherwise provide material benefits to Black neighborhoods. Blacks should impose standards and simply not permit any business to strip them of their financial assets and leave nothing of value. As Black people demand reciprocity and become more self-sufficient, they will be able to alter the uneven balance of trade deficit that comes from the continued practice of the Doctrine of Unequal Exchange.

Question 26. Is it possible for resource-rich Black Africa to become a world superpower?

Even though time is running out, Black Africa could become a world superpower—if they rise above tribalism, religious differences and the impact of the Berlin Conference (1884–1885) in which European colonial powers identified and took control of the parts of Africa they wanted and colonized the entire continent. Africa is the richest continent on this earth. It is on the verge of economic recolonization. Unfortunately, European powers have been draining the continent of its vital resources for centuries, and now countries from around the world are competing with Europeans to capture and export resources out of Africa. For 50 years, Black Africans have been visible in political leadership of African nations, but they are not in control of their nations' economies. European powers engage African politicians in practicing *comparative* economics instead of *competitive* economics. In comparative economics, African countries would bring raw materials to the marketplace and sell them to European corporations to be processed. Using comparative economics, Europeans process the raw materials then transform those products into goods which they sell back to African countries at a price quadruple what they paid for the raw materials. This trading practice leaves a balance of trade deficit that African nations cannot close unless they borrow money from the World Bank or the International Monetary Fund. This pushes those countries further into debt. Using *competitive* economics, African countries would keep their raw materials, manufacture consumer products, sell them to European and other nations, retain the profits and wealth and thereby prosper socioeconomically within the African continent.

In recent years, African countries have been overrun by countries like China, Japan and India, which are all in search of raw materials to supply their country's consumer demands. Those countries insert their people into the native African populations to specifically capture material resources and consumers, and build influence within African governments. They also exploit the people of Africa, destroy the continent's wildlife and deplete its natural resources. China is an example. It invests heavily in infrastructure in African countries in exchange for open-door access and control of Africa's numerous resources. China wields great influence in South Africa. The newly-approved South African National Constitution contains an Affirmative Action provision that grants preferential treatment for Chinese residents of South Africa, but does not allow preferential treatment for the nation's approximately 45 million African Blacks. African Blacks make up about 79 percent of the nation's population but own and control less than one percent of the nation's wealth, income and management positions. Why would Black political figure heads knowingly approve a National Constitution that denies preferential treatment to the impoverished majority Black population?

Nearly all of the major businesses and industries throughout Africa are owned and controlled by non-Blacks. Blacks in Africa are like Blacks in America in many respects. They are consumers and not producers. While non-Blacks are migrating into Africa to build businesses that produce wealth and power for their countries, African Blacks are distracted by internal fights based upon tribal or religious identification. Every month, thousands of African Blacks perish due to lack of food, water, medicine or war-related conflicts. Within a few years, foreigners will take control of the resources on the African continent and African Blacks will be locked into a permanent underclass—the same fate that looms for American Blacks.

Colonization of Africa allowed Europeans to control the enormous wealth from Africa's resources. Later, as the Black Civil Rights Movement was under way in the U.S., White colonial powers in Africa reluctantly began to surrender their open control of governments and political leadership to African Blacks. Just as they had done in other nations as they exited, however, White colonial powers established puppet leaders in high levels of government. By continuing to own and control the businesses, industries and resources in every African nation, Whites were able to continue to control the nations from distant lands.

Like Blacks in the United States, strength would come with greater African Black unity. Modern Africa could become a super power, if the individual political states could demonstrate a mutual transcontinental self-interest and organize to act as a single social and economic bloc that closed its borders to non-Black international exploiters. A number of efforts are currently underway to do just that and to reverse the effects of the 1885 Berlin Conference. The continent of Africa can no longer afford to be divided while their continent is plundered by foreign political interests. For nearly 130 years, the nations of Africa have been divided and within each African country there are hundreds of tribes and languages. In Nigeria, for instance, there are over 200 tribes and 256 different spoken languages. Once the various African nations achieve some degree of unity along social and economic lines, they will then be able to connect with people of African descent around the world and they would have to be recognized as an international superpower. When Africa is acknowledged as a superpower, respect and power for Blacks in America will increase. The fate of Blacks in Africa and the United States are linked in a way that has the potential to guide and uplift Blacks throughout the Diaspora.

Question 27. Why don't Whites have to march and fight for citizenship and civil rights?

In the mid-sixties, with an active Black Civil Rights Movement dominating the news, the nation seemed to be on the road to the realization of Rev. Dr. Martin Luther King, Jr.'s dream that someday Black children would be judged not by the color of their skin but by, "the content of their character." Fifty years later, our nation's streets continue to host race riots, Million Man Marches and Black Lives Matter demonstrations for justice and rights. In race matters, why is it that Whites do not have to march or fight for their rights in the streets like Black Americans routinely do? As simply as it can be stated, Whites do not have to march and fight for their rights because their rights are the foundational principles of this country. More specifically, the nation's founding documents blessed Whites with freedom, security and an abundance of happiness. They do not have to fight or demonstrate for their rights. Consider these facts:

1) The entire U.S. Constitution and its Amendments bestowed on Whites all of the rights, freedoms, protections and privileges of first-class citizenship;

2) The U.S. Constitution was crafted as the nation's first Affirmative Action Plan, and it was strictly for Whites;

3) The nation's first nationalization law of 1790 declared America to be a *White nation*, which was symbolized as the American Dream for European Whites seeking property and the rights to acquire free Native Indian land and free Black labor;

4) The nation's immigration laws are designed to ensure that Whites will remain the majority population, with dominance and control over everyone else's rights and privileges;

5) The U.S. Supreme Court has been filled with White jurists who historically render judicial decisions that preserve White superiority and advantages;

6) Slavery-based mal-distribution of nearly 100 percent of the nation's wealth and power into the hands of dominant White society determined opportunities and rights that still exist today, and;

7) Slave Codes, Black Codes, Jim Crow segregation and extra-legal organizations reinforced and protected White rights.

White Americans have a monopoly on *rights* in America. Blacks who march for their rights must do so with the full knowledge that only the civil rights laws and three constitutional amendments enacted during Reconstruction, but whose original intents were later corrupted by the U.S. Supreme Court, ever sought to guarantee rights for Black people. Most of today's problems that confront Blacks were created and sustained by Whites to protect their institutional rights and privileges and un-earned wealth. Equally as important is the reality that racial segregation was established and fought for because Whites believed they had the right to say who would be their neighbor, whom their children would attend school with, and who would sit beside them in a restaurant. Whites hold their rights to be constitutionally sacred and therefore are unwilling to share any portion with Black people, who the U.S. Constitution defined as property, three-fifths of a human and equal to field animals. It was the 13th and 14th Amendments to the Constitution that granted citizenship and paper, or illusionary, rights to Black ex-slaves.

With Whites viewing the Constitution as the Holy Grail, Blacks cannot rely on the Constitution as interpreted by Supreme Court jurists, who are the guardians of the status quo in race matters. Based upon the Supreme Court's historical rulings in Black-versus-White race matters, author Ian Millhiser, in his book, *Injustices*[35], appropriately described the Supreme Court as consistently, "Comforting the comfortable and afflicting the afflicted." Blacks' best hope for justice and rights is to have well-focused street demonstrations to reclaim the original intent of the 1866 Civil Rights Laws and the 13th and 14th Amendments that

---

[35]Millhiser, Ian. *Injustices: The Supreme Court's Histgory of Comforting the Comfortable and Afflicting the Afflicted.* Nation Books, New York, 2015.

Congress passed to specifically reverse the 1857 U.S. Supreme Court's Dred Scott decision. Chief Taney's Supreme Court decision declared that Blacks had no rights that a White man was bound to respect. The 10-year Civil War Reconstruction period began in the mid-1860s when Radical Republican members of Congress enacted civil rights laws and constitutional amendments to convey rights strictly to and for Blacks.

Reconstruction ended in the mid-1870s when the U.S. Supreme Court exercised assumed judicial powers to restore total White dominance and strip Blacks of those rights granted to them by Radical Republican Congressmen during Reconstruction. The Supreme Court ended Reconstruction by ruling that civil laws enacted for Blacks in the years between 1867 through 1875 were *unconstitutional*. Since the 1866 Civil Rights Laws have morphed into the Constitution's 14th Amendment, which could not be ruled as unconstitutional, the Supreme Court chose to corrupt the 1866 Civil Rights Laws by ruling that they were for everybody and not specifically Black people. If Blacks fail to challenge the Supreme Court's racist rulings and recapture original rights intended for them in the second U.S. Constitution (13th, 14th and 15th Amendments) and a series of civil rights laws, then Blacks have no legitimate constitutional rights in this nation.

Question 28. Was Washington, D.C. ever both the slave capital and the nation's capital?

The District of Columbia, situated between Maryland and Virginia, has been a showplace of federal government institutions, business enterprises and tourism throughout its history. But, most notably, before the Civil War, Washington, D.C. was the mistress of the enslavement industry. With its main streets studded with slave showrooms, slave depots and approximately 200 slave auction marts, it earned the title of being the nation's slave capital. It was the home of the most notorious and lucrative slave auction houses in the country. On a typical day, there were continuous parades of chained men, women and children being moved in the streets in funeral-like processions from one auction house to another. The slaves were held in pens and dungeons until they could be safely sold down the river into the Deep South.

"Roby's Pen Auction House, Washington, D.C."
Source: U.S. Library of Congress.

Washington, D.C., as the nation's capital, was distinctive because it was the destination of both enslaved and free Blacks. However, free Black persons living near or in the city were at risk of being kidnapped and sold back into slavery. Many reminders of the city's role in slavery still exist. One of the biggest and most infamous auction houses in the city was Roby's Pen Auction House, located near the U.S. Capitol. Its location was convenient for the slaveholders who also worked as government officials and wanted to move back and forth easily between the Capitol debates and slave auctions held on the Capitol steps. With the auction houses close to the seat of national government, the slaveholders could run the country and their slave plantations simultaneously. Thirteen of the nation's first 18 presidents were slave owners. Following the Revolutionary War, so were all of the members of the U.S. Supreme Court and most of the members of the U.S. Congress. When he was a member of Congress, Abraham Lincoln commented on how close Roby's Pen Auction House was to the Capitol and congressional offices. American slavery and government were the lifeblood of the District of Columbia and the nation. The race that held the slaves and whips 360 years ago holds the reins of government power today.

Question 29. Blacks didn't lynch Whites, so why did Whites routinely lynch Blacks?

My examination of historical records does not show a single instance of Blacks lynching Whites or members of any other group. Lynching is a form of terrorism used to frighten, punish, exploit and control Blacks. White extra-legal groups, such as the Ku Klux Klan, routinely lynched Blacks, especially Black men. Lynchings peaked in 1896 after the U.S. Supreme Court's *Plessey v. Ferguson* decision; again in 1918 when Black soldiers returned home from World War I and again in the 1930s, following the end of the Great Depression. Lynching Blacks was a recreational and festive activity for White men and it is not difficult to understand why. White men lynched Blacks primarily because: 1) they could; 2) they faced no prosecution by law enforcement; and 3) it was such an accepted part of the culture that nearly a century after slavery ended, U.S. presidents and congressmen refused to enact anti-lynching laws.

In a February 10, 2015 *The Washington Post* article[36], Mark Berman reported that the number of Blacks lynched by Whites had been under-reported through the years. According to Berman, 3,959 Blacks were

---

[36]Berman, Mark. "Even More Black People Were Lynched in The U.S. Than Previously Thought, Study Finds," *The Washington Post*, February 10, 2015.

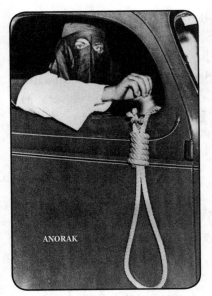

"Commonplace Lynching of Blacks by KKK and Extra-legal Groups."
Source: U.S. Library of Congress

killed in *terror lynchings* in just 12 Southern states in the 19th and 20th centuries. Lynchings in Northern big cities were equally as bad, if not worse. Tom Wicker, in his book, *Tragic Failure: Racial Integration in American*[37], stated, "Thousands of Blacks were lynched by Whites in the U.S. in the late 19th and 20th centuries for any or no reason at all. Race lynchings were conducted in Northern cities during the aftermath of race riots."

There were also pathological factors that drove White men to lynch Black men. Lynching is the murder of another human being in public so that everyone knows who did it. Besides killing the victim, the lynching act displays the power of the killer and the powerlessness of the victim. Since I could not find a single recorded instance of Blacks lynching Whites in my research, it seems a reasonable conclusion that Blacks were not driven to display revenge or race power by lynching Whites. Why Whites had such strong hate for Blacks would be a mystery, were it not for their determination to instill fear in Blacks and maintain control over them. For over a century, Black leaders and community groups lobbied presidents and the U.S. Congress to enact laws to stop Whites from lynching, burning alive and executing Blacks with crowds celebrating and witnessing the events. But, powerful White conservative political and social forces stopped all efforts to block legislation. In June 2005, the

---

[37]Wicker, Tom. *The Tragic Failure of Integration*, William Morrow and Company, Inc., New York, 1996, pgs. 37, 77.

U.S. Senate finally voted to issue a formal lynching apology. As many as 15 conservative Republicans who represented the North as well as the South, refused to endorse *any* anti-lynching resolution.

As abhorrent as it is now, less than half a century ago, lynching Blacks was so embedded in White culture that it was often perceived as a recreational event in both name and practice. In fact, the word *picnic,* according to some sources, is a coined expression for *Pick-a-Nigger.* From the end of the Civil War until the civil rights movement of the 1960s, a Black man was lynched on the average of one every two days. Black men were lynched inside and outside of the law, regardless of whether they were guilty or innocent. However, the practice of lynching is nearly as old as this country. The lynching practice started in America during the Revolutionary War, when Colonel Charles Lynch led a bunch of vigilantes to dispense their own brand of justice on British supporters and outlaws. Colonel Charles Lynch routinely used his Lynch Law on the British Loyalists in the Virginia colony. Later, White terrorist organizations held a monopoly on lynchings. White official power and authority gave groups like the Ku Klux Klan the right to conduct lynchings at the slightest provocation. Lynchings were used to kill individual Blacks, but the secondary purpose was to terrorize and intimidate all Blacks into *good behavior.* Good Black behavior meant Black dependency on and submissiveness to the control of Whites. Through the present time, few if any Whites have been legally tried, let alone punished, for lynching and terrorizing Black people.

The 10-year period between 1882 and 1892, provides a snapshot of how often lynchings occurred. Whites lynched over 2,000 Black men. By the early 1918, Booker T. Washington lamented that another 2,522 Black men were lynched for no justifiable reasons. Of the numerous offenses that White mobs used to justify lynching Black men, the following is a partial list: robbery, slander, uppityness, wife beating, cutting levees, kidnapping, voodooism, poisoning horses, writing insulting letters, incendiary language, political activism, gambling, quarreling, poisoning wells, swindling, jilting a girlfriend, organizing Negroes, throwing rocks, unpopularity, making threats, circulating scandal, gossiping, being troublesome, having a bad reputation, drunkenness, rioting, fraud, enticing a servant away, writing a letter to a White woman, asking a White woman for her hand in marriage, conspiracy, introducing smallpox, giving information, conjuring, concealing a criminal, slapping a child, touching a White woman, talking back to or sassing a White person, passing counterfeit money, owning a barking dog, failing to get off of the sidewalk so Whites could pass by, playing games with a White person, paying attention to a White woman, disobeying ferry regulations, running quarantine, being in the wrong place at the wrong time, being unwilling to work, reading a Black newspaper and accepting a job and simply doing as well as or better economically than Whites. Blacks suffered lynching and abuses from Whites, in large measure because of White population and power dominance.

There were also social as well as power reasons that explained why Blacks didn't lynch Whites. For centuries, White slaveholders and Black preachers socially conditioned Blacks to protect themselves and their families by playing *git low* and respecting White society's authority and code of etiquette. Even justifiably angry Blacks were persuaded not to seek revenge against Whites, but to instead forgive Whites and adhere to non-violence and religious passivity. White social acceptance became the ultimate goal regardless of what White society did to Blacks. Blacks did not lynch Whites for the very same reasons that they were willing to suffer 360 years of slavery and a century of Jim Crow semi-slavery. Blacks wanted love and acceptance from Whites. In all likelihood, neither slavery nor lynching would have endured and prevailed if the Black masses had in 1516, when slavery began, not accepted the brutalization of slavery, and instead demonstrated willingness to fight to the death, rather than to cooperate with the slave system.

Question 30. Why do Blacks always march to the Lincoln Memorial?

The Lincoln Memorial is the destination of Black marches because of the misplaced emotional linkage Blacks make between President Abraham Lincoln and Black enslavement. That attachment is based on the myth that Abraham Lincoln was the Great Emancipator who fought for and delivered Black Americans from slavery. The reality is quite different. President Lincoln fought the Civil War to save the Union, not to free Blacks from slavery. The fact that millions of Black adult demonstrators and schoolchildren visit the Lincoln Memorial, gaze starry-eyed at the Gettysburg Address and herald the Emancipation Proclamation, does not change the fact that Lincoln's proclamation did not, in fact, free a single slave. But, they leave Washington, D.C., with those false impressions. If they look at Lincoln as the savior, they miss the important roles Blacks played to free themselves through revolts, abolitionist activities and as Union soldiers.

Up until the mid-1850s, Lincoln had dutifully avoided the slavery issue. The record does not indicate that he identified with the issue of Black slavery during the 23 years he was a trial lawyer in Illinois. There is no record that he defended any runaway slaves or addressed the legal basis of institutionalized slavery. When he became president, Northern public officials were just as silent as Lincoln, and walked lockstep with him on race matters. On the issue of the Civil War and slavery, on July 21, 1861, Northern-elected officials expressed their feelings regarding the Civil War in a U.S. Congressional resolution, which declared, "This war is not being waged for the purpose of overthrowing the established institution of slavery, but to defend the U.S. Constitution and to preserve the Union." Clearly, Congress had no intention of disturbing slavery and neither did Lincoln.

"Kneeling Blacks Kissing Abraham Lincoln's Hand in Appreciation for Being Freed from Slavery."
Source: Pictorial Press, Ltd., Almay Stock Photo

In a meeting with President Lincoln, Hannibal Hamlin, the Vice President, urged Lincoln to make the aim of the war the freeing of Blacks and ending slavery, rather than saving the Union. President Lincoln, the *Great Emancipator*, refused, and responded, saying, "The war was to save the Union." Months later, Lincoln was under pressure to issue an Emancipation Proclamation, but at that time he refused, saying that, "to issue an Emancipation Proclamation would hurt our Union friends who were slaveholders and turn them against us." In an effort to aid his Northern slaveholding friends, President Lincoln sent a bill to the U.S. Congress that offered to pay $300 for each Black slave that Northern White slaveholders set free or emancipated[38]. When he finally decided to issue an emancipation document, his justification was politically practical. First, the Republican Party wanted to dissuade Europeans from entering the Civil War on the side of the South and second, it was important to Lincoln not to disrupt the agricultural production in the South. Lincoln knew that if slavery was abolished, there would be severe social and economic disruption.

The best-known myth about Abraham Lincoln is that his Emancipation Proclamation actually ended legalized slavery and freed millions of Black slaves, which is totally untrue. When Lincoln issued the Emancipation Proclamation, the Civil War was still in progress and his

---

[38]Perry, John C. *Myths and Realities of American Slavery*, Burd Street Press, Shippensburg, PA, 2002, pgs.189-196.

pronouncement had no authority in the South, which had seceded from the Union. He did have authority in the North and boarder states, but this Emancipation Proclamation did not apply to those slaves. In reality then, the Emancipation Proclamation did not free slaves anywhere in this country. Not until the Civil War was over and the 13th Amendment was ratified, did the entire nation accept the reality that institutional slavery had officially ended.

Venerating the myth rather than the reality keeps Blacks feeling obligated to Lincoln as their great savior. One of the nation's best-kept secrets is that the Northern states abandoned the newly-freed slaves and allowed the Southern states to recast them into Jim Crow semi-slavery for another 100 years. Until the present time, neither the spirit of Lincoln's Emancipation Proclamation, nor the original intent of the 13th Amendment of the U.S. Constitution, which required that Whites, *lift the legacies of slavery* from Blacks, has been adhered to in this nation's public policies. After centuries of marching to the Lincoln Memorial, Black Americans are still a hated out-group that mistakenly views Abraham Lincoln as the great emancipator and savior of Black people.

Question 31. What role did Black slaves play in building the U.S. Capitol?

Black people were the backbone of labor in America and built both the White House and the U.S. Capitol buildings. They also built everything from plantation mansions to government buildings to university campuses. Atop the dome of the Capitol stands the Statue of Freedom in the figure of a female warrior dressed in a star-festooned helmet and flowing robes. Jefferson Davis, Secretary of War during President Pierce's administration, oversaw construction. He opposed the original design of a woman wearing a French revolutionary's liberty cap. Secretary Davis was concerned that the liberty cap on the statue might inspire slaves, many of whom built the Capitol, to seek freedom and revolt. Davis wanted a statue of freedom on top of the Capitol dome that symbolized freedom for everyone, except Black people. The French liberty cap is on the freedom statue today.

The statue was designed for $3,000 by Thomas Crawford in Rome, Italy in 1856. In 1863, it was cast in bronze in Bladensburg, Maryland, at a foundry owned by Clark Mills, whom the government paid $23,736. Philip Reed[39], a slave owned by Mills, was given the responsibility of casting the Statue of Freedom and transporting it in sections to the east grounds of the nation's capital. Once the sections arrived, Reed and other slaves reassembled Freedom to make certain that all of her pieces fit together. Assembling Freedom took 31 days. Thus, the Statue of Freedom was disassembled, hoisted and reassembled by slaves. These slaves then hoisted the statue onto a pedestal in the Capitol dome so that she could signal freedom for *everyone*.

"Historical Drawing of Black Slaves Building the Capitol Building."
Source: U.S. Library of Congress.

In 1863, the White superintendent in charge of building the nation's capital building quit, complaining that eight dollars per day was too little

---

[39]Robinson, Randall. *The Debt: What America Owes to Blacks,* Plume; reprint edition, New York, 2001, p. 5.

money. He was replaced by Philip Reed, who supervised the construction. Reed was just one of hundreds of Black slaves and freedmen who helped build the U.S. Capitol, the White House and other monuments including the statue of Liberty. Like most slaves, Reed received no money, praise, plaudits or plaques. Clark Mills, Reed's owner, was paid for Reed's labor. Later on, European laborers and mechanics were imported to assist in the construction. They were paid market wages. When the work of the slaves was done, the U.S. Department of Treasury paid the Whites who owned the slave laborers. Archive volunteers recently examined the construction and pay records, and compiled a list of Capitol workers. They found 122 *Negro hires* referenced by their first names. Although most of the slaves were common laborers, the archive researchers were surprised to find the names of Black stonecutters, carpenters and painters. Slavery had produced an artisan class that worked on the Capitol building as well as in private construction projects.

Question 32. How was the 1954 school desegregation lawsuit switched from unequal funding to social integration?

The 1954 U.S. Supreme Court's decision in *Brown v. The Board of Education* was actually the culmination of several court battles filed by Blacks, including significantly a case that began in 1953 (*Briggs v. Elliott*) in Clarendon, South Carolina. The public policy on education in effect in South Carolina and across the South at the time was separate but equal. Because White schools were getting four to five times more funding than Black schools, Black parents filed suit, not because they quarreled with the fact that the schools were racially separated, but because the funding was unequal.

The NAACP joined in the suit. White school officials attempting to head off the Court's decision, offered massive increases in state appropriations to equalize funding of Black schools in a racially separate public system. The offer was unexpected by the NAACP. The organization was astonished that the state was willing to commit such enormous sums of money to Negro schools. The unexpected offer created a major difference between what the Black parents in Clarendon, South Carolina wanted for their children and what the NAACP wanted. The NAACP rejected the state's offer and the initial intent of the Black parents.

"South School Classroom in Pre-civil Rights Movement."
Source: U.S. Library of Congress

In his book, *Plural but Equal: Blacks and Minorities in America's Plural Society*[40], Dr. Harold Cruse comments on the devastating long-term effects of that shortsighted decision. He said of the NAACP, "The association negated in advance the possibility of Black political bases being fashioned around the important state function of public school funding and administration." Dr. Cruse further stated that when the NAACP advocated for full integration and rejected the Southern states' compromise gestures toward belated equalization of racially separate school systems, in effect the NAACP had done Black Americans a terrible disservice. The organization allowed school systems in Southern states to place the physical and financial burdens of implementing school integrating on the backs of Black Americans. Blacks lost their educational

---

[40]Cruse, Harold. *Plural but Equal: Blacks and Minorities in America's Plural Society*, Quill-William Morrow, New York, 1987, p. 199.

buildings, vehicles, equipment and so many school related businesses. More importantly, they lost their educational careers, employment opportunities and retirement funds. The effect of the NAACP's action was to convert the original goal of seeking equal funding and resources from the state to seeking, instead school integration.

Historian Dr. Benjamin Quarles expressed a similar assessment of the NAACP's commitment to social integration at any cost. Dr. Quarles wrote about the South Carolina funding offer and the thinking of the NAACP in his book, *The Negro in the Making of America*[41]. He observes that the state of South Carolina's huge financial offer would have rectified the issue of unequal funding, but the NAACP was so strongly committed to integration as a policy, that it changed the focus of the Clarendon lawsuit. It shifted the emphasis of the suit from funding and resources to eradicating *racial segregation* through physically mixing and integrating the races. The U.S. Supreme Court then ruled, as the NAACP had asked, that Black children must attend school together with White children, and all of the vestiges of Jim Crow Segregation must be dismantled with all deliberate speed. Dismantling meant dismantling Black schools, and that is what happened across the board, from Black elementary schools to colleges and universities.

According to Quarles, the NAACP's opposition to segregation meant it was also philosophically opposed to separate but equal Black neighborhood schools. This civil rights organization assessed that neighborhood schools were nothing more than the product of White-imposed segregation and needed to be eradicated. Quarles said that the NAACP felt the nation could only achieve quality education by putting White and Black children in close physical proximity, so it pushed for court-enforced school busing. An untold number of Blacks disagreed with the NAACP and wanted quality schools in Black communities. The

---

[41]Quarles, Benjamin. *The Negro in the Making of America*, Touchstone Books, New York, 1996, p. 276.

NAACP's Legal Defense Fund, however, which included a large number of well-meaning White lawyers, was intent on achieving social integration no matter the cost to Black America. The costs were enormous and so fundamentally destructive that Blacks will never totally recover. Black schools were closed down, Black teachers and principals were fired, large numbers of Black students were assigned to special education classes, and Black students were bused as unwanted minority guests into White schools and communities.

Dr. Benjamin Quarles observes that once the NAACP made a commitment to the policy of integration and the movement got underway, the organization did not want the White power structure to actually make good on its public policy of separate but equal. Black leadership did not want a dual system, even if it did allow Blacks to operate and control quality, competitive schools within their own communities. "The NAACP realized that providing Negro schools with better buildings, better equipment and better salaries for teachers, and changing the title *college* to *university* would only strengthen Jim Crow by establishing gilded citadels of segregation manned by Negro teachers and administrators who would have a vested interest in maintaining the status quo in racial education[42]." Black economic control over well-funded education systems in their own communities could have been the beginning of real unity, power and self-determination and could have provided a path up and out of Jim Crow segregation.

This was a case of the road not taken. The NAACP assumed that goodness was somehow a quality in Whiteness and did not see the goodness or value in Blackness. Its end vision was of a Black America that was dependent on and inextricably intertwined with Whites. Now 50 years down the path the NAACP chose in South Carolina, the evidence is in. Integration was an end in itself and was as far as the NAACP could

---

[42]Quarles, Benjamin. *The Negro in the Making of America*, Touchstone Books, New York, 1996, p. 276.

see. Blacks are now scattered under an illusion of social integration, even though Blacks and Whites are more residentially segregated in 2017 than they were in 1954. The imprudent social integration decision misled Blacks into giving up all of the positive advantages of segregation and propelled the entire race down a path toward group destruction. The social integration process destroyed Black communities and made Blacks uninvited guests in what Whites and other groups owned and controlled. Guests are expendable and have little power in dealing with their hosts.

Schools teach the values and goals of those who are in authority. Black parents should seek to control their schools and require that the education of their children be based on reality. An appropriate educational experience for Black children would be to recognize the unique background that Black children bring to school. Black children need basic skills, but they also need to learn to value Blackness and how to contribute to building a Black community that is strong and self-sufficient.

The 1954 Supreme Court's *Brown v. Board of Education* decision had far-reaching effects and unintended consequences. It reduced Black students to the position of being guests in schools, businesses and communities owned and controlled by Whites, who assigned racial inferiority onto Blacks. The decision itself addressed the separate schools issue, but the NAACP extended the Brown decision beyond public schools and into every aspect of the private and public sector. It was a fatal blow. What happened to Black schools also happened to traditional Black communities, businesses and institutions. They disappeared and Blacks joined the unemployment rolls. The NAACP apparently meant well, but could not envision the ruinous impact of social integration on Black America. The decision established an inappropriate model of self destruction for Blacks who, no matter how hard they strive, may never regain what they lost in the integration process.

PART VI
Politics of Race

Question 33. Which ethnic or racial group in America has a proven record of being the most patriotic?

Patriotism is the devoted love, support, loyalty and defense of one's country. It is ironic that after 24 generations of suffering slavery, Jim Crow segregation and Benign Neglect public policies, Black Americans hold a proven and unchallengeable track record of patriotism that stands head-and-shoulders above any ethnic, racial or religious group. They have proven themselves the oldest and most patriotic group in a number of ways. First, Blacks were the unpaid labor engine that drove the socioeconomic development of this nation. Blacks were the unpaid labor class that cleared the land, raised the crops and built the roads, bridges, canals and public buildings. Their blood, sweat, tears and overworked bodies forever connected them to this nation's land.

The second reason Blacks are the most patriotic group is that over 99 percent of them in America are direct descendants of slaves, which means they were here, building and fighting for this nation *before* 99 percent of the Europeans, Asians, Hispanics or their descendants ever arrived in this country. The third reason Blacks are the most patriotic group is that they are the only population group that has fought in every military engagement and major war in defense of this country since it was founded. Crispus Attucks, a Black man, was the first to die in the Revolutionary War of Independence. Today, in the 21st century military engagements, Blacks make up a large portion of the military. Fourth, and most notably, of all the major racial and ethnic groups in America, Black Americans are probably the only group whose countries of origin have not engaged the United States in a war. Through the centuries, the U.S.

has engaged in wars with Spain, England, France, Canada, Germany, China, Cuba, Puerto Rico, Mexico, Korea, Japan, Italy, Russia, the Islands of the Pacific, Vietnam, American Indians and a host of Middle Eastern countries. It has never been in a declared war with a Black African country. What other racial or ethnic group can make that claim?

Ironically, ethnic groups from all the countries that the U.S. has fought throughout history, can easily migrate into the U.S. and immediately rank higher in social acceptability than native Black Americans. During the Revolutionary War, World War I and World War II, Black Americans lobbied the government for the right to fight and die for the country that enslaved and Jim Crow segregated them. Unlike immigrants who legally and illegally enter the country, Black soldiers who returned home from combat in foreign lands still had to fight to be accepted as true Americans. Unlike others, Blacks did not voluntarily migrate to America, but they cherish the U.S. with all of its moles and blemishes, because with all of its flaws, it is the country that their labor built. America is the only home they have known.

Black Americans are models of what a truly patriotic group ought to be. White Southerners, as a class are disqualified, because their attack on the Union, triggered the Civil War, and made them the nation's first terrorists. Their continued affection for Dixie, denial of constitutional rights to Black citizens, and rhetoric of political secession, represents continued anti-American behavior, *not* patriotism

Question 34. Did Blacks build their own towns in an effort to escape the terrorism of Whites?

One of the first lessons that free Blacks and runaway slaves learned centuries ago, but experienced a memory lapse during the civil rights movement of the 1960s, was that they could fair better in their own communities with their own people. From the inception of slavery in the

"Photo Painting of a Maroon Town."
Source: Libary of Congress.

early 1600s, like Native Indians, runaway Blacks built their own separate communities, which they called *maroon towns*. The word *maroon* referred to a class of Blacks who preferred their independence, living separately from Whites, who sought to enslave them. During slavery and Jim Crow segregation days, Whites did not like the idea of Blacks living independently and would routinely search out and destroy Black maroon towns and other Black settlements. After World War I, Whites often became envious of the towns Blacks built and the successful businesses operating inside.

After emancipation, newly-freed Blacks tried different tactics to escape White hate and institutionalized racism. Wherever Blacks went in search of peace, Whites would shatter it. The most frequent pattern was for Blacks to migrate to the North or westward to build towns, villages and settlements that Blacks could live in and control. The sites of many of those old Black towns and villages are some of today's most notable residential and business areas, such as Seneca Village, New York; a part of Central Park in New York; the Five Points district that is today's Wall Street in New York; and the Freedman's Village in Virginia that is presently the Southern end of Arlington National Cemetery. Allensworth is now a state park in California. Rosewood, Florida; Tulsa, Oklahoma and Wilmington, North Carolina were burned. Blacks were killed and their homes and businesses were destroyed.

There were numerous lesser-known all-Black towns defined as generally residential areas with populations of at least 1,000, of which

95 percent were classified as Black. It is difficult to establish the dates the towns were built, however it appears there were four distinct periods during which those towns evolved: the pre-Civil War period, the post-Civil War period, the great post-World War I migration period and the post-World War II period. Although there are too many all-Black towns to name, here is a sampling of some of the names: Nicodemus in Kansas; Boley in Oklahoma; Mound Bayou in Mississippi; Brooklyn in Illinois; Lawnside, New Jersey; Robbins in Illinois; Fairmount Heights in Maryland; Glenarden in Maryland; Lincoln Heights in Ohio; Urbancrest in Ohio; Kinloch in Missouri; Grambling in Louisiana; North Shreveport in Louisiana; Richmond Heights in Florida; Samtown in Louisiana; Gredenwood in Alabama; Gifford in Florida; Pleasant Hill in Virginia; Saratoga in Virginia; Lloyd Place in Virginia; Bennettsville in South Carolina and Eatonville in Florida.

A White reign of terror always followed them. Ironically, Whites killed Blacks and destroyed Black towns because they did not want Blacks living too close to them and Whites killed and destroyed Black homes because they didn't want Blacks to migrate too far away from them. Whites have always been emotionally conflicted about proximity to Blacks. As per the Diversity Act of the 1705 Slave Code, Whites seem to want Blacks close enough so they can be monitored on a continuous basis.

Question 35. Were Blacks legally or symbolically emancipated from institutionalized enslavement?

Considering the fact that in the 21st century, Blacks are still treated as a socioeconomic underclass and political out-group, the real legal status of Blacks in America is unclear. History reveals that since the founding of this country, there were numerous emancipation proclamations that proposed to end slavery and set Blacks free. However, none in fact did. The nation's *first Emancipation Proclamation* was proposed by Lord

Dunmore, the British Royal Governor of Virginia in November 1775, on the eve of the American Revolutionary War. Lord Dunmore offered freedom to any slave who would take up arms against the colonies and fight with the British troops. Three months later, fearful of the harm armed and angry slaves would bring to European White colonialists, Lord Dunmore reconsidered and withdrew his Emancipation Proclamation to free Blacks.

Nearly a century later, in 1852, a *second Emancipation Proclamation* was drafted in response to Nat Turner's slave revolt. Turner's revolt shook the nation, especially the Southern slaveholding states. Frightened by the successful slave revolt in Haiti and Nat Turners' revolt in Virginia, many Southern slaveholders indicated a willingness to end Black enslavement and resettle Black slaves into Africa, Texas or the Caribbean Islands. Shortly thereafter, the mere thought of over four million angry, armed Blacks in the street quickly galvanized Virginia legislators to offer what constituted a *third Emancipation Proclamation* that proposed simply to abolish slavery. Ironically, nearly half of Virginia's legislators voted to abolish slavery in Virginia, the birthplace of Black American slavery. They came just a few votes short of ending slavery and preventing the Civil War that followed.

A few years later, on January 1, 1863, after the Civil War had begun, President Abraham Lincoln reluctantly offered the well-known *fourth Emancipation Proclamation* that did not free a single Black slave. Even though it was symbolic, it gave Blacks some sense of hope, which they recall annually on Juneteenth Day. Contrary to what so many Blacks believe, Abraham Lincoln signed the well-known Emancipation Proclamation in an effort to save the Union, not out of love and compassion for Black slaves. Lincoln's proclamation was a propaganda ploy to lift the spirits of the tired Union troops as well as expectant Blacks. The proclamation announced that all persons held as slaves within any state in rebellion against the United States were henceforth and forever free. President Lincoln had no control over the rebelling Southern states and no constitutional authority to abolish slavery in loyal states. Consequently, Black slaves actually had to wait until the end of the Civil War and the passage of the 13th Amendment to the U.S. Constitution before they gained some quasi-freedom.

A *fifth Emancipation Proclamation* was proposed by the Southern Confederacy in the closing months of the Civil War. Some of its most prominent leaders wanted to use their Emancipation Proclamation to recruit Black slaves to fight the Civil War on behalf of the South. General Robert E. Lee and Jefferson Davis, the president of the Southern Confederacy, announced in their Emancipation Proclamation, willingness to free the slaves in exchange for official recognition from the North that the South was an independent and sovereign territory. The North refused. Even so, the Southern Confederacy finally decided to set Blacks free, but by then it was too late. The war was over and the Southern Confederacy had lost. Five different Emancipation Proclamations were proposed, but none of them actually ended slavery.

Each of the above five proclamations was issued for a specific purpose of the issuer, but none ever went into effect nor ended slavery. The proclamations excited Blacks but did not free them. This is the reason the 13th Amendment to the U.S. Constitution was necessary. Even then, the freedom offered was tenuous, qualified and led to Jim Crow semi-slavery.

Question 36. Blacks have experienced segregation and integration, which should they choose?

Blacks should not choose either segregation or integration. Although segregation had some positive socioeconomic advantages for Blacks, neither strategy was designed to make Blacks fully independent, self-sufficient and socioeconomically competitive in America. To achieve these missing conditions, Blacks should establish communities and use them as platforms for *Ethno-aggregation*, a PowerNomics® term for coming together for empowerment by pooling Black America's various group-based resources. Ethno-aggregation is a proven model used by ethnic, racial, religious and cultural groups to strengthen and self-empower their groups. Ethno-aggregation is different from segregation and integration.

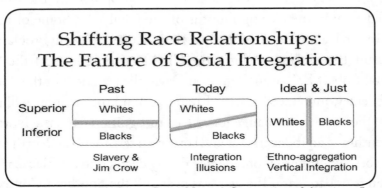

Source: Dr. Claud Anderson, PowerNomics® Corporation of American, Inc.

Segregation benefited Blacks because it forced them into communities where they had to live, work and play together. They built businesses, employed each other, and circulated money within their communities. However, Blacks abandoned the base of the functional communities that they had begun to construct during the 100 years of Jim Crow segregation. Factors that kept Blacks marginal during segregation were both tangible and intangible. During segregation, Blacks had physical communities, a sense of community and a code of conduct. What they lacked was sufficient wealth, an independent Black political party and a competitive group self-interest. The Black Codes and other Southern laws deprived Blacks of these essential resources during slavery and Jim Crow segregation. The primary purpose of slavery was to mal-distribute nearly 100 percent of this nation's wealth, land, businesses, rights, resources, privileges, and political assets into the hands of the dominant White society. To overcome the lack of resources imposed on them by slavery and segregation, Blacks must play as a team and Ethno-aggregate or pool all of their assets and reverse the negative impact of centuries of those destructive systems. Blacks cannot compete while owning only one-half of one percent of anything of value in the richest nation on earth.

More than 60 years after the civil rights movement marched Blacks toward racial integration, history has proven that goal to be a tragic failure. Social integration did not correct the legacies of slavery nor make Blacks a more competitive group. In a nation where power and wealth follow the numbers, the integration process required Blacks to become scattered, minority, unwanted guests within a dominant White society. While Whites were required only to give Blacks limited access to their communities, institutions, and businesses, Blacks volunteered to divest themselves of their culture, history, speech patterns, material resources, religion, schools, businesses, communities, music, sports teams, group identity, racial unity, and most importantly, their group self-interest. These divestitures made Black Americans vulnerable, dependent and more noncompetitive than they had been since slavery.

Integration scattered Blacks and destroyed their sense of community, peoplehood, unity and the economic foundation upon which they could have built competitive and self-sufficient communities. Integration did not provide Blacks with economic resources, in the form of land, businesses, industries and inheritable wealth. Integration offered immeasurable opportunities to get along, cooperate, be acceptable and physically close to Whites in what they owned. But, social integration had certain rules. Blacks had to give up all that was Black in order to integrate. They had to give up their unity, their togetherness, their schools, and their professional business class of doctors, lawyers, dentists, plumbers and carpenters lost their exclusive customer base. Integration stripped from Blacks, the few resources they had managed to accumulate during segregation. Blacks exchanged the few tangibles they had accumulated for symbolism like streets named Martin Luther King, Jr. Boulevard, Rosa Parks Avenue and placement of a few Blacks in high positions in White corporations. Blacks were encouraged to subordinate all forms of Blackness under politically correct public policies. In his book, *The Debt: What America*

Owes to Blacks[43], Randall Robinson quotes former President Bill Clinton, who commented on the willingness of Blacks to accept symbolism as political payment. President Clinton said, "The Black people love me. I don't really know why, but all they seem to care about are the symbolic things like cabinet appointments." When Blacks accepted integration, they gave up Blackness, disappeared into multicultural diversity and still did not get the resources they needed.

Blacks got sidetracked and bamboozled. There was a disconnect between the problem they needed to solve and the solution they chose. There is little connection between rights and resources. Blacks had legal rights awarded to them in the 13th, 14th and 15th Amendments. When Blacks chose integration, Whites began acquiring the cultural and physical assets that Blacks were abandoning or made accessible to Whites. These substantive losses took Blacks backwards, because they received little in return. After centuries of institutional slavery and Jim Crow segregation, the question ought not to have been whether they preferred segregation or integration. That question is never put before Asians, Arabs, Jews, Hispanics or American Indians. Blacks should have publicly proclaimed that they did not want either socio-political process. The foundation upon which Black Americans should now build their communities is the PowerNomics® principle of Ethno-aggregation, which means pooling group resources, whether monetary, political, population or votes, and then playing as a team. Once Blacks gather together their group-based resources, the group should build vertically to control all of those resources from the bottom to the top of the process.

As Blacks try to build new communities, they must remember two things; 1) to make deliberate self-interest group choices, and 2) to avoid past mistakes. When Blacks marched from segregation to integration it was a horizontal move, which failed to empower them. Power comes

---

[43]Robinson, Randall. *The Debt: What America Owes to Blacks*, Plume; reprint edition, New York, 2001, p. 101.

from moving vertically and controlling all the steps from the bottom up to the top of a political or economic hierarchy. Blacks have struggled to get out of the ditch they are in, but they lurch from one philosophy to another, with faint measurable goals. Before undertaking any marches, demonstrations or campaigns, the purpose, goals and the tangible benefits to the race Blacks hope to achieve ought to be clearly formulated and stated—with *measurable* milestones. In the civil rights movement this was rarely done. Integration goals were intangible and non-measurable.

What indicators would Blacks use to measure social integration, freedom, equality and equal opportunity achievements, when these are all terms that are intangible in terms of definition, and are not quantifiable. Measurable milestones would include, for instance, a decrease in the number of unemployed and imprisoned Blacks; an increase in the number of Black businesses and vertical industries, which would mean an increase in Black manufacturers and suppliers; an increase in Black-owned trade schools and magnet schools established in Black communities.

In an effort to avoid repeating the failures of social integration, it is critically important that Blacks have a national plan for a socioeconomic movement with goals, milestones and timetables. If they are going to re-build Black business communities, a coordinating Black organization or network must identify the most appropriate cities; sources of capital; kinds of businesses and industries; professional personnel; marketing strategies; domestic and international partnerships; investors and dependable suppliers of consumer products and raw materials. Blacks built functional businesses and communities before, and they can do it again. This time, perhaps there will be less resistance from White and other ethnic groups, especially if the Black businesses are located within marked and closed Black business districts. The overall goal of building new Black communities should be to make them self-sufficient and competitive socioeconomic enclaves.

Segregation might have been forced upon Blacks by Jim Crow laws and public policies, but in response Blacks built and maintained their own communities, institutions and professional class of leaders. They were producers as well as consumers and owned 10 times more businesses per 100,000 Blacks than they do today. Most importantly, they supported, protected, bought from each other and played as a team. Having tried both segregation and integration, it is time for Black Americans to try *Ethno-aggregation.*

Question 37. Are Blacks too race conscious?

Blacks are not too race conscious. In reality, they are not race conscious enough, as demonstrated by their dogged pursuit of social integration over the past 50 years while the rest of America was balkanizing along ethnic and racial lines. Today, an increasing number of Black Americans are imploring Blacks to rebuild Black communities and spend their money with Black merchants. Clearly, the mere fact that Black Americans have to be encouraged to do what Whites and other ethnic groups do instinctively indicates that Blacks are not race conscious[44] enough to have a self-interest that puts their own people first. Unlike Whites, who identify and unite around their Whiteness, Blacks lack a sense of oneness and solidarity that is needed for group-based socioeconomic empowerment. Blacks have had short spurts of race consciousness in which they tried to come together to pool their resources in their own best self-interest, but those periods did not last long and Blacks rarely played as team long enough to prosper.

During 360 years of slavery, Blacks could neither move nor assemble freely and unsupervised. It was difficult, at best, for Black slaves to develop a sense of unity when they lived in monitored cabins on scattered farms and plantations throughout the Southern states. Slave drivers and plantation overseers conditioned Black slaves to see life and the world

---

[44]Fukuyama, Francis. *Trust: The Social Virtues and the Creation of Prosperity*, A Free Press Paperbacks Book, New York, 1995, pgs. 295-306.

through the eyes of White society, in general, and White slaveholders in particular. Without protection of the law, many Blacks tried to protect themselves by professing love for their masters and all forms of Whiteness. Just as it is in present-day society, slaves were conditioned to believe that by advancing the interests of the master and White society they were advancing the interests of slaves collectively or themselves as individuals.

During the post-Civil War period, millions of newly-freed Black people, for the first time, focused on being Black and coming together in a sense of oneness. They could see the world through the eyes of a Black consciousness instead of through the eyes of the slaveholders' Whiteness. They began transforming their lives from usable property into exceptional human beings with special gifts. They used their new sense of group oneness to build Black churches, schools, businesses, newspapers, social organizations, banks, insurance companies, funeral homes and burial associations, broom factories, mattress factories, movie theaters, factories for Black hair-care products and independent communities. It was within these quasi-communities that Blacks successfully stored their history, culture, pride and businesses. An unintended result of Jim Crow segregation was that it forced Blacks to do what they should have done normally and they owned and operated more businesses during segregation than they have under the illusion of social integration.

During the 20 years between 1915 and 1935, race consciousness emerged again. Aggressive Black visionaries, like W. E. B. Du Bois, called for Black politics; Marcus Garvey for Black economics; Carter G. Woodson for Black culture and Black education; Elijah Muhammad for Islam and a Black nation; and the Harlem Renaissance celebrated Black artists and entertainment. The sense of Black race consciousness was prevalent and profound, but it was short-lived. When the Great Depression ended in the late 1930s, institutionalized Blacks (i.e., civil rights leaders, ministers and newspaper owners) felt there was too much Blackness or race consciousness and called for Black Americans to seek inclusion in mainstream society. They urged the visionary Black leaders and their respective organizations to shift their focus from race consciousness to *universality*, another name for social integration. The march away from race consciousness and toward social integration progressed into the 1960s civil rights movement. The civil rights movement, led by institutionalized Black leaders, clashed with younger Blacks, who organized the Black Power Movement and demanded more Black consciousness.

The Black Civil Rights Movement's push for social integration garnered more attention, acceptance and respect within mainstream society, because Whites felt more threatened by the Black Power Movement. In response to White anxiety of Black consciousness, the government intervened and destroyed the Blackness movement by distorting its activities and criminalizing its leadership. A few years into the civil rights movement, Black leadership abandoned Black race consciousness, and pledged their commitment to public policies of political correctness involving immigrants, women and various other fabricated minorities. Did Black leaders truly believe that Whites would voluntarily give up their own race consciousness, sense of oneness and White togetherness? Racism is a team sport, which means a group must play as a team or risk losing by default. Civil rights leaders, ministers and elected public officials soon abandoned all forms of exclusive Blackness. They joined mainstream White society's focus on fabricated classes, minorities, diversity and open-door immigration policies. They thereby allowed White society to capture and corrupt the civil rights movement, pervert its language and goals, use Dr. King's concept of a color-blind society to extract race out of racism and demonize all forms of Black consciousness. Just like during slavery, Whites were more at ease with Blacks who were color-blind and accepted the racial status quo.

Slavery and Jim Crow semi-slavery in the United States did more than rob Blacks of their individual dignity, it robbed them of their social cohesiveness and pride and discouraged cooperative behavior. Race consciousness is essential for self-sufficiency, but there are no mainstream incentives or rewards.

Question 38. Should Blacks form and support their own independent, national political party?

Most definitely, Blacks should form and support their own independent, national politcal party. Voting is based on the core premise of Quid Pro Quo, which means something for something. The delivery of a group's bloc vote should give the group the leverage to demand benefits to improve the lives of group members. Blacks then should cast their votes *only* to support a candidate that has promised benefits specific to their group. They ought not support anybody or anything that does not socioeconomically advance their group collectively.

"Build a Black Independent Party."
Source: PowerNomics® Corporation of America, Inc.

Whites have perfected shifting political parties according to what is best for their group self-interest. After the Civil War, Blacks flocked to the Republican Party and Whites left and joined the Democratic Party. In the 1940s, President Truman integrated the military and Senator Strom Thurmond led the exit of Whites out of the Democratic Party to the Republican Party. More Whites left the Democratic Party when President Kennedy was elected, because he was pro-integration, and

Blacks swarmed into the party. Whites choose political party affiliation based upon what is best for them. Blacks tend to stay loyal to a political party, even if they receive nothing in exchange for their support. Neither national political party, Republican nor Democratic, has delivered specific material benefits to Black Americans in the last 150 years. Some might say, "But Lincoln freed the slaves." Freeing the slaves was incidental to Lincoln's desire to reunite the nation. Freedom for slaves was a collateral benefit. Political party affiliation is a diversion and straw man. It is not the real issue. From the 1500s to the late 1860s, nearly five million enslaved Blacks did not belong to any party. From the 1860s to the late 1940s, approximately 20 million Blacks belonged to the Republican Party and were Jim Crow segregated. From the 1950s to 2016, 44 million Blacks belonged primarily to the Democratic Party and they remain beneath a public policy of Benign Neglect. They are ignored, displaced and treated with hateful indifference. National party affiliation does not make a difference in the way that Blacks are treated.

Some suggest that there are benefits to Blacks splitting their allegiance between the two national parties. However, that does not strengthen Blacks as a group. They are already a planned minority. The White majority voters combined with White ethnic immigrants out-number Black voters nine to one, which implies a no or low chance of Blacks winning or being considered. Whites do not need the Black vote to get a voting majority to approve whatever it is they want. The only way Black voters can be recognized, respected and become a powerful voting bloc is to form a national, independent Black political party, according to PowerNomics® principles[45]. The way for Blacks to acquire greater voting power would be to: 1) withdraw from both the Democratic and Republican Party; 2) run no candidates for public office; but 3) proclaim a willingness to vote as a solid national bloc for any political party, or its candidate, regardless of color, that promises and delivers the most

---

[45] Anderson, Claud. *PowerNomics®: The National Plan to Empower Black America*, PowerNomics® Corporation of America, Inc., Maryland, 2001, pgs. 214-218.

benefits to Black Americans. The mere possibility that the Black vote might be in play; that they would have to be courted with promises and follow through; that their vote might no longer be predictable and that 44 million Blacks might vote as a bloc, would make it difficult for any political party or candidate to ignore Black voters or take them for granted.

In Chapter Seven of *PowerNomics®: The National Plan to Empower Black America,* I discuss the importance of Blacks having a national political party and explain that the two major parties do not need or respect Black voters. They only use Black voters to shift the balance in a close major election. Democrats feel Black voters have no place to go and no leader to take them there, so they are ignored and taken for granted by the Democrats. Author Tom Wicker, a retired White political columnist for *The New York Times,* echoed my position in his book, *The Tragic Failure of Racial Integration in America*[46]. Wicker said, "Both political parties are reliant on, indebted to, and protective of powerful corporate interests. The Republicans are devoted primarily to serving the immediate wishes of the mostly White middle-class. The Democrats are the *me too* party, with neither the power, nor the vision, nor the political courage, to advance the interests of poor African-Americans."

After Blacks make a declaration of political independence and form their own national Black political party, they must learn to carefully articulate and then demand measurable benefits and use their leverage to reward and punish politicians. They must get out of their political rut and, if a candidate does not say their group name–which is *Black* not *minorities, poor people* or *everybody*—then they should not give that candidate their vote. Should Blacks form an independent political party? The answer is in a line from a popular song from the 1940s, "Mama may have, Daddy may have, but God bless the child that's got his own."

---

[46]Wicker, Tom. *The Tragic Failure of Integration,* William Morrow and Company, New York, 1996, p. 37.

Question 39. Did the Slave Codes of 1705 intentionally inflict psychological damage on Black people?

The Slave Codes were laws that severely restricted slave behavior and were intended to prevent slave uprisings and rebellions. The Slave Codes imposed harsh physical punishment on the slaves. The Black man was a particular target. Black men were the natural guardians of the race and the family, but the success of slavery depended on the ability of the slaveholders to crush and control the Black man. Slavery was successful.

Slaveholders developed effective techniques to control the behavior of a male slave, techniques that would cripple his children and their children for generations to come[47]. The Slave Codes formalized many control techniques, but left much room for creativity. The Black man was totally helpless before his White master, who used the psychology of harsh physical punishment to encourage the Black man to submit to slavery, to break his independent will and to shape the attitudes of the Black boys in the slave pipeline. The slave owners did this by demeaning the man in front of his family so that it was clear that the Black man could not protect them, that he was totally helpless before the White man and that he could never be anything other than a slave.

It has long been the role of males in most cultures to provide for and protect the family and to provide leadership and training to the children. When African men were brought to these shores, slavery interfered with and perverted their normal masculine behavior patterns. Commercial enslavement was primarily a gender-specific industry. The slaveholder feared the Black man more than he feared the Black woman. Until the early 1800s, nearly 80 percent of the slaves brought into this country were Black men. In the 1600s in the Virginia colony, both White women and Black women were out-numbered by their male counterparts four to one.

---

[47]Greenberg, Kenneth S. *Honor and Slavery*, Princeton University Press, Princeton, New Jersey, 1996, pgs. 33-37.

White slave owners wanted the strongest slaves that they could find and worked them to death before they were 40 years of age. African women became important as breeders when the Constitution outlawed importing slaves after 1808. It was true that Black women—having a higher birth rate; greater longevity; less harsh life style; and being in a protected class with less chance of being killed—allowed the number of Black women to catch up to and surpass the number of Black men.

The Slave Codes had a psychological basis. The purpose was to create a population of slaves that were docile, compliant and would never rise up against the slaveholders. Slavery also had an effect on those who imposed the harsh treatment. They became dehumanized and conditioned to inflicting pain. Thus, the Slave Codes had psychological effects that lasted for generations on both the Whites who imposed the treatment as well as the recipient Blacks. That conditioning is on display today in many ways, for instance, when White police officers use excessive violence and even kill unarmed Black men. The Slave Codes crippled 15 generations of people. They kept Black men from fulfilling the role of responsible fathers and husbands, degraded Black people, made them hopeless and non-productive for anything other than slave duties and criminalized nearly every normal behavior.

It is unconscionable for society to look at Black people today, criticize their behavior and ignore the permanent harm Whites, the Slave Codes and similar laws intentionally inflicted on an entire race of people. While the slaveholding ancestors designed the system of slavery and applied the pain and degradation, Whites today enjoy the benefits. When the psychological damage is added to the fact that Blacks *could not* benefit from the resources found in this county, in fact *were considered* a resource, it is a wonder is that any Blacks have managed to rise above the legacy of slavery. Blacks will need resources from the dominant society to rehabilitate their race. The call for reparations should come from fair-minded people. It should not come only from Blacks.

Question 40. Why was it a criminal offense to teach Blacks to read and write?

The European colonists opposed educating Black people because they knew that educated Blacks, like educated Whites, would not tolerate being enslaved, brutalized and exploited. An educated person would fight back and revolt. Whites knew that the best way to protect their financial investment and their lives was to impose ignorance on Blacks. They therefore instituted public policies that stipulated that any White person caught teaching a Black person to read and write would be fined $100 and suffer 39 lashes with a whip. Later, there are numerous recorded instances where Blacks were lynched for carrying a book or newspaper, especially in the South. Teaching people to read and write was a crime *only* when it applied to educating Blacks. Schools were established and operated for immigrants and American Indians, making Blacks the only people who for centuries were subjected to imposed ignorance.

The last thing White America, and especially the South, needed were Black slaves capable of reading, writing and challenging the nation's socioeconomic system. Whites in the North harbored the same fears as their Southern counterparts, and education for the majority of Blacks in the country was nearly non-existent as a matter of practice. In the North, segregation in schools was the practice, if not the law. Segregation in the South, however, was both law and practice. The law was clear; it was illegal to teach a slave to read and write. White Southerners believed that educating or teaching slaves to read or write only ruined them as laborers. Prevailing sentiment in the South was that Whites had the responsibility to take every measure possible to ensure that no light ever entered the brain of a Black person.

In some of the Northern states, where it was against the cultural norms, but not state law, some Quakers and philanthropic Whites did educate a few Blacks and trained them to perform a few household and simple business tasks. Following the Civil War, Black ministers and business owners assumed the responsibility of educating newly-freed slaves. They worked together and built public and private schools for Blacks. However, only in rare instances were Black schools permitted to educate their students in highly skilled areas, such as medicine, engineering and the practice of law. Howard University in Washington, D.C., was one of those rare exceptions. Howard was built for the Black offspring of White members of Congress, and its students were mainly mulattoes. Oliver O. Howard, who had been a distinguished general in the Civil War and was a member of Congress, was the founder of the University. Howard students received a higher quality education than Black children with undistinguished parentage in other schools. In almost all other cases, in both public and private schools, Black students were relegated to an education that made sure they were noncompetitive with White students.

Following the Great Depression, public policies made it acceptable to provide Blacks at least a marginal education, usually in what was called *manual* or *industrial arts*. But, it was still dangerous to be educated, even in manual arts. Following World War II in the late 1940s, in Southern states it was normal for Black teachers to be insulted and beaten and to have their schools burned down. There were instances in which Blacks traveling in Southern states were beaten and even lynched just for reading a Northern Black newspaper, which was considered contraband. The Ku Klux Klan, America's premier White supremacist organization, was the anti-reading enforcer. Klansmen were assigned to monitor trains and bus stations, watching to find Black porters and travelers who were reading. They confiscated any Black newspapers they found. Even though many Klan members were uneducated and most could not read, they knew enough to believe that educated and informed Blacks were a greater threat to White society and the Southern culture than uneducated Blacks. During slavery, Jim Crow segregation and into the Black Civil Rights Movement, Black people learned to dumb down to protect their lives and jobs, especially in Southern states. The 1954 Supreme Court *Brown v Board of Education* case forced the issue of Black education, and Whites pushed back to keep the races separate, but it was a losing legal issue. Consequently, Whites decided to move away from Black people rather than to fight them. They retreated from urban centers and relocated their businesses, wealth, jobs, schools and middle-class lives into newly-constructed, all-White suburbs.

By 2017, it was no longer necessary for Blacks to pretend to dumb down. In many urban areas the schools, public and private, are under-educating Black children. There are reports in some districts that there are schools that: 1) do not even have basic school supplies, like textbooks, paper and pencils; 2) have buildings that are not physically well-maintained; and 3) allow up to 50 percent of Black students to graduate from high school without basic skills in reading, writing and math. If those reports reflect the educational conditions for Black children across the country, then there is little difference between criminalizing the education of Black children and the failure of responsible people to educate Black children.

Question 41. Is the Statue of Liberty an outdated immigration symbol?

The Statue of Liberty is among the most recognizable monuments in this country and around the world. Millions of people visit the statue annually and identify with it emotionally, viewing it as the symbol of hope that it was for their European immigrant ancestors. No Statue of Liberty or symbol of hope greeted the millions of kidnapped Africans brought into this country as slaves. Black Americans are the nation's only non-immigrants, even so-called Native or American Indians migrated across the Bering Straits around 5,000 years ago. The millions of immigrants that came before the Civil War came to get a part of the American dream of free land and free labor, and to be the ownership and management class over the millions of Africans imported to be the free labor class. African Blacks, the ancestors of 99 percent of today's native Black Americans, were shipped from Africa to the Caribbean islands then to the United States. Most entered the country through Jones Island, James Island and Sullivan Island, destination ports located in the harbor of Charleston, South Carolina. From there they were shipped to other locations.

Unlike the Statue of Liberty in New York's harbor, arriving slave boats and their human cargo were met by slave drivers, slave pen owners and auctioneers who stood on the display platforms to sell the slaves. The notorious slaveholding platforms were removed from town centers in South Carolina in the 1970s, the Statue of Liberty still stands although the reception center for European immigrants was closed nearly 60 years ago. Since the 1960s, the number of Europeans migrating to America has significantly decreased. The majority of today's immigrants, both legal and illegal, are entering through this nation's Southern borders. They too, like European immigrants of yesteryear, come into the country in search of unearned benefits and opportunities as promised in the American Dream.

An increasing number of Blacks as well as White Americans, however, are sensing that this nation can no longer afford to receive an unlimited flow of immigrants and are demanding immigration reform. They want this nation to close its doors for a while, improve the immigrant vetting process and alter the words on Ms. Liberty's bronze plaque, written by Emma Lazarus in 1883. The sonnet urged the world to send, "…your tired, your poor, your huddled masses yearning to breathe free," to the U.S. Lazarus wrote the *Liberty Poem* as part of the effort to raise funds to construct a pedestal for the statue on Ellis Island. (It is quite ironic, though not a well-known fact, that the model for the statue of Liberty was a Black woman.) Although Blacks were, "…the tired, the poor and the huddled masses yearning to breathe free," after slavery, times have changed. Today, both Black and White Americans are tired, growing poorer and more apprehensive about uncertain social and economic conditions in this country and around the world.

How do the words on the Statue of Liberty connect with immigrants from Middle-Eastern countries that are fighting 1,500-year-old religious holy wars, or refugees fleeing drug wars in Latin America? Since 1965, most immigrants have received support from private or government subsidies, whether grants from their home countries, subsidies from the U.S. or church programs. European and Asian immigrants are not exceptionally poor. The personal net worth of Mexican immigrants doubles and triples when they become citizens of the United States. So, today's immigrants are not generally the, "wretched refuse" of any country's teeming shores, but they still come here seeking the American Dream and the many unearned benefits made available to them because they have been classified as minorities. President Barack Obama extended invitations to an even greater number of immigrants and provided increased benefits. But, Blacks who are stuck in the urban centers seeking to escape poverty, gang warfare, poor education and unemployment in their own country, do not have even the same access and assistance to the American Dream as immigrants and refugees. It is illegal and immoral for this nation's government to classify immigrants as refugees and give them civil rights, privileges and benefits that are not even available to suffering urban Blacks. The U.S. focused on correcting the historical, government-imposed injustices to Black Americans for a few years in the 1960s, but never finished the job. Immigration is not, nor should it be, classified as a civil rights issue. Immigrants as a class have not been abused, subordinated, enslaved or Jim Crow segregated in this country by the American government.

Blacks are now the nation's official, abandoned labor class buried beneath the continuous torrent of immigrants, who rank higher in social acceptability in a politically correct society. It is time for native Black people to demand that the nation carry out its obligations to them first. A good beginning point would be for the government to acknowledge that the symbol of the Statue of Liberty is no longer relevant. The next step would be for the government to acknowledge that the U.S. first has an obligation to prioritize and correct the economic and social problems of native Blacks, whose ancestors built the country but were never allowed to profit from their work, *before* extending unearned benefits to immigrant newcomers. For 500 years, native Blacks have been the tired, hungry, poor, the, "huddled masses yearning to be free." This is a political issue that will only be addressed if and when Blacks demand that it be done.

Question 42. Is there a voting guide for the average Black American voter?

The Dilemma of the Black Voter: No Quid Pro Quo

Source: PowerNomics® Corporation of America, Inc.

Chapter Seven of my book, *PowerNomics®: The National Plan to Empower Black America*, released in 2001, offers Black voters strategies they can use to maximize the effect of their group vote and gain the greatest group-based tangible benefits. When Blacks play American politics, based upon the needs and interests of other groups, they are not playing to win, they are *playing to play;* to be accepted; to get along and to get nothing in return for their efforts. The 1870 Code of Conduct was the Maryland law that codified the political behavior Whites expected Blacks to exhibit. It described the rules of how Blacks would play in the game of politics, but only play. Politics, however, is socioeconomic Darwinism, the survival of the fittest.

The PowerNomics® guide for voters is a new Code of Conduct for Blacks based on the assumption that they will play to *win* for self and team. These principles require a group change in behavior and will demonstrate to all that Blacks as a group will no longer abide by the 1870 Code of Conduct; that they are instituting a new Code of Conduct in politics and that Black interests will now come first. To implement new strategies, Black voters should begin by cleaning their own house first. They must no longer tolerate Black elected officials or others who purport to represent Blacks, but actually want only to *play* in the game of politics. These officials want to be seen in a positive light, as generally friendly and cooperative but do not want to deliver benefits to Black supporters, preferring instead to deliver benefits to competitor groups. Too often Black officials oppose or refuse to stand up for issues specific to Blacks and cause the group to lose, although the officials themselves may personally profit. The PowerNomics® action steps below are a guide to Blacks for implementing new political strategies. The new Code of Conduct in politics also informs Whites of the changed behaviors they can now expect from Blacks. The PowerNomics steps are a guide and new Code of Conduct in politics that Blacks should follow. These PowerNomics principles in politics are narrowly focused to address the needs and interests of Black Americans and should be used as criteria to analyze candidates, political parties and ballot issues.

PowerNomics Political Principles

1) **Play to Win**
   Politics is a game that decides what groups receive which benefits. Blacks should not participate in a game in which they can never win. Vote to win and to get group benefits or withhold the group vote.

2) **Negotiate Quid Pro Quo Agreements with Candidates and Parties**
   Create a list of tangible and measurable benefits your group expects to receive from candidates and political parties in return for the group votes. Vote only for those candidates who promise and deliver the

most material benefits to Black Americans for their votes. Do not even consider support of candidates who insist on using all-inclusive terms, such as *everyone*, *minorities*, *diversity* and *people of color* while they are specifically seeking the Black vote.

3) **Aggregate Group Resources: Vote as a Racial Bloc**

Voting is a team-based activity in which the majority wins and rules. Blacks are a planned permanent minority. Power and wealth follow the numbers. Build an independent party that uses the Black block vote to extract group benefits from political candidates, regardless of the race of the candidate. Once elected, use your bloc vote to hold elected officials accountable. If no candidate promises group benefits, also withhold the Black bloc vote. If politicians win because of the Black vote but fail to deliver measurable benefits specifically to the group, discipline that politician by using the Black bloc vote to recall them or to defeat them in the next election.

4) **Vote the Economic Interest of Your Group First**

What Blacks own and control determines their rights and opportunities. Use your group vote to control economics and to influence and control politicians and political parties. Prioritize and vote the economic interests of your group before looking out for the interest of others.

5) **Support Only Those Who Support Black Americans**

Do not support any political party, political candidate or business, regardless of color, which will not publicly support Black America. Demand explicit support. Under the new Code of Conduct in politics, it will no longer be acceptable to send Black politicians to office to look out for *everyone*. Candidates who get Black support must deliver. Inappropriate behavior or betrayal by elected Black officials or others will be unacceptable.

The new code will also apply to corporations and ethnic businesses established in Black neighborhoods. Blacks must require those businesses to marshal their political resources to help eradicate the systemic problems of housing, unemployment, lack of top quality schools and poor food. It will no longer be politically acceptable for these businesses to extract money out of Black neighborhoods without making a substantial contribution to the well being of the Black consumers.

6) **Reject Intangible, Symbolic Measures as Payment for Your Votes**
Demonstrate rejection of the 1870 political Code of Conduct by demanding explicit support, material and measurable resources that can be touched, counted and have monetary value. Do not accept implicit, unspoken, assumed or symbolic support. If the Black vote puts a politician in office, do not accept a basketball court, a street or building named after a Black person as adequate reward. If the Quid Pro Quo political benefit cannot be measured or deposited into the bank, it is unacceptable as an exchange for votes.

The 1870 political Code of Conduct defined the behavior of Black elected officials and unfortunately still guides the behavior of them, even today. The code conditioned the politicians, but it also conditioned Black voters, and taught them to *not* vote for their own interests in politics. It conditioned Whites to expect that Black voters would not speak for or even name their own group or articulate the needs of the group. It is unconscionable that today, in 2017, Black politicians and voters have not publicly rejected the conservative behavior required by the old Code of Conduct. PowerNomics® principles, however, guide Blacks to disavow the 1870 Code of Conduct; to speak and vote in a way that benefits their group and to hold accountable all those who benefit from Black political action. Blacks should use their vote to elect people who will take positive action for their specific group and to impose consequences on those who will not.

PART VII

Profiling Presidents and Authorities

Question 43. What is the link between U.S. presidents and marijuana/hemp?

In the mid-1980s, President Ronald Reagan's wife, Nancy Reagan, led a national anti-drug campaign, telling the nation and young people that in regards to drugs, "Just say no." Today, nearly 40 years later, marijuana growing and selling marijuana have the potential of becoming one of the nation's greatest wealth-building industries. Since President Ronald Reagan and Nancy Reagan departed from the White House, many popular entertainers and athletes have admitted their recreational use of marijuana and an increasing number of states have legalized its use and possession. Within the last 25 years, even three American presidents contributed to the growing public acceptance of marijuana by admitting their use of it. Bill Clinton made his public admission in the 1990s. Barack Obama surprised many people when he confessed in his autobiography and on national television that he had smoked marijuana. In January 2015, Jeb Bush, ex-governor of Florida and brother of ex-president George W. Bush, began to clear away personal debris as he prepared to run for the presidency, telling reporters for *The Boston Globe* newspaper that he had smoked marijuana. The public may be accustomed to hearing about entertainers and marijuana, but they ought not be that surprised about U.S. presidents and other public officials having a relationship with marijuana. There is a long history between them. The only thing that is new is high-level government officials publicly admitting their involvement with this particular drug.

Marijuana played a central role in the lives of not only modern U.S. presidents and other public officials, but the nation's Founding Fathers and other prominent historical figures who were also involved with the hemp plant and other drugs. For centuries, the hemp plant was a basic raw material used in numerous industries to produce a variety of consumer products. It was prominently grown, especially on Southern plantations, and used recreationally and medically as well.

Large slavery plantations grew marijuana for consumer items and for use on the plantations. As examples, George Washington, Thomas Jefferson and Benjamin Franklin, who each owned hundreds of slaves, were large hemp plant growers and reputed smokers. Even President Abraham Lincoln allegedly used marijuana recreationally as well as for a painkiller. The marijuana hemp plant was legal tender, used even to pay taxes, in colonial society until the mid-1800s. Fibers from the hemp plant were used to make ropes, canvas, twine, string, paper and clothes for Black slaves. Various pharmaceutical companies used the liquid to produce medicines. According to the U.S. Census, in 1850 there were 8,327 marijuana plantations. By 1883, marijuana-smoking parlors were legally opened in major urban cities. New York City alone had over 500 smoking parlors. By the late 1800s, marijuana and hemp were so popular, cities and towns were named after them. There were Hempstead, Long Island; Hempstead County, Arkansas; Hempstead, Texas; Hemphill, North Carolina; Hempfield, Pennsylvania and many other towns and streets bearing the name.

Although Blacks were never the major producers or commercial users of the hemp plant when it was legal, they were stigmatized by the possession and use of the plant after it became illegal. Instead of blaming White owners of large farms that produced the plant, Blacks were blamed for the increased use of marijuana between 1910 and 1930s. Public officials in New Orleans charged that marijuana smoking was making Blacks think they were as good as White men. Some members of the White overclass believed marijuana was to blame for the assertiveness of Black activists and the loud laughter of Blacks when Whites gave them orders.

By the time Presidents Bill Clinton and Barack Obama confessed their marijuana smoking, it had gained acceptability and was nearly politically correct. With rising acceptability, like the Phoenix, marijuana production and use will rise again and become the biggest wealth producer of the 21st century. A number of states and federal institutions began issuing licenses for legally growing marijuana beginning in 2013. However, in all likelihood, just as in previous centuries, Blacks will wind up being consumers of the product rather than producers and will most likely not be the beneficiaries of the wealth it generates.

Question 44. What will be President Barack Obama's greatest and most memorable legacy?

In a speech to the Congressional Black Caucus on September 18, 2016, President Barack Obama told the assembled Black audience, "I will consider it a personal insult and an insult to my legacy, if the Black community does not support Hillary Clinton's candidacy so that she can continue my legacy." Donald Trump however was elected as President of the United States of America. In a shocking reversal of voting patterns, Black voters gave Donald Trump three times the number of votes they gave the Republican Party in the past 65 years of presidential elections. Black voters who switched their political loyalties from Hillary Clinton and the Democratic Party to Donald Trump sent up a distress signal. These Black voters did not want continuation of President Barack Obama's legacy nor the traditional way Hillary Clinton and the Democratic Party have viewed and treated Black Americans. Blacks wanted a change in their socioeconomic conditions, conditions that Obama did not address during his two terms.

Black voters gave Barack Obama nearly 100 percent of their vote in both of his national elections, but the quality of life gap between Blacks and Whites widened while Obama served as President. Courtland Milloy, a columnist for *The Washington Post*, in an article on August 2, 2011, lamented Black sadness. Milloy said, "Black America is crying the blues like no time since the Great Depression. Black households, on average, have lost more than half their worth in just a few short years, and the wealth gap between Blacks and Whites is at a historic high.[48]" What Milloy neglected to say was that racial disparities widened across the socioeconomic spectrum under President Obama's administration. White unemployment dropped, while the Black structural unemployment rate remained at nearly 50 percent. The poverty rate for Blacks increased to nearly 37 percent and their median family incomes declined. Black imprisonment remained above 51 percent. Black student achievement levels and college enrollment dropped, and the FBI continued reporting that approximately 67 percent of the nation's hate crimes are committed against Black Americans.

With social integration and the Black Civil Rights Movement having failed to significantly eradicate racial disparities, a host on the American Urban Radio Network[49] asked President Obama, what, as the most powerful man on earth, were his plans for relieving the suffering and desperate conditions within Black America. President Obama quickly responded, "I can't pass laws that say I am going to help Black folks. I am the president of the entire U.S. What I can do is to make sure that I am passing laws that help all people, particularly those who are most in need." These are glorious but misleading statements but show weakness and indifference toward his own people. If his intent was to help *all* the people, then he should have helped Black Americans. All means all. Further, Obama chose to give special assistance to Hispanics, Arabs, Jews, American Indians and LGBTs without, "passing laws for them." In the

---

[48]Milloy, Courtland. "Black America Still Celebrates Obama, if not His Policies," *The Washington Post*, article, August 2, 2011.

[49]An official White House interview of President Barack Obama by April Ryan, a Black reporter for the American Urban Radio Network, conducted on December 21, 2009.

instance of American Indians, the Harvest Institute Freedmen Federation filed a lawsuit in 2007 and asked President Obama not to *pass a law*, but simply to *obey* the 1866 Indian Treaties. A treaty, an agreement between sovereign nations, is supposed to be the highest law in the land. The 1866 Treaties mandated that Black Indians and those Blacks formerly-owned as slaves by Indians, be treated exactly as non-Black Native Indians are treated. For eight years, President Obama and his administration ignored the 1866 Treaties and the benefits those treaties mandated for Black Indians and Black Freedmen, but he used the same laws to settled more than 100 pending legal suits filed by non-Black Native Indians. President Obama made the front page of major newspapers in 2016 as the tribes celebrated their victory and thanked Obama for remembering the promises he had made to them and kept.

To Black Americans, he had made no promises, therefore there were no promises to be kept. Throughout two years of campaigning and eight years of being the most powerful man of earth, President Obama rode the racial fence and used flowery rhetoric in the hopes of magically achieving the impossible. He tried to take race out of race matters and racial inequalities. Instead of providing wheelchairs to Blacks, historically crippled by mainstream society, President Obama chose to provide wheelchairs to other more socially-preferred and less-afflicted groups. He left Blacks to hobble on their own. President Obama continued the Benign Neglect public policies and practices that President Richard Nixon instituted on Black people in 1970. In Benign Neglect, the government excludes Blacks from public policies by name, but gives the public illusion that they are included within the broad categories of *minorities, people of color and diversity*. Over the course of the past 50 years, these public policies have transmuted into hateful indifference toward Blacks people.

President Barack Obama's turning a blind eye toward Black Americans will be a model for all future presidents. In the closing months of his presidency, an increasing number of Blacks, as well as Whites, were asking why President Barack Obama had so judiciously avoided identifying with and aiding Blacks. Some speculated that it was because Obama was the first African American, not *Black* American president. Raised outside of the continental U.S. and not having the experience of Black enslavement or Jim Crow semi-slavery in his family, could be a partial answer. Others speculate that since he attended Harvard Law School and taught constitutional law, he knew the risks of associating with Blackness, yet chose to ignore the principle of electoral politics, Quid Pro Quo—something for something; you vote for me, I owe you. Many Black voters are feeling betrayed, remembering that Obama placed his hand on the Holy Bible and promised to, "represent, protect and serve," all the people, yet he ignored identification with loyal Black voters. He chose instead to identify with and direct resources, not to Blacks, but to lower-risk groups, such as ethnic immigrants, religious groups, LQBT and gender minorities.

In reality, there were no incentives for Barack Obama to identify with and represent Black Americans, since he did not campaign in Black neighborhoods and promised them nothing for their votes and loyalties. President Barack Obama was a color-blind president who was a master of using soaring rhetoric and supporting symbolic activities that were emotionally gratifying to Black Americans. Therefore, Black Americans must bear some of the blame for the behavioral indifference that President Obama exhibited toward his own people. For too long, Black Americans have been satisfied with receiving nothing or just emotional satisfaction when a Black person is elevated into a high-level position *because* of their support. Blacks must exercise greater critical thinking and evaluate Black public officials based upon what the officials do—or do not do—in measurable terms for Black supporters.

President Obama will have two landmark legacies. First, as a president, Barack Obama showed that Black candidates are qualified to hold the highest office in the nation and can be relied upon to do exactly what any White person holding the office would do in regards to racial matters. Second, Barack Obama will go into the history books as a model for all future White presidents who, in race matters can say to Black Americans, "If a Black man who was in the White House for eight years did absolutely nothing to help his own people, why then should a White president feel obligated to do anything? If a Black man is color-blind to Blackness, why shouldn't Whites also be blind to Blackness." Such a legacy will be difficult to explain to future generations of Black voters who grew up hearing about the power of the vote and the importance of getting Blacks elected to high levels of government.

Question 45. In 1870, what Code of Conduct in politics did Whites impose on Blacks who sought public office?

The 15th Amendment to the U.S. Constitution was specifically designed to grant suffrage rights to Black people. The amendment stipulated that the rights of Blacks to vote, "Shall not be denied or abridged by the United States or by any state on account of race, color or previous condition of servitude." Blacks assumed that this new law meant that as newly-freed slaves they would have unrestricted opportunities to vote, run for public office and politically exercise an interest in addressing the needs and aspirations of their own people. The Radical Republicans, who were the congressional liberals in those days, enacted the laws that freed Blacks and gave them voting rights. However, White conservative political forces still needed a subordinated Black labor and consumer class. Southern Whites were unwilling to relinquish control of Blacks, who were anxious to enter electoral politics. Blacks got their chance in the late 1860s, after the Civil War, when Southern states had to comply with the Reconstruction Act of 1867. This act required every former Confederate Southern state to host a constitutional convention and to craft a state constitution before it could rejoin the United States of America.

"The First Black Congressional Representatives Elected During Reconstruction." Source: Libarary of Congress.

To ensure that the new state constitutions contained all of the post-Civil War constitutional amendments and the 1866 Civil Rights Law, Radical Republicans used their congressional powers to push both Republicans and Blacks to attend the Southern constitutional conventions and actively participate in the planning sessions. In South Carolina, which was one of the most conservative Southern states, Blacks not only attended and participated in the committees, they constituted the majority of those attending South Carolina's constitutional convention. The participation of Blacks in the state conventions frightened White conservatives, who were already concerned that Radical Republicans were giving Blacks entrée to government employment by appointing them to low-level jobs, such as clerks, postmen, sheriffs and school employees at the federal, city and county level. There was an even greater concern about Blacks seeking high-level state and federal elected positions. Conservative Southerners contrived a plan that enabled them to neutralize Blacks' newly-acquired political power and simultaneously conserve employment, income and power opportunities for Whites.

With the legal controls of slavery gone, conservatives instituted numerous formal and informal codes of behavior to protect the group-based interests of Whites in maintaining the racial status quo. Conservatives established political Codes of Conduct, many unwritten, that they imposed on Blacks seeking to be elected or appointed to public office. Some states did formalize their political codes of conduct into laws. Whether written or unwritten, those codes have stood as sacred understandings between Blacks and Whites for centuries, and endure until the present time, especially in Southern states. These codes plainly told Blacks the political behaviors from them that Whites would consider inappropriate and unacceptable. The three primary elements of the Code of Conduct ground rules for Blacks seeking public office were: 1) Blacks in high public office could not use their position to publicly encourage, support or direct causes to alter Black economic conditions; 2) Blacks in high public office could not encourage Black people to act as a unified group; and 3) Blacks in high public office could not advocate holding Whites accountable for slavery or ill-treatment. The particulars of the Southern behavior codes and what Whites expected of Blacks were conveyed through person-to-person contacts, written media and by public proclamation of legal and extra-legal organizations, such as the Ku Klux Klan and White Citizens Councils. When Reconstruction ended in the mid-1870s, the Radical Republicans abandoned Blacks and withdrew back to the North.

The unofficial Code of Conduct for Blacks in elected politics is visible today in the behavior of Black politicians who try to take race out of race matters or try to avoid involvement in the topic altogether. This behavior management tool imposed on Blacks has been in place for 150 years, but does not apply to other racial, ethnic, religious or gender groups of people. It applies only to Blacks. It is inconceivable that White, Asian, Native American or Jewish elected officials would be instructed to avoid taking public positions on issues of importance to their specific group. Fearing the consequence of breaking the Code of Conduct, Black elected officials today still shy away from using their office or a public platform to address and remove the historical barriers that prevent their people from being self-sufficient and competitive. Expectations of the political Code of Conduct have become so engrained in Blacks, in general, and Black voters, in particular, that they do not even expect leadership or material support from Blacks in high levels of government or corporate America.

As the authentic period of the Black Civil Rights Movement was ending in the late 1960s and early 1970s, a few activist Black elected officials defied the Code of Conduct. They entered politics for the specific purpose of using their offices to improve the socioeconomic conditions of Blacks in their jurisdictions. They defied the political code and took public positions on Black issues, worked for the good of the group, treated Blacks as White politicians treated White constituents and began to deliver benefits to their constituents. Mayor Harold Washington of Chicago, Illinois; Mayor Coleman Young of Detroit, Michigan; Mayor Marion Barry of Washington, D.C.; and Mayor Maynard Jackson of Atlanta, Georgia are some of the mayors who used their positions to ensure Blacks were included in contract, grant and employment processes. As a result, Blacks in those cities accessed and profited from economic opportunities that had not previously been available to them.

Black voters who elect candidates to public office have a right to expect benefits. It is apparent that there is a missing connection between electing a Black person to a public office and Black America receiving proportional social and economic benefits in return for their votes. There is a good chance that Black voters could change the game, if they established a Black Code of Conduct that rewards or punishes Black elected or appointed officials who become color-blind and can no longer see their people's suffering.

Question 46. How were programs like the Great Society and the Freedmen's Bureau subverted from their original intent to help Blacks?

The Great Society Program of the 1960s and the Freedmen's Bureau, 100 years earlier, were both created to correct Black problems that stem back to slavery. These programs are just two instances where solutions to *Black* problems were distorted and resources redirected to benefit other, non-affected but more preferable groups. The pattern and strategy of diversion have been used throughout the history of this country and are still effective today. It is important to recognize and understand these strategies and patterns. Examination of the life cycle of the Great Society Program and the Freedmen's Bureau show how well intentioned programs to help Blacks are diverted to help minorities or everyone.

Great Society Program

President Lyndon Johnson's 1964 Great Society Program, as proposed, was a comprehensive package of socioeconomic programs, created during the midst of the civil rights era, in response to the misery Johnson saw in Black communities and requests from the civil rights community. The $3 billion-dollar package deal that passed Congress, however, reflected the country's social construct on race, and the benefits were soon spread broadly to *everyone*. The Great Society Program contained social and educational components, but the centerpiece was economic opportunity and jobs in both rural and urban areas. Some of the more notable Great Society Program were the Job Corps, the Neighborhood Youth Corps, the Peace Corps, Model Cities, Upward Bound, Community Action Programs, the Food Stamp Program, Head Start, Medicare, the Office of Economic Development and the Regional Development Commissions.

Although unevenly distributed, the entire nation benefited from the Great Society Program. In a program designed to correct racial inequalities, Blacks should have received disproportionately higher assistance than Whites. In math, if the same function is performed to both sides of an equation, nothing changes. Whites received a disproportionately high share of the funds for economic opportunities, such as business development and the majority of the administrative jobs created in the Great Society Program. Poor White communities, especially in the Appalachian Mountains, received special, targeted economic benefits. The benefits Blacks received, especially in the urban cities, were primarily in the area of education—Head Start, Upward Bound, Distant Horizons and a number of college studies programs. These educational programs disproportionately helped Blacks, along with students of all races, but to correct the mal-distribution of wealth, Blacks needed economic and business development resources even more than social and education benefits. Those resources were not directed to them. The lack of direct economic assistance and Black business development was no accident.

Freedman's Banks

History is prologue and often repeats itself. The pattern of diversion is similar for the Freedmen's Bureau created at the end of the Civil War in 1865, and the Great Society Program of the 1960s. After the Civil War, Radical Republicans, liberals of the day, pushed through civil rights laws as well as the 13th, 14th and 15th Amendments to the Constitution to give former slaves rights of citizenship that all non-Blacks already had. These Radical Republicans declared publicly that Black ex-slaves could never be free men if they did not have an economic base and legal protection from their previous White owners. The Freedmen's Bureau was therefore established to place newly-freed slaves in a protected class and to give them the minimal amount of economic resources that they would need to live as free people—40 acres, a mule and $100. But, true freedom and self-sufficiency was not to be. Some Blacks acquired a few acres of land on Southeastern offshore islands. The Black masses never received the promised economic stake because of opposition from anti-Black Southerners, angry over losing the Civil War, their land, slaves and their livelihoods, who convinced Congress to corrupt the initial intent of the Freedmen's Bureau by including poor Southern Whites as well as the old plantation owners as beneficiaries.

The Freedmen's Bureau was initially charged with distributing the land captured during the Civil War to the slaves, along with food, clothing and a few dollars. The corruption of the Freedmen's Bureau redirected nearly all of the limited resources and land into the hands of the same plantation owners from whom the Union had taken them. The plantation owners, Southern citizens and Confederate soldiers received nearly all of the Freedmen's Bureau's money, clothing and food that were intended to provide Black ex-slaves an initial economic stake. With the Bureau's funds and resources redirected, the former slaves were forced to survive with no land, food, weapons, tools, animals, education, culture or institutions. Southern Whites depleted the resources of the Freedmen's Bureau. Once they had the land back, what did they need? Free or cheap labor. The agency established to *lift the burdens of slavery from Blacks*, did not come close to fulfilling its mission, and the Union did not want the slaves to come North. The South then was allowed to implement the Black Codes that mandated, among other things, that ex-slaves must be in possession of a signed job contract at all times or be incarcerated. This created the free or cheap labor supply Southern Whites needed and the former slaves were often forced to return to work for their old masters or risk being jailed as vagrants. Since Blacks were denied education and could not read, they could not consummate contracts in their own behalf. This fact alone produced the free or cheap Black labor supply that Whites needed in domestic service and on the old farms, and justified Blacks being sent to prison farms and road gangs, which were the approved vehicles thorough which Whites acquired free Black labor.

Diversion Technique

Both the 1960s Great Society Program, designed to transition Blacks out of Jim Crow Segregation, and the 1860s Freedmen's Bureau, designed to transition Blacks out of slavery, were created to provide access to resources that Blacks had been denied. The main elements of the diversion process were the same in both programs. The main elements of the pattern were to:

1. Initially address a horrible problem peculiar to Blacks;

2. Immediately expand the pool of beneficiaries to more preferred groups; and

3. Allocate the majority of program resources to those other groups, leaving Blacks again with the least and the same unsolved problems.

Fast-forward 100 years from the 1860s and the end of reconstruction to the 1960s and the end of Jim Crow. Watch how the technique was applied. President Johnson was sympathetic to and responded to the demands of Black civil rights organizations for government assistance through the Great Society Program. Southern politicians opposed any government assistance to Blacks, just as they had when they opposed and corrupted the Freedmen's Bureau in 1865. Johnson was a strong politician and his opponents failed to kill off the program, but they watered it down by including and prioritizing poor Whites, women and others over Blacks.

Conservative political factions wanted to reduce public attention on racial conflicts and strategically promoted the Great Society Program as a War on Poverty. Underfunding the program and shifting focus to eradicate poverty among all population groups allowed conservatives to give the pretense that the program would help Blacks, but the substance did not match the rhetoric. When President Johnson announced his program he acknowledged the compromises he'd had to make when he said, "We have created new avenues of opportunities through jobs, education, and expanded access to health care for seniors, the poor and Americans with disabilities." Blacks received less than half of one percent of the $3 billion spent on the Great Society Program. Blacks got the bill without the thrill of getting tangible benefits.

Both the Great Society Program and the Freedman's Banks were intended to address the specific unique needs of Blacks, which resulted from centuries of slavery and Jim Crow segregation. In those rare instances where politicians do have the courage to target a problem peculiar to Blacks, there are so many others who work to ignore the problem or to only offer Blacks symbolic benefits, while the tangible, unearned benefits go to groups other than Blacks. It requires vigilance to detect the old sleight of hand trick of diverting resources from one group to another.

Question 47. Did Black Americans receive the same economic benefits as Whites in Franklin D. Roosevelt's 1930's New Deal?

In President Franklin D. Roosevelt's 1932 New Deal Program, Black Americans, the people who had suffered the most during the Great Depression, received the least in benefits. The stock market crash in 1929 triggered the Great Depression that stalled economies around the world, closed factories and businesses and brought hard times to everyone's front door. This nation's general unemployment rate was pushed to 25 percent for Whites, and was two-to-three times higher for Blacks. One-third of the nation was ill-fed, ill-housed and ill-clothed. These conditions propelled Roosevelt, a strong believer in the role and power of the federal government, to campaign for the Office of President of the United States.

In his 1932 presidential election campaign, Roosevelt, a Democrat, used rhetoric that gave Blacks the impression that he was sympathetic to their economic needs. Roosevelt's slogans expressed a deep concern for the *forgotten man* and pledged a new deal for *the people*. Black Americans naturally, but erroneously, believed the broad terms forgotten man and the people either referred to or included them. At that time, the majority of Blacks belonged to the Republican Party, a continuation of their allegiance to Abraham Lincoln. But, in the 1932 election, Blacks abandoned the Republican Party and threw their votes to Roosevelt, who won the election with their support. Once in office, Roosevelt and his administration designed a New Deal Program for the working class and poor. However, as it turned out, Roosevelt's New Deal program did not have Blacks in mind. The New Deal did not address the government and culturally-imposed reasons Blacks were so poverty-stricken in the first place, and provided them only a few low-level jobs, limited health care services and minimal welfare benefits. Within a few short years of implementation of the New Deal, national surveys and social discomfort indicators revealed that in the midst of the Great Depression, economic conditions for Blacks grew worse and the gap between them and Whites grew even wider. Eleanor Roosevelt, the wife of Roosevelt, was sympathetic to the conditions of Blacks and tried to provide them an entrée to her husband. She organized an informal group called the *Black Kitchen Cabinet* to meet with her and to advise her on Black issues, which she presented in her own way to the President.

By the 1940s, a significant number of Blacks had lost faith in Roosevelt and began to call his New Deal the *Dirty Deal*. Blacks had experienced a political lesson: that in our competitive race-based society, the social construct on race does not allow equal footing. White privilege is structural and, whether conscious or subconscious, the socioeconomic outcomes are foreordained by race.

Question 48. Does Black America need a World War II-type Marshall Plan?

Black Americans entered the 21st century as an impoverished and politically abandoned people still suffering from socio-economic pathologies and the legacies of slavery. Astronomically high rates of unemployment, homicides, failing schools, incarcerations, drug addiction and dysfunctional families will be made worse by an apathetic majority society that is fixated on supporting immigrants and class minorities. Black America needs a World War II-type of urban Marshall Plan to address its dilemma just as this country invested $12 billion and relocated 300,000 European Jews in the late 1940s to aid Germany's recovery. Even in the fall of 2016, President Barack Obama's administration continued World War II efforts in support of European Jews, and approved $24 million for Holocaust survivors in the U.S. living below the national poverty line. While this was a generous gesture, no similar level of concern seems to have been made to relieve the distress of the more than 50 percent of Black American families who live on incomes below the national poverty line, 156 years after slavery officially ended. The protracted problems that Blacks endure today in America are similar in nearly every respect to conditions in Germany following World War II, conditions which were justification for the aid the U.S. gave to the nation that it had just fought for four years. The U.S. wanted to take whatever measures possible to help Germany develop industries, businesses and consumer products and return to a normal functioning country, otherwise there would be no political stability and no assured peace in Germany. This is the same message that Black Lives Matter marchers have carried across this nation in recent years. Their banners and chants proclaim *No justice, No peace*. The urban centers where Blacks are the majority population need to be economically redeveloped and industrialized to become politically stable and peaceful. Blacks need industrialization not gentrification or displacement by immigration.

The goals and strategies of the World War II Marshall Plan are good models because, by all accounts the plan was enormously successful in rebuilding Germany and war-torn Europe. An urban Marshall Plan for Black America should provide federal funds targeted to 10 majority-Black populated urban centers. Such a national Marshall Plan should primarily focus on economically redeveloping and industrializing those centers for the specific benefit of this nation's historically underserved Black population. Just as this nation has implemented programs to address problems peculiar to immigrants, women, gays, ethnics, and the handicapped, it is time for it to prioritize and fully address the protracted socioeconomic dilemma of the nation's official underclass, Black Americans. Because of their unique historical oppression, Black Americans should not have to queue up with fabricated class minorities for corrective government assistance. The goal of such assistance should be to complete the short-lived efforts begun in the 1960s to correct the historical legacies of slavery.

In summer 2012, *The Harvest Institute Report*[50] asked President Barack Obama to structure an urban Marshall Plan for Black

---

[50]"A Letter to President Barack Obama." *The Harvest Institute Report*, Semi-Annual Newsletter, Summer 2012, pgs. 1-6. www.harvestinstitute.org.

America. Unfortunately, Obama did not acknowledge nor did he or his staff respond to the request and Black people and their respective neighborhoods continued to deteriorate. But, where there is life, there is hope, even though Black Americans are without functional communities, a competitive economy and are an underclass. An underclass group is one that has faded from the public consciousness and, by the very nature of its socioeconomic conditions and political powerlessness, will always struggle for survival. However, Blacks did not become an underclass overnight. An urban Marshall Plan for Black America still holds the potential to reverse deteriorating conditions within Black America and their neighborhoods. The question is from whence will come the needed measure of national concern and economic assistance?

Question 49. Why is the pattern of Black men killed by White law enforcement personnel so acceptable and so entrenched in society?

For centuries, America has been a killing field for young Black men, especially by White law enforcement. Although a long historical pattern, incidents in recent years have been troubling. In nearly every instance, courts and grand juries allow those who profile, beat or kill young Black men to go unpunished. Why? Because the underclass status of Blacks, which caused them to have unique historical experiences, is codified in this nation's revered founding documents. The Constitution of the U.S. and the Bill of Rights declare America a land of exceptionalism, the cradle of democracy and a nation that values immigrants. Blacks were exceptional, too. They were the nation's only non-immigrants. They were valued only as human property, entitled to be treated just like field animals. This lack of respect for a Black man's life, rights and contributions became infused into the nation's national spirit and codified into the legal and political infrastructure. America's perception of Black men was framed by the U.S. Supreme Court's infamous *1857 Dred Scott* decision.

A Black slave declared he was a free person because he had visited and temporarily lived in a free state. The Supreme Court ruled, however, that, *"A Black man* has *no rights which a White man is bound to respect."* This infamous ruling, never reversed in over 150 years, has been locked into the culture and collective American psyche and passed down from generation to generation of ethnic Whites. The first lesson immigrants learn when they come to this country is that they are prized and valued over native Black Americans. This prevailing attitude impacts every aspect of how our political and law enforcement systems view and treat Blacks.

"Slavery Plantation Police Badges Issued to Protect Whites and Property."
Source: *Lest We Forget Slavery Museum, Philadelphia, Pennsylvania.*

"Ku Klux Klan Badges."
Source: *U.S. Library of Congress.*

This nation's public policies of Benign Neglect and political correctness further depreciated the value and rights of Black Americans. Those policies were constructed to kill off the Black Civil Rights Movement of the 1960s and to make all forms of Blackness invisible. The policy of Benign Neglect took the focus off of Blacks, and over the course of the next half-century, morphed into political correctness and diversity—polices that do not distinguish or aid Blacks. The views of law enforcement and society in general carry the legacies of slavery, Jim Crow semi-slavery and the Dred Scott decision. Having relinquished the few concrete gains made during the civil rights movement, Blacks have slid back into a powerless underclass status. Blacks, however, should not be treated as guests in America. This nation was founded on the blood, sweat and labor of millions of Blacks who were denied their very humanity and the fruits of their labor. The newly-fabricated class groups, especially immigrants, inherit *unearned benefits*, respect and rights to which Blacks were entitled but never received. The larger society adds further insult to injury when it participates in public dialogue that gives the false impression that all people and groups have contributed equally to the development of this nation. That is a convenient myth.

The racial problems between law enforcement and Black men will not abate until this nation addresses the exceptional history and achievements of Black Americans. Police power is freely exercised against Black men who are perceived as obsolete and powerless to do little more than march or riot. The larger society has a responsibility to resolve the long-standing dehumanization of Blacks that is contained in our foundation documents, and to erase the emanating legal precedents.

The tension between law enforcement and Blacks will never abate as long as Whites own and control 98 percent of all of the nation's wealth, income, businesses, land, privileges and all levels of government. The mal-distribution that slavery produced and the cultural effects of the Dred Scott decision must be considered in any serious efforts to analyze the relationship between Blacks and law enforcement. Calls for healing, no matter how sincere, will not correct the problem. Understanding the historical context, however, would be a better beginning point. At least both groups would understand the importance of reversing the holding of Dred Scott and the contribution of the U.S. Constitution to the problem.

PART VIII

Immigration and Naturalization

Question 50. Why are the doors of immigration open to Hispanics, but closed to Haitians?

The primary reasons immigrants from Haiti are treated differently than Hispanics are skin color and the country's historical role in the development of the Western world. The welcome mat for immigrants has always been based upon a ranking order of skin color, ethnicity and country of origin. Hispanics, whether in Europe or the Americas, have always been classified as Whites speaking Spanish, therefore, entitled to preferential immigration into the U.S. from any country of origin. For Haitians and other persons of African descent, the welcome mat did not exist, except as slaves. The bias against Haitian immigrants and refugees has a deep-seated historical element that caused great fear in Whites in the U.S., for Haiti was the world's first free Black nation in the entire Western Hemisphere.

When Black slaves in Haiti successfully revolted against their French slaveholders, they became a free, independent nation, the first and only instance where slaves were ever able to break free and establish their own independent nation. No other Black nation on earth had ever rebelled and overthrown their White colonial powers. The slave revolt in Haiti hit hard in America. President George Washington and Secretary of State Thomas Jefferson, who were slave owners, supported France in its efforts to suppress the Haitian slave revolt, but to no avail. It is remarkable that Black Haitians defeated Napoleon Bonaparte's army, which was France's most effective military force. They also defeated the military forces of England and Spain. White slaveholders in the U.S. feared slave revolts would ignite physical hostilities between White society and the millions of Blacks they held as slaves.

The military success of the slaves in Haiti did have a profound effect on slavery and a lasting impact on the way the United States treats Haitians today. Slavery was legalized as an official institution in 1789 with ratification of the U.S. Constitution. Two years later, in August 1791, Haitian slaves revolted and took control of the island. Four months later, on December 8, 1791, frightened American slave owners persuaded the U.S. Congress to enact the 2nd Constitutional Amendment that granted White citizens the right to have militias and required all White males between 18 and 45 years old to bear arms in case of slave revolts. The fear of possible slave revolts was omnipresent and triggered Southern states to organize militias. There were a few slave revolts in the U.S., but none of them succeeded. The key point in this historical recitation is that the fear generated by the successful Haitian revolt produced a hate and fear in Whites toward Haitians. Haiti paid a high price for its military successes. The country was reviled, feared by all White nations of the world precisely for its successful slave revolts and Haiti was therefore isolated and crushed into deep poverty.

The difference between the treatment of Hispanics and the treatment of Haitians seeking citizenship in America reflects racism and the lasting memories of the astounding victories in the Western Hemisphere by the poor, almost defenseless, dark people in the most isolated nation in the Americas. The punishment to Haiti for its military achievements and the embarrassment that it inflicted on world superpowers is incorporated into America's enduring international policy. For instance, the 1823 Monroe Doctrine defined any intervention by external powers in the politics of the Americas as a potentially hostile act against the U.S. This prohibits Haiti from getting much foreign political aid from other countries. They cannot help themselves and the U.S. will not allow others to help them. As recently as May 2017, *The Washington Post*[51] reported that President Donald Trump's administration was treating Haitians in this country differently from other immigrants. To decide whether Haitians here in

---

[51]Kay, Jennifer and Licon, Gomez. "Haitians Fear Wrenching End to U.S. Immigration Protection," *The Washington Post*, article, May 10, 2017.

Temporary Protected Status should be allowed to stay in the U.S., the administration is taking the unusual step of seeking data on criminal background and Haitian use of welfare benefits.

The First Naturalization Law of 1790 permitted immigration only by Europeans. In the 1960s, Congress modified that law and immigration policies. It replaced skin color preferences with country of origin, rank-ordered based upon the historical number of immigrants who had migrated from Europe, Asia, the Middle East and African countries. Since the ancestors of Black slaves were never officially classified or registered as immigrants, the immigration quota for persons from Black nations, like Haiti, was set at less than one percent. Civil rights leaders, who had started making the shift from Black to *minority, people of color* and other euphemisms, went along with the change in immigration law from European White to country of origin. The civil rights leaders did not have the support of sophisticated think tanks and were unable to foresee the devastating impact the new immigration policies would have on native Blacks. The new immigration policy gave preferences to persons from Mexico and poor Central and South American countries seeking political asylum rather than economic opportunities. Using the new immigration focus, in the 1960s the John F. Kennedy administration initiated and approved a Cuban Refugee Program, which opened the floodgates to millions of Cubans, who obtained citizenship in America for political as well as economic opportunities. Nearly 100 percent of Cuban refugees were classified as White. Only a few dark or Black Cubans entered the United States.

Haitian refugees have been treated with extreme prejudice. Their escape boats have been intercepted, pushed back into the water, the people left to drown. Those who made it to the U.S. have been deported, incarcerated and rejected because of the interpretation that they seek economic opportunities rather than political asylum. Until Haitian refugees are reclassified and treated in a similar manner to Hispanics, including Cubans, an ethnic group within the category of Hispanics, Haitian refugees will continue to be treated with extreme bias. The 40 million legal and illegal Hispanic immigrants who came to this country did not come to seek asylum. They came here seeking money and a better life.

The basis for rejecting Haitians is historical fear, inherent racism, Haiti's abysmal poverty, its African-based culture, low education levels and most importantly, because an increase in Haitians could increase the political and economic potential of Black Americans. The nation's doors are not now and have never been open to all who seek the American Dream.

Question 51. Is America now, or has it ever been, a color-blind society?

America is not a color-blind society nor has it ever been[52]. It has always been color conscious and color-specific even before it existed as a formal entity. High-minded talk about color-blindness and individual merit maintains the racial status quo and reinforces a historical pattern of race-based exclusion. Rev. Dr. Martin Luther King, Jr., mistakenly thought the Constitution was color-blind, when in fact it was very color-specific[53]. The drafters knew they were consigning Blacks to be property, equal to field animals. They intentionally denied Blacks the fruit of their labor, education, votes and personal movement. So, when King and the civil rights movement pushed for a color-blind society, it was lofty rhetoric and they could not have imagined how those words would be used against their cause. Conservative social forces captured the concept of color-blind equality and perverted the meaning to take color out of

---

[52]Millhiser, Ian. *Injustices: The Supreme Court's History of Comforting the Comfortable and Afflicting the Afflicted*, Nation Books, New York, 2015, pgs. ix-xv.

[53]Steinhorn, Leonard and Diggs-Brown, Barbara. *By the Color of Our Skin*, Plume, New York, 1999, p. 8.

race. This well-meaning but unwise rhetorical phrase gave Whites a tool to destroy corrective efforts for Blacks.

The color-specific Articles of Confederation and the U.S. Constitution were designed to be the nation's first Affirmative Action plan for the specific purpose of enriching, empowering and valuing White skin by distributing to them nearly 100 percent of the nation's wealth, land and privileges. The second purpose of the founding documents was to control, exploit and subordinate all who did not possess White skin. As the nation's need for free labor, and later cheap labor, increased, a ranking order of skin color preferences emerged and institutionalized itself in the social fabric of the society and its immigration policies. The intentional allocation of everything of value into the hands of Whites created racial inequality, which was used to justify separating Whites from Blacks in all things. Color-blind rhetoric allowed Whites plausible deniability for responsibility for the socioeconomic conditions of Black America.

Skin color was at the heart of the 1896 case of Homer A. Plessey, a light-skinned Black man, who believed he had the right to sit in the White section of a rail car, but was ordered to move to the Black section. Plessey's response was to file a major lawsuit, *Plessy v. Ferguson*, a case that eventually worked its way to the U.S. Supreme Court[54]. The responsibility of the Supreme Court is to uphold the U.S. Constitution, therefore it has always functioned as the guardian of the racial status quo in America. The Court carried out its charge and ruled against Plessey, saying he lacked the required skin color qualifications to sit in the privileged and best seats on the train. This Supreme Court decision further institutionalized racism and legally marked the beginning of Jim Crow Segregation laws. Justice John Marshall Harlan, the only dissenter, wrote the minority position in the Court's ruling. He argued that the U.S. Constitution, "… ought to be color-blind," based upon the 13th and 14th Amendments to the Constitution. That was the first use of the term color-blind in

---

[54]Fireside, Harvey. *Separate and Unequal*, Carroll & Graf Publishers, New York, 2004, p. 22.

the law. Justice Harlan was ignored and mainstream society was racially segregated by law for another 50 years. Affirmative Action skin-color preferences and privileges were maintained for Whites. During that time period, those with White skin continued to own and have access to the best communities, schools, food, housing, medical services, clothing, employment opportunities and control of government.

With the Black Civil Rights Movement of the 1960s came a demand from Black citizens for Whites to share and redistribute some of their ill-gotten privileges, preferences and resources. Blacks wanted an Affirmative Action plan to restore the damages done to Black people. Like Justice Harlan, they wanted a color-blind society that did not consciously exclude and abuse Blacks based on skin color. Instead, they wanted Whites to recognize Black skin in a positive way and redistribute resources to them based upon a skin-color preference. Conservatives were not to be out-smarted. They went back to the original social construct of the founding documents and flipped the script on Blacks. Whites began to champion the words of Dr. King's dream of Blacks being, "Judged by the content of their character rather than the color of their skin." Conservatives pretended that society was already color-bind and it would be a travesty to show preference to Black skin. Some Blacks mounted weak dissent, but as a group, they were out maneuvered. Policy and laws, therefore, remained very color conscious in favor of Whites and color-blind toward Black Americans. The concept of color-blind makes Blacks invisible and unnecessary.

Question 52. Prior to the 1960's civil rights movement, what was the stance of Black leaders on immigration policies?

Black leaders and activists unilaterally expressed opposition to the nation's open-door policy on immigration throughout the 19th Century. These conscious Black leaders expressed concern that immigrants were reinforcing the subordination of the native Black population, as well as usurping the access of Blacks to rights, privileges, employment education and wealth-building opportunities. The negative impact of immigrants worsened after the Civil War when millions entered the country. After slavery, there was a labor shortage and one would have logically expected the former slaves, who had been skilled tradesmen—carpenters, blacksmiths, cooks, artisans and farmers—to fill those jobs. But, the country recruited and imported European immigrants instead. The pattern was just beginning. For more than a century, Black leaders had struggled and challenged the White power structure to close the nation's immigration doors. In his famous 1895 Atlanta Exposition speech, Booker T. Washington pleaded with White industrialists, businessmen and politicians not to look to European immigrants to develop skills and work in their businesses, but to look instead to native Blacks. Washington pointed out that many already had the skills, attitudes and experiences to meld into the mainstream society. W. E. B. Du Bois was against immigration and spoke frequently about the downside for Blacks of 40 million White immigrants coming into the country, doing the jobs of former slaves and being automatically elevated into an overseeing White management class.

When the Black Civil Rights Movement commenced in the late 1950s, the new Black leadership dismissed or ignored the opinions of their predecessors. One can only speculate as to the reasons. Perhaps they did not have the foresight to fully understand the politics of displacement that was occurring; were unknowledgeable about this nation's immigration history; wanted to demonstrate altruism; or they simply preferred to ignore or forget history and go along to get along as much as they could. Whatever the reasons, the new Black leadership switched from the anti-immigration stance of their predecessors to pro-immigration. While the reason for the change in position is not clear, it is clear that they made the switch without fully understanding that providing unearned rights and benefits to immigrants chasing the American Dream caused native Black Americans to be neglected, disadvantaged and rendered invisible in all respects. The old Black anti-immigration fighters must be turning over in their graves.

Black civil rights organizations and politicians began to *presume* alliances[55] with newly-arriving immigrants. Those alliances, especially with Hispanics, did not and do not exist. Hispanics firmly deny that such alliances exist and it takes little analysis to determine that any alliances Black leaders presume, are one-sided. Black leaders even support policies that benefit immigrant groups at the expense of Black people. Many Black leaders, for instance, support increased immigration, but immigrant groups such as Hispanics, Asians or Arabs do not commit to or give support to Black issues. There is no reciprocity and immigrant advocate groups not only do not represent the interests of Blacks, the very purpose of their advocacy is in outright opposition to Black interests. Why is it that after all these years, leading Blacks cannot recognize circumstances that are harmful to their people? Why is it that the people permit those whom they have accepted as leaders, to continue doing them harm?

Question 53. How do immigration policies specifically injure native Black Americans?

Throughout the history of North America, waves of immigrants have entered the country to take advantage of the considerable economic opportunities extended to them and to enjoy the elevated status, respect and privileges they automatically receive over Blacks in the labor force. Since the Black descendants of slaves are not immigrants, they are excluded from the privileged status, benefits and rights extended to immigrants and must compete with every immigrant for basic rights and life resources. Immigrants and Blacks compete for space, rights, economics and privileges. Reaching America has been a dream come

---

[55]Vaca, Nicolas C. *Presumed Alliance: The Unspoken Conflict Between With Black Americans*, HarperCollins Publishers, New York, 2004, pgs. x-xii, 194-196.

true for immigrants, but it has been a nightmare for many native Blacks and their forefathers.

"Uncle Sam Teaching White and Ethnic Immigrants While the Black Child Cleans Windows." Source: Puck Magazine, U.S. Library of Congress.

Space

Although a growing number of legal and illegal immigrants are located in the suburbs, most immigrants find residential and commercial space in urban areas. Once they establish a toehold in the urban centers, they then mark and close the space, using their language, culture or religion as barriers to encroachment. Within the confines of their closed communities, they concentrate their resources and build socioeconomic enclaves or niches. Immigrant niches can be found in most urban areas like Detroit, Miami, Los Angeles, Philadelphia, New York, the District of Columbia, San Francisco and Chicago. After closing their territories, they mark them in their cultural images as Korea Town, China Town, French Town, Japan Town, Little Cuba, Greek Town and Mexican Town. As their numbers grow, they spread out and gentrify Black areas, such as Harlem in New York City; Overtown, Liberty City and Coconut Grove in Miami; Inglewood, Compton and Watts in the Los Angeles area and Sweet Auburn n Atlanta. All these formerly Black dominated cities are now occupied predominantly by Hispanic immigrants.

Numerical displacement means diminished economic and political influence by Blacks in mainstream society. Since 1900, the Hispanic population increased from 100,000 to 55 million in 2016. They have surpassed and made Black Americans a minority-minority. Hispanics boast that they are now the nation's new majority-minority and will gentrify urban residential areas along with Whites and Asians, displacing Blacks.

Economics

The economic impact of immigrants on native Black Americans is quantifiable. For every 10 percent increase in the number of immigrants, native Black income is reduced by three-tenths of one percent. Blacks had an earnings ratio of $0.56 to every dollar earned by Whites in the 1950s. Because of the Black Civil Rights Movement, in the 1970s Blacks' earnings ratio rose to 66 percent against every dollar earned by Whites. However, between 1970 and 1990, there was a 300 percent increase in the number of legal and illegal Asians and Hispanics that entered the country, and the ratio of Black earnings to White earnings dropped from 66 percent to 57 percent, where it was nearly 40 years earlier. In short, the nine-point economic gains due to the Black Civil Rights Movement were wiped out by the 300 percent increase in immigrant population that occurred between 1970 and 1990.

Employment

Whether the job categories are skilled or unskilled, this nation has a long history of displacing Blacks to make employment opportunities for incoming immigrants. According to a U.S. Department of Commerce survey conducted in 1865, over 100,000 of the nation's 120,000 skilled artisans were Black Americans newly-freed from slavery. During the same time, 55 to 65 percent of all Southern farmers were Blacks and former slaves. Instead of Lincoln's administration mainstreaming the five million former slaves, he and his administration chose to enact immigration reform that attracted 26 million Europeans into the country to replace the Black farmers and artisans. Initially, newly-arriving immigrants replaced Northern native Blacks in the lowest paying and dirtiest jobs. Later waves of immigrants replaced native Blacks in the South as well as the North in skilled trades, artisan crafts and agricultural-based occupations.

For those who would argue that immigrants do not displace Black Americans in jobs and employment opportunities, why are so many of the jobs that Blacks used to hold in hotels, retail sales, restaurants, airports, trash collection, banks, other local businesses and all levels of government now staffed by Hispanics, Arabs and other ethnic groups? Many Blacks were displaced by immigrants in businesses and public offices because they could not speak Spanish or other languages. The actual hidden or structural unemployment rate for Black Americans is nearly 50 percent. According to a report from the Center for Immigration Studies, matters were made worse between 2006 and 2016, when approximately 50 percent of all new jobs went to Hispanics. Where is the economic justice for Black Americans?

Education

The U.S. Supreme Court's *Brown v. Board of Education* decision was supposed to have corrected damages inflicted on Black students for more than 400 years of zero schools and poor schools. But, before any major educational improvements could be made, the immigration reforms of 1965 brought in a massive influx of immigrant *minority* children who began to compete with native Black children for resources. There are no constitutional mandates to give newly-arriving immigrant children, legal or illegal, accompanied or unaccompanied, educational advantages *over* Blacks. Prevailing policies and laws, however, give immigrants preferential treatment over Blacks.

Affirmative Action

Affirmative Action programs were originally designed to correct injustices to one race of people, Blacks, by another race of people, Whites;

and to eliminate the legacies of slavery and Jim Crow segregation. Today, Affirmation Action programs have been converted into preference programs for immigrants, though most categories of immigrants are White and have never been negatively impacted by the racism and racial conditions that caused these programs to be necessary. This error can be traced to the Immigration and Reform Control Act of 1986, which effectively required employers to treat immigrants exactly like native-born citizens. Since nearly 90 percent of all immigrants are classified as White on their immigration records and drivers' licenses, why aren't immigrants treated like Whites and *excluded* from Affirmation Action programs? Why are they categorized with Blacks *only* in the instance of Affirmation Action?

Putting apples and oranges into the same categories sets up a situation where immigrants of any race displace Blacks from the very programs designed to help them. It is not possible to justify including Hispanics, Arabs, Asians, other immigrants and women (who are a majority) in Affirmation Action programs. Yet, in 2016, Black civil rights leaders, elected officials at the highest levels and other members of the Black overclass publicly supported immigration reform and granting citizenship to 12-to-20 million illegal immigrants that had entered the country since 1990. The Black overclass agreed with those who wanted to reach out and invite even millions more immigrants. Our federal and state governments may have reasons to support increased immigration, but they have a moral obligation to avoid and correct the devastating harm it causes native Black Americans.

Question 54. Are global diseases that are linked to immigrants a threat to native Black Americans?

Any plant, animal or human that relocates into an entirely new physical environment represents a potential danger to the natural or native habitat. The easy global movement of people who may be infected with diseases or who come into contact with infected people, presents biological dangers, not only to Black Americans, but also to all Americans. In the U.S., there have been increases in drug-resistant microbes, rebirth of diseases once under control, and exposure to non-native diseases through global travel and legal and illegal immigration into the United States[56]. These traveling diseases pose a particular threat to Black Americans, because many immigrants move directly into the nation's major urban centers, where approximately 70 percent of Black Americans reside. Introduction of foreign diseases to urban areas allows the diseases to spread quickly. Those urban centers often lack adequate medical facilities, hospitals and have lower rates of medically-insured populations. Immigrants intimately interact with the native population, performing babysitting and domestic chores in homes and they become part of the food chain as migrant workers in the agricultural belt, harvesting produce, working in fast-food restaurants, hotels, entertainment centers, restaurants and offices, often without having health examinations for diseases and other infectious bacteria.

The National Institutes of Health (NIH) and the Centers for Disease Control and Prevention (CDC) alert the public to contagious diseases that can or have been imported into the United States by visitors and tourists that have traveled to countries that harbor infections. Recent alerts include diseases such as Ebola, Zika and drug-resistant TB. The CDC website, www.cdc.gov, has a list of diseases by country of diseases travelers might encounter and from which immigrants may bring diseases of concern to the U.S. In addition to new diseases, the United States has also experienced a resurgence of diseases that were once under control in the native population, diseases such as pertussis, measles, smallpox and polio. When imported diseases suddenly appear, they have imposed crippling financial hardships on hospitals, communities and municipalities. In

---

[56]"Medical Alert," *The Harvest Institute Report*, Winter 2006, p. 1. www.harvestinstitute. org.

addition to the diseases listed above, there are other new and reemerging diseases, such as avian flu, severe acute respiratory syndrome, West Nile virus, malaria, blood disorders, AIDS, leprosy, cholera, chagas, hookworm, tapeworms and hepatitis. Black neighborhoods have been severely weakened by 50 years of social integration, and medical resources are not sufficient to serve their normal health needs. With so many new immigrants with so many health problems, Blacks face dilution of already inadequate health care.

Dangerous diseases migrate from all parts of the world and in many ways, but the 14- to 20-million illegal immigrants are often direct sources. Most are poor, have had inadequate health care in their countries of origin and many enter the U.S. without health evaluations for communicable and infectious diseases[57]. The CDC labels the border states of Texas, New Mexico, Arizona and California as hot beds for diseases that are common in Mexico, Central and South America.

Immigrants that are ill or have serious health issues become a costly challenge. Approximately 43 percent of those under 65 years of age have no health care insurance, although several of Barack Obama's immigration programs, such as the *Dream Act,* contain provisions for low-cost or free medical coverage for some. A high percentage use emergency rooms for regular medical and dental care, again forcing native Blacks to compete with immigrants for services that are meager to begin with. The costs of uninsured immigrants are passed on to taxpaying Americans, which further strains the health care community and has contributed to severe financial stress at some of the nation's finest emergency medical facilities, hospitals and medical practices.

Governments, especially local and state, should stop turning a blind eye to the costly impact that immigrant health issues and reemerging diseases are having in urban and rural areas. Immigration has had few

---

[57]"WHO Lists the Most Dangerous Superbugs and Urges Action to Combat Them," *The Washington Post*, February 28, 2017, Economy & Business Section, p. A11.

meaningful parameters because corporations and various political forces want the doors to stay open. However, Black leaders should publicly identify health as an issue, demand protective measures for Black neighborhoods and see that stringent health certification is mandated for immigrants entering the country. These measures would provide at least a modicum of protection to native Black Americans in the neighborhoods in which they live. Additional information regarding immigrants and health care can be found in the Medical Alert article, in the *Harvest Institute Report,* Winter 2006, or at www.harvestinstitute.org.

PART IX
Sites and Signs of the Times

Question 55. What is the special history between the District of Columbia and Blacks?

Washington, D.C., aka the District of Columbia (D.C.), and Black slavery were bound together at the very founding of this nation. The city was founded by the U.S. Constitution in 1787, and has been embroiled in slavery and race matters ever since. It was carved out of two major slaveholding states, Virginia and Maryland, and was given a combined name after two slave promoters, George Washington and Christopher Columbus. It became the national center for greed, slave trading and politicians, whose ceaseless rhetoric was pure mockery. Slaves were displayed daily in slave pens and sold from auction blocks on the White House lawn, within the shadows of the Capitol Building. The city's numerous monuments, squares, streets, statues and public edifices stand today in hypocritical testimony to the nation's espoused beliefs in freedom, justice and equality for *all*.

One of the most infamous slave pens in D.C. was the Franklin and Armfield Auction House on Duke Street in what is now Alexandria, Virginia. Isaac Franklin and John Armfield were probably the nation's most active slave traders. They controlled nearly half the coastal slave trade, from Baltimore, Maryland to New Orleans, Louisiana. They took advantage of the relatively low price of slaves in D.C. and sold them for high profits in the deep South. They walked their chained slaves more than 1,000 miles, all the way from their headquarters in D.C. to their Forks-of-the-Road headquarters in Natchez, Mississippi just to save shipping costs. The Franklin and Armfield Auction house still stands in Alexandria and is still connected to Washington, D.C., and Black Americans. It is now the headquarters for the National Urban League and the New African American Museum is just across the Potomac River, in the nation's capital.

Southern states wanted the nation's capital to be located close to their slaveholding, agricultural enterprises. Benjamin Banneker, a Black man, is also a connection between the District of Columbia and slavery. Banneker was a free Black surveyor who worked with Pierre L'Enfant, the chief architect who designed the District of Columbia and who before completing the project, resigned and returned to France. Banneker had memorized L'Efant's plans and was commissioned to finish the architectural design of the District. Black unpaid laborers also built the government buildings and universities, many of which stand today. Ironically, there were both slaves and free Blacks in the District, which remained a major center for migrating Blacks.

During most of the 1900s, the District was a majority-Black populated city and was later affectionately often referred to as Chocolate City. However, the intense gentrification to which the District has been subjected since the late 1980s, has reduced the Black population to less than 49 percent. The special relationship of Blacks with the District of Columbia, diminishes each year and its status has begun to change from Chocolate City to Vanilla City.

Question 56. What were some of the famous resorts built in America by Blacks during the 1900s that were killed off by social integration?

History chronicles how Black slaves escaped plantations to find or build safe havens called maroon towns and villages. Sometimes they built places to be together just to feel free and have fun. After slavery and well past the mid-1900s, Black Americans continued to build resort towns across America. Brighton Gardens and Idlewild in Michigan; American Beach in Florida; Martha's Vineyard in Massachusetts; and Highland Beach in Maryland were some of the more notable communities established for and by Black Americans who wanted to live with, spend their money on, have fun and party with their own people. These communities were grand in size and rich in spirit. Brighton Gardens, an approximately 40-acre community, boasted of having the deepest freshwater lake in Michigan. American Beach's 200 acres extended along the beautiful sandy beaches of Florida's Amelia Island and offered Blacks in the Southeastern states relaxation without humiliation. Martha's Vineyard, an island off the Southern coast of Cape Cod, Massachusetts, offered high-quality recreational opportunities to the likes of Paul Robeson, Adam Clayton Powell and the Rev. Dr. Martin Luther King, Jr., as well as the elite of the Northeastern states.

However, the premier resort and recreational area that was known as *the* vacation spot that segregation built was in Idlewild, Michigan. Idlewild was initially established by White developers in 1912, but was turned over to Blacks in 1921. Like the other resorts, Idlewild began to be celebrated as a place for Black Americans to invest their new-found wealth and pride, and in turn, became the most famous Black resort and recreational area in America. From the early 1920s through the 1950s, Idlewild was referred to as the *Black Garden of Eden*. Idlewild offered a high-quality living experience with summer homes, lakes, lodges, motels, bowling alleys, grocery stores, restaurants, nightclubs, taverns, riding stables and a golf course.

Idlewild's famous Paradise Club, Flamingo Club and Purple Palace provided high-end entertainment and showcased such Black stars as Sammy Davis, Jr., Bill Cosby, Moms Mabley, T-Bone Walker, Fats Waller, Billy Eckstein, Billie Holiday, Count Basie, Sarah Vaughan, Cab Calloway, Louis Armstrong, Della Reese, Dinah Washington, B. B. King, Aretha Franklin, the Four Tops and countless other entertainers. The Who's Who of Black America owned lots and cabins in Idlewild, including Dr. Daniel Hale Williams, W.E.B. Du Bois, Madame C. J. Walker and Joe Louis. Social integration of the 1960s killed most of the Black resorts. When Blacks were given a chance to sit with Whites in Las Vegas, Reno and Miami Beach, they quickly abandoned their own recreational communities. As recently as the late 1990s, a group of Blacks who realized the value of what was lost sought to rebuild Idlewild, Michigan. Although there has been a modest revitalization, it is unlikely that Idlewild will ever be restored to its former glory. In the minds of most Blacks, integration was the pot of gold at the end of the rainbow and Blacks believed White ice was colder. When they gave up their Black resort communities, however, they gave up yet one more group of assets that once released can almost never be recaptured.

Question 57. Should abolitionist John Brown be studied as an example of courageous behavior in pursuit of justice?

Black Americans should view John Brown's identification with and commitment to Black people with the highest regard. His unselfishness allowed him to sacrifice his entire family in hopes of ending slavery and achieving racial justice for Black Americans. John Brown, a determined abolitionist, should absolutely have a special place in history. When asked to name their greatest heroes, Black Americans generally offer names of well-know personalities, such as Rev. Dr. Martin Luther King, Jr., Abraham Lincoln, and Frederick Douglass. Very few name John Brown, who was totally committed to mobilizing Blacks to free themselves from slavery. Brown did not just talk the talk, he drafted revolt plans and tried to recruit Black leaders from across the nation and Canada. In his Christian belief of an *eye for an eye,* he avenged the death of Blacks killed by slaveholding Whites. In an attempt to confiscate weapons and arm Black slaves, Brown sacrificed himself and five members of his family in his attack on Harpers Ferry, Virginia in 1859. Most White historians called Brown a fanatic madman, because a White man would have to be *crazy* to give his all to free and protect over five million enslaved Blacks.

John Brown's selfless actions sensitized the nation to the evils of slavery and ignited the great Civil War. John Brown was bold and forceful. The White power structure feared him. Many even considered him to be above the law. Brown was so popular in the North, the government feared that arresting him would trigger riots. When President Buchanan put a price of $250 on Brown's head, Brown responded by putting a bounty of two dollars and fifty cents on President Buchanan's head.

Having no fear of the government, John Brown moved freely across the country. In the summer of 1859, under an assumed name, he rented a farm in Maryland from the heirs of Booth Kennedy, the great-great-grandfather of President John F. Kennedy. His plan was to obtain military weapons and ignite a slave revolt, then retreat into the Appalachian Mountains with his armed band of former slaves. The rented farm was a good hiding place for Brown and his supporters to plan an attack on the Marine Corps armory in Harpers Ferry, West Virginia, only a few miles away.

Brown knew that a successful revolt depended on the number of participants who were involved. Consequently, Brown tried, unsuccessfully, to have some visible Black leaders like Frederick Douglass and Harriet Tubman to join him and help call the Black slaves into an insurrection. Tubman was ill and Douglass admitted his fear. Undeterred, Brown and his children rode into Harpers Ferry to secure weapons from the armory on the evening of October 16, 1859. Brown never got the chance to attack the town. He did not get the weapons and he did not have the voice of a strong Black leader to rally the slaves to revolt. Brown was captured in the fire station and eventually hanged. His raid and hanging set the stage for the Civil War that followed two years later.

Dedicated to his religion, John Brown held Whites accountable for what they did to Blacks. He and his followers included his children and a few Black members all of whom sacrificed their lives for what they thought was right. For his courage and actions, he should have a memorial of recognition. In 1949, the historic farm site where Brown planned his attack was purchased by a Black minister, the Reverend Leonard W. Curling from Hagerstown, Maryland. After owning it for a short time, Curling sold the farm to South T. Lynn, a White private developer, who restored it to its 1859 appearance and registered it as an historical landmark with the National Park Service. John Brown should indeed be recognized as an example of unusual courage. On December 6, 1859, the state of Virginia hung Brown and made him the first American since the founding of the nation to be hanged as a traitor. Let it be known that abolitionist John Brown, a White man, was a great protector and a friend, with no parallel, to Black America. In truth, John Brown not only predicted, but triggered the American Civil War.

Question 58. What were sundown towns?

A sundown town was an organized jurisdiction that enacted public policies and practices that kept Blacks from being in their all White towns after certain hours. Although there have been some changes over the course of 100 years, the proclamation of racial harmony and successful social integration has proven itself an illusion. It legitimizes and hides racial hatred and the exclusion of Blacks in American society. Whites responded to social integration after the 1960s by moving away from physical proximity to Blacks, and built suburbs for Whites only. In similar fashion following the legal end of slavery, Whites openly organized towns and enacted public policies that forbade Blacks from living in or spending the night within the jurisdictional boundaries of sundown towns.

These sundown towns and communities publicly boasted about having hanging trees for Blacks. The traditional South had some independent sundown towns, but most were in middle America and Northern states. Blacks across the nation responded to the fact that Whites did not want to be around them by building their own towns and resort areas. Many of their communities or towns were located at the edge of sundown towns because Blacks were dependent upon the daytime jobs that the sundown towns offered them.

a

"Dr. Claud Anderson views town Billboard." Source: Author's Personal Collection.

After the Civil War, Jim Crow was instituted, further racially polarizing the North and South. Some sundown towns posted conspicuous signs and billboards in public places that notified Blacks that they were not allowed to enter or were only allowed to enter for short periods during specified times and only after posting bond. The message on billboards in one sundown town boldly said, "Nigger, if you can read this, you'd better run; if you can't read this, you'd better run anyway!" The Ku Klux Klan and similar *community-spirited* organizations enforced the warnings and expressed the town's restrictions to the unwanted guests. The civil rights movement of the 1960s brought down most of the conspicuous signs and billboards that warned Blacks, but did not erase the sentiments.

Although most of the sundown towns disappeared after the 1960s, a few lingered a while longer in Texas and other Southern states. Texas had the most sundown towns, such as Cumby, Grand Saline, Vidor and Alba. As the nation entered the 21st century, the sundown towns in Texas had the reputation of being the worst in America[58]. A sign at the Alba city

---

[58]Loewen, James W. *Sundown Towns: A Hidden Dimension of American Racism*, The New Press, New York, 2005.

limits, for instance, once warned Blacks—not minorities, people of color, or women—but Blacks—to stay out. The word *Alba* means *daybreak* in Spanish. Alba was founded in 1881 with an all-White population of 50. By 1910, the town's population had increased to 2,595 and was ethnically diversified. The ethnic mix was reportedly 2,225 Whites, seven American Indians and 68 who were Mexicans, Bohemians or Armenians. Alba had diversity, but zero Black residents. Racism in Alba and similar sundown towns was directed strictly at Blacks. On the other hand, those sundown towns welcomed Asians, Arabs, Hispanics and European Whites. The Center for American Progress, in a research publication, *The Failures of Integration*[59], found that 85 percent of Whites indicated in a poll that they did not care whether they lived in an area where most of their neighbors were White or where most were Black. However, in other questions in the same survey, 85 percent of Whites also said they actually lived in areas where they had few or no Black neighbors. The majority of Whites indicate they support integration, but most Americans do not live in that reality. One wonders what is the difference between the sundown towns of yesteryear and today's suburban cities that surround Black inner cities?

Question 59. Did Uncle Tom's cabin really exist, and if so, what happened to it?

Uncle Tom's cabin really did exist and still does. It has been restored and opened to the public. The former slave, Josiah Henson, was the real-life model for the character Uncle Tom in Harriet Beecher Stowe's novel, *Uncle Tom's Cabin*[60]. Josiah Henson's home, his cabin, is today incorporated

---

[59]Cushin, Sheryll. "The Failures of Integration," The Center for American Progress, June 15, 2005.

[60]Stowe, Harriet Beecher. *Uncle Tom's Cabin*, The New American Library, Bibliographic copyright 1981.

into a modern home on Old Georgetown Road in Rockville, Maryland. Born in Charles County, Maryland in 1789, Henson was five years old when Isaac Riley sold him at an auction to Adam Robb, who brought him to Rockville, Maryland. Henson's health began to deteriorate in Maryland, so he was sent back to live on Isaac Riley's farm. Riley agreed to pay Henson for his labor so that he could buy both his and his family's freedom. Henson worked for over 30 years before he earned enough money to buy his freedom from Isaac Riley.

"Uncle Tom's Cabin in Rockville, Maryland."
Source: Author's Personal Collection.

However, when Henson attempted to buy his freedom, Riley demanded more money and threatened to sell Henson's family down the river. Henson gathered his family and escaped to Canada via the Underground Railroad. In 1849, he published his autobiography, upon which Harriet Beecher Stowe based her groundbreaking novel, *Uncle Tom's Cabin*. The cabin where Uncle Tom or Josiah Henson lived was privately owned by a White couple for many years, but was purchased by the Montgomery County Planning Board around 2003 and made into an historical site.

Question 60. How did Blacks know how to find accommodations and travel safely during Jim Crow segregation?

Whether it was during slavery or Jim Crow segregation, safe travel was a primary concern of Black people and required careful planning to get from one point to another, especially in the South. Black people were always sensitive to the physical dangers associated with leaving their communities and entering non-Black communities. They had to determine the best mode of travel as well as how best to find food, shelter and other consumer items while traveling outside of their communities. The U.S. Congress enacted a highway law, known as the Enforcement Act of 1870, which on paper provided a limited amount of safety and comfort to Black travelers. Unfortunately, within a decade after passage, the U.S. Supreme Court again exercised authority which the U.S. Constitution never gave it (see Question 21), and nullified the Enforcement Act as unconstitutional. Fully aware of their vulnerability, Black Americans took responsibility for their own personal safety on the highways while traveling. Without weapons, the best resource that Black travelers had was *The Negro Motorist Green-Book* published and distributed by Victor H. Green and Company in 1936. It was not only a travel guide, it was also a vacation and recreation guide that listed amenities in every state across the country, whether Blacks were driving, riding a train or taking a bus. It listed hotels, boarding houses, restaurants, beauty shops, barbershops, drugstores, groceries and gas stations where Blacks would find acceptance. The Victor H. Green Company, an early travel agency, maintained a reservation office to assist Blacks with their travel plans.

The Negro Motorist Green-Book was widely distributed through religious groups, sororities and fraternities, and other Black groups that planned conferences and various kinds of gatherings. Interested travelers could secure a free copy by writing directly to the Victor H. Green Company. The *Green-Book* contained advertisements for the Ford Motor Car Company, which helped to defray the cost of publication.

It was regularly published up until the 1950s, when social integration began across the nation and Blacks were not so fearful about traveling via automobiles and finding food, gas and sleeping quarters.

Question 61. Why did runaway slaves view Detroit as an ideal terminal city?

Big cities in so-called free states in the North long served as powerful magnets for slaves who contemplated running away from plantations and Southern enslavement. Large cities, like Detroit had some friendly White abolitionists and enough Blacks that runaways could easily blend into crowds. It was also just across the river from Canada. In Canada, there was a mixture of slave and free Black populations in which runaways from Detroit could also easily mingle with the local Black population. Runaway slaves could sail or swim across the Detroit River to Canada in the summertime with little difficulty. In the wintertime, they could walk or drive a horse and buggy across to Canada. Located on an international border, Detroit gave runaways an option, even though, Detroit had more than its share of White slaveholders.

On September 22, 2005, the headlines of the *Detroit News* blared, "Racial divide haunts Metro Detroit." So, what's new? Detroit, Michigan has a unique racial history and many of the symbols remain unchanged, even though the city is presently an 86 percent majority-Black city. Detroit is unique as a Northern city because of its location and because it tolerated slavery in defiance of the law. Slavery existed in both Michigan and Canada, and prominent citizens in both places owned slaves. Detroit was a pit of confusion for a slave who escaped from the South, then sought freedom in the North. There must have been traffic jams on the river as Canadian and Black slaves from Detroit criss-crossed the same river seeking freedom on the other side. Detroit was not a promised land for either runaways or free Blacks. It was a Northern city with a Southern slave society mentality. In the 1800s, there were approximately 1,650 enslaved Blacks in the city of Detroit.

In Detroit, there was much to make a runaway slave wary. Slaveholders were venerated. The city's major streets, schools, parks and county seats of government were named after prominent slaveholders like Joseph Campeau, John R. William and Lewis Cass. A small city within the boundaries of Detroit was named after the slaveholder John Hamtramck. Since William Macomb was the largest slaveholder, a county was named after him. Woodward Avenue, Detroit's major and longest street, was named after a judge, Augustus Woodward, who was known for his harsh rulings against slaves. The Northwest Ordinance of 1787 banned slavery in Michigan, but there was the case of Peter and Hannah Denison, who sued in court in 1807 to free four of their children who were being held as slaves. Judge Woodward ruled that all slaves born before 1793 must continue to be slaves for the rest of their lives.

Question 62. What is the story behind the Good Darky statue in Natchitoches, Louisiana?

The primary purpose of statues and memorials is to reflect cultural values considered positive for the time and to honor individuals who behaved in a manner considered pleasing to the public. When Uncle Jack, a Black man who had been a lifelong servant to a White family, died in 1926, his death left such sadness with the family that they sought to express their deep feelings by commissioning a bronze statue in Uncle Jack's image. In 1927, the Natchitoches City Council voted to erect a public statue of Uncle Jack, later known as the Good Darky statue, at the foot of Front Street. The inscription on the base of the statue read, "Erected by the City of Natchitoches in Grateful Recognition of the arduous and faithful service of the Good Darkies of Louisiana." The city's Rotary Club followed the Council and adopted a resolution that connected the statue to slavery. It read:

"Resolved that the faithful and devoted service rendered by the old Southern slaves, in working and making crops and taking care of the [White] women and children, while their masters were away for many years, fighting to keep them in slavery, has never been equaled. Those who are old enough to remember can tell you how the slaves remained at home and took care of everything and worked and made crops as they had always done."

Of course, Whites and Blacks viewed the statue differently. Blacks believed the statue reinforced behavior required of slaves, but slavery had ended 50 years earlier and such behavior was totally inappropriate for free Black Americans. Consequently, Blacks publicly protested and demanded that the statue be removed from its public site and destroyed. Whites, on the other hand, did not have a problem with the statue, felt it was appropriate and saw nothing racially wrong with a public image of a Black man, holding his hat in hand, smiling and bowing in an accommodating manner. The Good

"The Good Darky Satutue in Louisiana."
Source: U.S. Library of Congress

Darky statue reinforced the desired demeanor White Southerners wished to see in Blacks—compliant, humble, meek, unaggressive, loyal, faithful and servile. The statue gave a sense of position and comfort to White society in the 1890s. Most importantly, it reminded the Black man that the way to win approval was to stay in his place, and to act according to the Southern codes of etiquette.

Hard feelings were expressed on both sides in regards to the Good Darky statue, but the racial temperatures lowered when the city chose to relocate the statue to the Rural Life Museum at Louisiana State University in Baton Rouge. It became a tourist attraction portraying a model for Black behavior and a symbol of White approval of racial subordination.

Question 63. What lessons should Blacks take from the book, *Uncle Tom's Cabin?*

Harriet Beecher Stowe's renowned pre-Civil War novel, *Uncle Tom's Cabin,* first published in 1852, contains numerous teachables and warrants a reading by all Americans today. One of the first important things this book did was to focus the nation's attention on the cruelty, moral evils and dehumanizing realities of Black enslavement. The second teachable was the author's personality study of the main character, Uncle Tom, as a principled man who expressed his willingness to die before inflicting harm on his own people. Lastly, the book presented a character study of the opposite of Uncle Tom, Sambo, a Black slave driver who would do anything to gain the White slaveholder's acceptance and love. The lessons in *Uncle Tom's Cabin* are as relevant in real life today as they were when the book was released.

Uncle Tom's Cabin originally appeared in an abolitionist newspaper under the title, *The Journal Story of Uncle Tom.* Harriett Stowe's lead character, Uncle Tom, was based on the life of a former Black slave named Josiah Henson, who related his story to her and shared his journal. The magazine article about Uncle Tom was an instant hit. It was rewritten as a book, and it became so popular that it sold more than 300,000 copies in its first year alone. Harriet Stowe became the nation's first author to write a national bestseller. She achieved significant recognition, too, as the first writer to bring dignity to nearly five million enslaved Black people. She presented Black people to the world as being as human as White people. When President Abraham Lincoln met Harriet Stowe several years later, he said, "So you are the young lady whose book has caused a Civil War across this land." Most importantly, for Black Americans, her novel offered numerous illustrations of what constitutes appropriate versus inappropriate behavior for Black Americans in race matters.

The first lesson for Blacks from *Uncle Tom's Cabin* would be to unlearn the inaccurate popular images of Uncle Tom. During the latter part of the 1800s and the early 1900s, it was the trend to paint the Uncle Tom character as a despicable Black man constantly trying to curry favor with Whites. Uncle Tom in the novel, was weak and overly religious, but he was not a bad man. Uncle Tom had deep personal integrity and refused to mistreat his own people. When slaves ran away and crossed the river, Uncle Tom refused to tell where they would hide. When a slave was short of his quota of cotton to pick, at the weigh-in Tom would put cotton from his own sack into the sack of the slave who was short, just to keep him from being beaten. Tom also refused to beat Black women to make them pick more cotton to make their quota.

Simon Legree, the White slaveholder, decided to break Uncle Tom's spirit and stop him from trying to protect the other slaves. Simon Legree told Uncle Tom that he would have Sambo beat Tom every night until he started revealing where the slaves would hide and proclaim that Legree was his lord and master. Uncle Tom told Legree that he would die before hurting other slaves or call Legree his lord and master. Sambo, who faithfully followed Legree around, said he would gladly beat Uncle Tom and show the White master where the *coons would hide*. Uncle Tom would not give in, so Sambo finally beat Uncle Tom to death. The real culprit in the story was Sambo, not Uncle Tom. Uncle Tom was the hero and a model for the behavior that Black America needs more often in its Black men and women.

The name *Uncle Tom* did not become a derogatory term until the 1940s when it acquired the meaning of a fawning, submissive and compromising Black person. In the last part of the 1900s, however, usage began to change as I explained the difference and urged Blacks to replace the term *Uncle Tom* with the more accurate term *Sambo*. Joseph Boskin, in his book, *Sambo: The Rise and Demise of an American Jester*[61], underscored the importance of using an accurate name for inappropriate Black behavior, saying, "As his name is, so is he." Just like the Sambo character in *Uncle Tom's Cabin*, in real life, the Sambo label signifies a self-hating, conservative or liberal Black person who inflicts pain on members of his own race to gain recognition, acceptance and personal benefits from Whites.

---

[61] Boskin, Joseph. *Sambo: The Rise and Demise of an American Jester*, Oxford University Press, New York, 1986, p. 17.

PART X
Black Economic Empowerment

Question 64. Should Blacks ally with liberals or conservatives?

In truth, it makes little difference with which ideological group Blacks identify, because there is scant difference between liberals and conservatives. Neither is willing to drastically alter the socioeconomic structure to benefit Black Americans. Consequently, if Blacks choose either side, they would still wind up in the same spot—at the bottom of a ranking order of acceptability—powerless and impoverished. Conservative racial tactics are open, direct and demonstrate their determination to conserve White privileges, political advantages and nearly 100 percent ownership of all wealth and resources. Conservatives do not intend to share the unearned prosperity that their ancestors gained by migrating to America, prosperity that came from Black enslavement and Jim Crow segregation. Conservatives are well aware of the purpose of the racial norms established in the Diversity Acts of the 1700s—that Whites would be the dominant and controlling population. Conservatives do not believe in sharing or surrendering power or resources. Conservatism comes from the root word *to conserve,* which means to hold on to what one has. When Black Americans have never had more than one-half-of-one percent of anything of value in the richest nation on earth, and suffer from a disproportionate share of social pathologies, what do *Black* conservatives think they are conserving? Food stamps, public housing, welfare, or criminalization? Conservatives will sink a Black boat while liberals will attempt to comfort Blacks as the boat sinks to the bottom.

Liberals espouse diversity and multiculturalism without understanding how those terms came about or how they are used against Black Americans. Inside of broad terms such as *minority, diversity* and *multicultural*, Blacks are either downgraded or totally excluded. Even those leading the Black Civil Rights Movement did not seem to understand that the political correctness of diversity caused liberals and the public in general to turn a blind eye on the unaddressed needs of Black Americans. In a society that no longer chooses to deal with race, diversity forces Blacks to compete with all the *fabricated minorities* that liberals have added to the pot in a Kumbaya effort to share the wealth with everybody. Liberals impede Black socioeconomic progress by using euphemisms and equating Black suffering to discrimination experienced by other self-perceived aggrieved groups. Once these groups are created, they are offered to both the private and public sectors as a menu from which to select for Affirmative Action and other preferential treatment programs. Since the American ranking order of social acceptability puts Blacks in the lowest position, government agencies and private businesses will usually choose women and ethnic immigrants over Blacks.

When the menu of preferred groups and the national policy of Benign Neglect were first introduced in the mid-1970s to take the focus off Blacks, both conservatives and liberals were amazed that Black leadership did not push back or take to the streets in protest. The federal government issued a registry that reclassified Hispanics and women as minorities, and added American Indians, Eskimos, Asians, Arabs, Pacific Islanders, Sephardic Jews, and poor Whites as minorities eligible to compete with Blacks in Affirmation Action programs. None of these groups needed the Emancipation Proclamation, or the 13th, 14th and 15th Amendments to the Constitution in order to be accepted into mainstream society. If they had needed them, they would have pursued them. Liberals and conservatives worked as a team in a manner that inflicted pain on Black Americans and compounded the injustices they had endured. By the late 1970s, liberals gave up their focus on Blacks, deciding that aligning with Blacks was probably a losing cause, but that the newly-fabricated minority classes could cloak themselves in the historical negative treatment endured by Blacks and pretend that they, not Black Americans, were the victims of racism. There is no constitutional, legal or moral basis to equate the experiences of these new minorities to the unique oppression of Blacks or to queue them up in the same benefits line. Both liberals and conservatives show their indifference to Black Americans by accepting diversity and political correctness concepts that displace Blacks.

History shows that neither conservatives nor liberals can be depended upon to protect the rights of Blacks or to take action to see that Blacks are placed in a protected class based upon their exceptionality and unique historical oppression. Blacks must not only do their own political thinking, but also place their own group's self-interest first and foremost.

Question 65. Is Black exceptionalism the unused key to Black self-empowerment?

Blackness has had special importance and impact in America and the world. For centuries, the American public and politicians, in particular, have proclaimed that America's democratic values, freedoms and immigration policies make it an exceptional nation among societies and is therefore due special recognition, respect and an elevated status over all other nations. Exceptional means something that is different, unique, rare, unusual and remarkable. In the case of a group, it means the members have been treated in an uncommon manner from all others. What group of people, in America in nearly every respect, have been viewed and treated in a more egregious manner than Black Americans?[62] Black Americans are an exceptional people in this nation in many ways. It is time for Black Americans to demand compensation, recognition, appreciation and respect for what their exceptionality created in America

Because of Black exceptionality, it is an affront and disrespectful for this nation and the Black overclass to continue relegating Black Americans

---

[62]Wicker, Tom. *Tragic Failure: Racial Integration in America*, William Morrow and Company, 1996, p. 181.

to broad and ambiguous groupings such as *minorities, poor people, people of color, diversity, disadvantaged* and *multicultural*. Inclusion into those categories not only denies Blacks recognition for their achievements, it gives the misleading impression that all categories of *class minorities*— immigrants, Native Indians, gays, transsexuals and women were enslaved, denied free land and wealth, lynched, castrated, denied to benefit from their own labor, denied human rights and love and were as maltreated as Black Americans. They were not. None of those groups have been treated like Black people. Blacks are a very special people.

Black exceptionalism is the missing factor needed to ignite a movement to change the bottom-rung status of Blacks. A fundamental premise of my PowerNomics® concepts urges Blacks to build group self-sufficiency and competitiveness upon its advantages and exceptionalities. PowerNomics principles are the best hope that Black Americans have to survive and prosper in America. However, the window of opportunity is very small and closing quickly. In my book, *PowerNomics®: The National Plan to Empower Black America*[63], I correctly projected that, when compared to other population classes, Blacks would be a permanent underclass by 2013. Underclass status is measured by a group's standing on social discomfort indicators such as measures of health, employment, poverty, income, wealth, education, criminalization and business ownership. These data show Blacks are fixed at the bottom of every negative indicator and bear a disproportionate share of social pathologies. Underclass status is evident when in public discourse or policy, Blacks are ignored, no longer mentioned or acknowledged by name, as a group. Black Americans must use their exceptionalism to change direction. They have devoted nearly 500 years to running away from Blackness as a negative, but they must now turn to their exceptionality, view it as a positive and proclaim it based upon the exceptional treatment and history they have experienced in American society.

---

[63] Anderson, Claud. *PowerNonics®: The National Plan to Empower Black America*, PowerNomics® Corporation of America, Inc., Maryland, 2001.

To use group exceptionalism as a positive focus, it is necessary to know what makes them exceptional and distinguished from other groups in society. The following is a partial list of the ways Blacks are exceptional in the U.S. Black people were the:

1) First people on earth and ancestors of all mankind;

2) The first people in North America, the Folsom people and the Moors;

3) Only people enslaved by the U.S. Constitution, the U.S. Supreme Court, and state Jim Crow laws;

4) Only people classified as property, three-fifths of a human and *a peculiar species*;

5) Only people made a permanent minority and underclass by the 1790 nationalization laws;

6) Only people excluded from the billions of acres of free land granted to White immigrants;

7) Only people not paid for their labor, therefore they could not acquire assets to pass on to their descendants;

8) Free labor that along with free Indian land became the definition of the American Dream sought by immigrants;

9) Only people for whom it was illegal to attend school or learn how to read and write;

10) Descendants of slaves and were in America before 99 percent of all other people arrived here;

11) Most patriotic people and fought in every major war since the nation's founding;

12) Creators of music, dance and slang copied and confiscated by every nation;

13) Pawns over which the North and South fought the 1860s American Civil War of brother against brother;

14) Only people who created the need for a second U.S. Constitution, the 13th, 14th and 15th Amendments and civil rights laws;

15) Southern labor class whose images were displayed on Confederate currency;

16) Only people in America who were denied the humanity of loving, nurturing, building and protecting their own families;

Reflection upon the exceptionalities listed above should lead readers to question how different the U.S. would look today, if:

1) Blacks had been a paid labor force that cleared the land, built the roads, bridges, canals, government offices and universities?

2) Blacks had been members of the Founding Fathers, participating in writing the nation's Constitution, allowed to vote, hold public offices and express a group self-interest?

3) Blacks had ownership of some of the thousands of acres of free land upon which to build mega farms and ranches and extract the minerals, oil, gas, lumber and other resources and the opportunity to accumulate wealth from the generous land give-aways?

4) Blacks had been allowed to economically benefit from their inventions, music, dances, culture and communities?

5) Blacks had received the land, money and tribal membership mandated in the 1866 Indian Treaties?

6) Black ownership rights had been preserved to land in Florida according to the Adams-Onis Treaty?

7) Blacks had received the $50 million stolen by Whites from Freedman's Bank?

The exceptionality of Black Americans is their best, but so far unused pathway to socioeconomic competitiveness, independence and self-sufficiency.

Question 66. How does the 1819 Adams-Onis Treaty relate to Black people?

The Adams-Onis Treaty of 1819 was a treaty between the U.S. and Spain that sold the Spanish territory of Florida to the United States. The Treaty also settled the fights that the two countries had long waged over slavery and the rights awarded to Black people who settled in Florida. Some Black settlers had always been free and others had escaped from slavery. For 300 years, Spain had claimed the Florida territory that stretched from the Atlantic Ocean and along the Gulf Coast to mid-Texas. During that period, the Spanish government and the Catholic Church proclaimed Florida to be a haven for free Blacks and runaways who escaped Southern plantations to become Spanish citizens. Spain's offer of citizenship included physical protection and free land for Blacks accepting Catholicism. After a number of costly military conflicts, Spain fell on hard times and by 1819 agreed to sell Florida to the U.S. for a mere $0.05 an acre or approximately $15 million. The sale was formalized in the Adams-Onis Treaty signed by Secretary of State John Quincy Adams and ratified by the Senate in 1821. The terms of the sale should have protected Blacks, who were made U.S. citizens by the Treaty, which conferred upon them ownership of the Florida land they had worked. Alas, that did not happen.

The Adams-Onis Treaty is another instance in which Whites one-sidedly benefited from circumstances and assets created by Black people. The Adams-Onis Treaty expanded this nation's land mass and provided the opportunity for Whites to steal land and benefits that had rightfully belonged to Blacks. Whites not only stole land ownership and freedom from Blacks, but also severely punished them. Treaties are the highest laws of the land and have the strength of international law when they are made between sovereign nations. The Treaty stipulations required the U.S. to honor the protections and rights that the Spanish Crown had granted the slaves, free Blacks and Native Indians. It required the U.S. to treat people with African blood living free in Spanish Florida the same way it treated Whites. The language of Article VI of the Adams-Onis Treaty specifically bound the U.S. to these conditions, stating, "The inhabitants of the territories which his Catholic Majesty cedes to the U.S. shall be admitted to the enjoyment of all privileges, rights and immunities of citizens of the U.S." It is clear that the terms of the Treaty guaranteed *all* Black settlers freedom, U.S. citizenship and rights to their Florida land. It also gave them the right to migrate to any territory owned by Spain.

Years before the Adams-Onis Treaty, the U.S. was under great pressure from White slaveholders, who wanted their runaway slaves returned. They also wanted the Florida land that the runaway slaves, free Blacks and Native Indians owned there. Black settlers' ownership was by Spanish decree and Natural Law. It was estimated that Black settlers owned approximately 40 percent of the land across north Florida. Slave owners petitioned General Andrew Jackson to use his military forces to help them seize the land and the slaves. General Jackson, a slave owner himself, was sympathetic and obliged the slaveholders. He made several illegal military incursions into the Florida territory to capture runaways, take their land and to destroy the Black maroon towns and Seminole Indian villages that were protecting Black settlers. Jackson had no military, executive or congressional authority to invade Spanish Florida and to kill its Black and Indian citizens. His actions nearly threw the U.S. into war with Spain over the incidents. The only reason Jackson's military invasions did not trigger a war at the time was that Spain was so financially weak that it preferred to sell Florida to the U.S. rather than to get into another fight.

As stated earlier, after the Treaty was signed in 1821, Florida became an American territory and the inhabitants became U.S. citizens. However, that did not stop General Jackson from breaking the law. He committed numerous additional reprehensible acts to aid the White slave owners. He repeatedly used the U.S. military to capture Blacks in Florida and delivered them to the slaveholders. In so doing, Jackson violated the U.S. Constitution that declared it illegal to bring slaves into the country after 1808. These intentional illegal actions on the part of Jackson and the complicity of the U.S. government because it let those illegal acts occur, raise numerous questions. The answers to those questions create legal pathways to remedies for reparations for today's Black Americans. In the following section, I am intentionally framing detailed legal arguments that should be used to compel the U.S. government to provide reparations, to Black Americans, as a group.

Violations of the Adams-Onis Treaty provide a strong statutory basis for reparations that Blacks should pursue. The following legal issues arise out of Articles Four, Five, Six and Nine of the Adams-Onis Treaty. These articles articulate the citizenship and land rights granted by Spain to all Black settlers and the rights that transferred with them upon the sale of Florida. To pursue reparations based on this Treaty, Blacks must develop a comprehensive legal strategy. The first step Blacks must take is to demand the U.S. government provide an historical investigation into each legal issue I have identified and make a formal claim. The most appropriate investigators should be the U.S. Department of the Interior and Congress. Second, given the realities of history, Blacks must organize their legal scholars and elected officials to monitor government progress and to identify descendants of Black Spanish settlers. Third, Blacks must make restitution from the Adams-Onis Treaty a political issue and organize the masses.

These facts below are some of the legal issues that Blacks today must demand answers to as they pursue reparations based on the Adams-Onis Treaty:

1. General Andrew Jackson and the United States accepted ownership of Florida as a new state, but ignored the numerous provisions of the Treaty that Spain had made for free Blacks, runaways and Black Seminole Indians.

2. What compensation is due to the descendants of the free Blacks in Spanish Florida that General Andrew Jackson killed or shanghaied and delivered into slavery more than a generation after 1808, the date after which the Constitution, as ratified, prohibited bringing slaves into the country?

3. Why didn't Black Spanish citizenship and land ownership convert into citizenship and ownership in the United States as required by the Treaty?

4. When Indians and Black settlers were removed from Florida by the United States government, why weren't the millions of acres of Florida land owned by Black settlers and Black Seminoles held for them in accordance with the Adams-Onis Treaty? What happened to the ownership of that land?

5. Do the descendants of Black land owners still have entitlement to that Florida land? They owned land based on Spanish decree and Natural or Devine Law, but did not have paper documents such as deeds.

6. If the terms of the Treaty are *invalid*, then the state of Florida still belongs to Spain. Nearly two centuries after the U.S. Congress signed the Adams-Onis Treaty, it is necessary to track ownership of the many Florida lands that had been owned by Black Spanish settlers whose land rights should have followed them after the

U.S. purchase. If the Treaty is *valid*, then the obligations to Black settlers must be honored.

7. What happened to the sovereignty rights of free Black settlers who had lived throughout Florida for centuries and were forced into slavery or were later marched along The Trail of Tears with Native Indians to the Oklahoma Territory? What happened to their land? Were the owners compensated? Were their descendants compensated, or is that a bill still waiting to be marked PAID IN FULL by the U.S. government?

Question 67. Did a real-life monopoly game replace slavery as the primary generator of wealth power?

A monopoly by definition implies exclusive and total control of a commodity or service. Slavery was an economic system in which one group of people had absolute power and control over another group of people for the specific purpose of enriching themselves at the expense of the subjugated group. The wealth from institutional slavery became the foundation for real-life monopoly. On the eve of the Civil War, the private sector had invested more capital into slavery than all levels of government had invested in the entire nation up to that point in time. Slave owners profited without having to work. Their return on investment was high, about 500 percent for each dollar. Typical expenses for a slave cost the owner about $12 a year, while each slave was expected to produce at least $55 a year, yielding a profit of $43 a year per slave. In today's economy, $43.00 would equal about $10,000, thus ownership of 100 slaves would be an asset worth $1 million in today's market. The labor of a slave produced the money for the slave owner to invest in all forms of property and assets for even more profit.

Slave power and monopoly power are similar in market impact and wealth building. Both produce massive profits from absolute control of assets. Slave owners had absolute power over labor, controlled agriculture, wealth building and political power and therefore had monopolies. In the early 1900s, the board game Monopoly was created as an educational tool to illustrate the impact of the concentration of wealth, land and power. In Monopoly, the winner of the game is the player who has acquired the greatest control, wealth, power and possession of entire groups of assets that generate unearned profits from passive investments. The American economy, a vast pool of wealth and power, was built by the labor of enslaved Blacks and when formal slavery ended, after 360 years, the accumulated wealth was transferred into businesses and industries on the New York Stock Exchange on Wall Street. The Stock Exchange was a mechanism for pooling wealth to finance even bigger industries.

Under slavery, Black labor was a commodity just like cotton, tobacco and grain. A slave was moveable personal property, which could be collateralized. The value of a slave was usually consistent in the region, but as the value of slaves fluctuated, so did the prices of the slave-made products that were sold on the stock exchange and in the general market place. The value of a slave reflected the value of labor and an expected return on an investment. Playing the stock market was seeking additional unearned income from slaves and the products of their labor. The same hands that held the plantation whips were able to monopolize wealth building in the nation's marketplaces. Slavery-generated wealth became the foundation for the nation's banking, insurance, real estate, telecommunications, transportation, manufacturing, agricultural and processing industries. Wall Street was literally founded on slavery. Slavery built Wall Street. Slave labor provided the capital and the financial structure of Wall Street that remains a key pillar in upholding racial inequality and socioeconomic oppression today.

Descendants of Black slaves do not have the financial capacity to compete in a real-life monopoly game. They never acquired it. They were not allowed to participate in the wealth-generating land grabs at the beginning and were denied the essential tools to generate capital and never received the promised 40 acres and a mule. It is impossible for Blacks to play and win in a society in which they own practically nothing.

Slavery compares to life's monopoly game in that all Blacks are forced to play the game of capitalism without the benefit of capital and monetary assets. They were not allowed to stand in line when the land and resources were doled out to Europeans. The land aggregated by Whites at the beginning of the country has been passed down from generation to generation, doubling in value every 20 to 30 years. Today the average White person has 3,500 times more wealth than the typical Black person. Just like in the game, without money to play, a Black player must roll the dice of life and hope to land on Free Parking, Income Tax Refund or a Social Service Payment. However, if the Black player's dice throw lands him on expensive property or a business that is owned by another player, the Black player must pay up, go bankrupt or go to jail. In real life, if you are alive, you have no choice but to be in the game, but if you have no resources, you have fewer choices and you cannot win, unless you apply PowerNomics® principles to your game strategy to win the game.

Question 68. Why is Black unemployment always higher than that of Whites?

A number of factors cause unemployment to be higher among Blacks than Whites or other population groups in the U.S.[64] Some factors are structural and some are economic and societal trends affecting the entire world. Although most things are beyond their control, there is one thing over which Blacks can exercise some control. The U.S. Bureau of Labor Statistics reported in November 2016 that the national unemployment rate for Black Americans was 10 percent, or twice as high as the unemployment rate of 4.4 percent for White Americans. These statistics under-report Black unemployment and do not explain why it

---

[64]Katznelson, Ira. *When Affirmative Action was White*, W.W. Norton & Company, New York, 2005, p. 13.

is consistently much higher than unemployment among other groups. Blacks need to know why. The reasons are related to emerging societal or worldwide trends and are structural.

The two most impactful social trends that affect general unemployment, and particularly Blacks, are technology and immigration. The massive application of technology brought about by advances in the capacity of computers, robots and artificial intelligence has had an enormous job-killing effect on both skilled and unskilled employment. Blacks, who are already at the bottom of the job hierarchy, often simply fall off the job grid. Following technology, is the impact of globalization and the influx of legal and illegal immigrants who enter America at a rank higher in the nation's social order of acceptance and because they are preferable, displace Blacks in the economy.

Several factors in Black unemployment are structural:

1. **Economic Theory**

   The first structural factor in Black unemployment is the economic theory that guides our national employment policies, which is called the Non-Accelerating Inflation Rate of Employment. It is the level of unemployment that does not cause *inflation* and intentionally tolerates a structural unemployment rate of four-to-six percent. According to this theory, our national economy functions best with a certain percentage of built-in unemployment to control inflation from year to year. Therefore, the government's goal is not *full* employment for everyone. Some people must be classified as expendable. It is critically important that Black Americans understand the importance of and the role of this structural unemployment percentage. Any group with an unemployment rate that is in the four-to-six percent range is viewed as having full employment. Therefore, as far as the government is concerned, unemployment for Whites, Hispanics, Arabs and Asians, which is below five percent, is within the policy definition of full employment and there is no need to create job producing programs for them.

Black Americans, however, have a hidden national unemployment rate of 35 percent that rises to 48 percent in Detroit, 48 percent in Baltimore, 49 percent in Pittsburg and over 50 percent in New York for Black men. The only time Blacks have had full employment was during slavery. After slavery and Jim Crow semi-slavery, the need for and the importance of Black labor decreased so substantially that Black Americans became an obsolete labor class.

2. **Race**

Race is the second structural employment factor. Andrew Hacker, in his book, *Two Nations: Black and White, Separate, Hostile, Unequal*[65], highlights the major role that racism plays in keeping Black unemployment high. Hacker wrote, "For as long as records have been kept, in good times and bad, White America has ensured that the unemployment imposed on Blacks will be approximately double that experienced by Whites. Stated simply, if you are Black in America, you will find it twice as hard to find or keep a job." Hacker underscored the familiar rule that Blacks are the last hired and the first fired. Throughout the nation's history, if White or other business owners had job openings, they would first hire members of their own group. Unfortunately, there are no incentives or benefits for Whites or others to gain from providing jobs for Blacks. In the public sector, nearly 70 percent of the nation's employed Blacks work in some level of government—federal, state and local. The trend of downsizing government has resulted in many Blacks being downsized out of work or forced

---

[65]Hacker, Andrew. *Two Nations: Black and White, Separate, Hostile Unequal*, Charles Scribner's Books, New York, 1992, p. 102.

into retirement. As Blacks are forced out, positions are filled by incoming immigrant groups. Downsizing government meant de-employing Blacks and helped to increase Black unemployment.

3. **Lack of Business Ownership**

The third structural factor that drives up Black unemployment, and perhaps the most important, results from the failure of Black Americans to own businesses, a natural source of employment for their own people. Only two percent of Blacks find jobs in the few Black businesses. Moreover, the few Black businesses that do exist typically employ only 1.5 persons. An important cultural trait that holds down the unemployment rates in White, Asian, Arab and other immigrant communities is that they hire their own people in their own businesses; they do not need to seek employment outside their group. Their businesses on average employ five to six people. Compare that set of facts to the circumstances of Blacks. Black Americans have some control over this unemployment factor. They could do what other groups do normally: build businesses and hire members of their own group. While immigrant group behavior can be instructive to Blacks in America, building a business has its own set of problems. The majority of Whites, Asians, Arabs and Hispanics work in their own businesses within their own communities. Blacks live in neighborhoods, not communities and they are conditioned to *look* for jobs rather than *make* jobs. Blacks look for jobs outside of their neighborhoods.

These trends and public policies ensure that the unemployment rate of Blacks will be twice that of Whites. This nation needs a positive race-specific employment policy to correct these structural defects and to protect Blacks in accordance with the Equal Protection provision of the 14th Amendment.

Question 69. Should Blacks withdraw from Affirmation Action programs and instead pursue racial reparations?

Affirmative Action, one of the most contentious public policy issues for nearly 50 years, provides, benefits to women, immigrants, LGBT, the handicapped, American Indians and religious groups, but only minimal benefits to Blacks. Reparations should be corrective actions framed *only* for Blacks. The initial intent of Affirmative Action was to correct the government-approved acts that damaged Blacks as a group of people. To date, Affirmative Action has defended and preserved the inherited privileges, wealth and advantages of the dominant White society, especially White women. According to Sally Kohn, in her article in *Time* magazine, on June 17, 2013, Affirmative Action has helped White women more than any other group. They have received more benefits even though they are not a minority; they are a majority-majority. Consequently, present-day Affirmation Action programs and policies are on questionable legal grounds, because they intentionally target women and class groups that are more socially acceptable than Blacks. These groups receive unearned and greater benefits from these programs than Blacks, resulting in the debt to Blacks remaining unpaid and making them invisible instead of a top public policy priority. Gender and ethnic groups profit from the exclusion and maltreatment of Black Americans.

The fact that the historical maltreatment of Blacks was authorized and legalized by government is the moral basis and justification for preferential treatment to correct the damages inflicted on Blacks. Government has no historical practice of excluding, maltreating and systematically exploiting women and immigrants. Consequently, Blacks should not have to queue up in Affirmative Action programs with fabricated classes of gender and ethnic minorities. Blacks should be restored to the protected class status they had when the Freedmen's Bureau was established.

Conservative Whites, the primary beneficiaries of Black subjection, are the primary opposition to Affirmative Action specifically for Blacks. They argue that slavery was not that bad and that Blacks benefited from the enslavement system, were treated as well as *other* immigrants and the nation has already gone too far in its social commitments to Blacks. If Blacks were not the victims of 360 years of slavery and 100 years of Jim Crow semi-slavery, then who were the victims? Who benefitted from the exploitation of Blacks and the mal-distribution of the nation's resources? These questions are rarely asked or answered. So, in the context of Affirmation Action, Blacks are the only legitimate beneficiary group. At the same time, the unearned, structural racial preferences and skin-color advantages for Whites should not go unchallenged and unquestioned.

Affirmative Action has not worked for Black Americans for several reasons:

1. The targeted groups for Affirmative Action benefits are intentionally non-specific and ambiguous.

2. Women were intentionally included in Affirmative Action to become the dominant beneficiary group even though historically they have been in a protected class as stipulated by the U.S. Supreme Court in the 1860s. Women constitute a majority in terms of population, wealth, educational achievement, and voting power. Women are not a minority in a majority-win society. White women receive the largest proportion of Affirmative Action benefits.

3. Newly-arriving immigrants are included in Affirmative Action even though there is no record of them being abused nor exploited by the U.S. government.

4. Affirmative Action policies are intentionally targeted to areas such as higher education admissions, contract bids and representation in employment rather than to correction of the mal-distribution of the nation's land, wealth, material resources, preferences, privileges and controls of all levels of government in White society.

5. Black leaders and liberals surrendered to the realities of racism and political correctness and abandoned Blacks for inclusion in a movement for all people irrespective of how they have been treated historically.

6. Most importantly, the number of benefit groups was intentionally expanded, because White society was unwilling to surrender or share its inherited privileges or the wealth received from Black enslavement and the preferential treatment of Whites.

As evidence that Affirmative Action was not corrective action for Blacks, racial disparities between Blacks and Whites continue to widen in the 21st century and Black America is sinking deeper into a permanent underclass status. An underclass group is one, which by its nature, is at the very bottom of socioeconomic conditions and has no means of escape. Black Americans and their unique socioeconomic dilemma have been rendered invisible by various decisions of the U.S. Supreme Court, the de facto guardians of the nation's racial status quo, with conservatives historically dominating the bench. The Court has narrowly interpreted the U.S. Constitution and civil rights laws to strip out the nation's debt to Blacks.

Blacks have never been any more or any less than what White society has wanted or made them to be. If Blacks are going to change their status and become self-sufficient and competitive, it is time to use a new strategy. They must begin to demand correction for injustices of the past based upon group exceptionality and unique historical experiences in America which no religious, ethnic, gender or immigrant group can claim. Exceptionality must become the base for *Black reparations*. Black Americans should extract their group out of sham programs and policies that are not corrective action for them.

Until race is re-inserted as the primary corrective focus, Blacks ought to boldly disengage and withdraw from Affirmative Action and diversity programs. Until race is re-inserted as the primary corrective focus, Blacks should jam up the system by filing lawsuits and staging nationwide protests then proceed directly to mobilizing a new strategic movement to demand national reparations for *native Black Americans.*

White America owes a debt to Black Americans. Reparations is payment made in compensation for wrongs committed against a group of people, such as reparations paid to Jews for the Holocaust or American Japanese for their internment in camps during World War II. Reparations for Blacks should be in the form of cash awards, community redevelopment funds, redevelopment banks, land grants and fulfillment of the Adams-Onis Treaty. Reparations based upon the exceptional historical experiences of Blacks, and *only* Blacks, is a more specific way for America to repay its debt to Blacks than Affirmative Action programs that benefit nearly everyone.

Question 70. Have labor unions been an ally of Black workers?

The first unions in America can be traced to the colonial period when European immigrants began forming trade unions. The early European immigrants were forming unions at the same time that leaders of the country were institutionalizing Blacks as slaves. Over the course of several centuries, the relationship between White unions and Black workers mirrored and reinforced how White mainstream society viewed Black Americans. White unions have consistently used their collective powers and relationships with White-owned businesses to maintain the status of racial disparities. Black workers did gain some benefits from union activities during the 1960s Black Civil Rights Movement. The only time in this nation's history that Blacks had full time employment opportunities was during slavery, as slaves. For Blacks to get full union membership and benefits in the short time period between the mid-1950s and 1960s, as the nation's industrial economy was declining, is a bit like being invited to a major buffet dinner after the food has been picked over and the guests are leaving. Black workers had been caught up in an employment catch 22.

After slavery officially ended, Blacks have had limited or no access to jobs. In post-slavery, when Blacks had slightly improved access to jobs, unions and blue-collar businesses began disappearing[66]. Exclusion by White unions led to two periods in history when Blacks formed their own separate unions, after the Civil War and again after World War I. Prior to the Civil War, five out every six craftsmen in the South were Black. They were the skilled slaves who did the farming, and were the blacksmiths, furniture makers and tailors. At the close of the Civil War, so many European immigrants had been recruited to the country that only one out of every 20 working craftsmen was Black. Because Europeans were no longer forced to compete with *free* labor, their unions began to grow. Blacks offered to join the evolving labor unions but were rejected. White workers pressured unions and employers to drive Blacks totally out of skilled jobs. Without union membership, Blacks were marginalized and consigned to the dirtiest, harshest work and lowest-paying jobs. Regardless of where or when they were lucky enough to find work, they were paid one-third to one-half of what White workers were typically paid.

Throughout the history of unions, Blacks responded to lack of support and actual opposition from White unions by forming their own unions. In 1870, they established the Bureau of Labor, a national labor organization that supported local chapters under the aegis of the National Labor Union. Within four years, the Bureau of Labor had a 90,000 Black membership. However, White employers marginalized and misused Black unions and Black workers. There were numerous times, for instance, when Black workers were intentionally hired and set-up as strike breakers by White businesses. The National Labor Union effort soon folded. The American Federation of Labor, the largest and one of

---

[66]Steinhorn, Leonard and Diggs-Brown, Barbara. *By the Color of Our Skin*, Plume, New York, 1999, p. 105.

the oldest White unions, promised to accept Black membership and treat Blacks fairly, but by the turn of the 20th century they bowed to pressure to exclude Blacks from membership. For the next 50 years, or up until the late 1950s, White unions did not consider Blacks at all and Blacks were unsuccessful in organizing and managing their own unions. At the same time, labor unions began to weaken, and Blacks began seeking civil service jobs. By the mid-1970s, nearly 67 percent of Black Americans were working in some level of federal, state, county or city government. That precipitated a conservative backlash against the number of Blacks employed in government jobs. Conservative Whites had viewed unions and government civil service jobs as positive opportunities when they were exclusive to Whites. Anti-union and anti-government sentiments reflected an anti-Black bias. Increasingly, as Blacks are displaced by Hispanics, Asians and Arabs, those groups will become more prominent in and will dominate unions and civil service. When that happens, conservatives will no longer be anti-union and anti-government.

In a final analysis, from prior to the Civil War of the 1860s until the 1960s Civil Rights movement, White unions and businesses collectively used a number of tactics to eliminate or limit Blacks as a competitive work force in the market place. According to Benjamin Quarles, in his book, *The Negro in the Making of America*[67], unions used techniques and tactics such as: 1) denying union memberships to Blacks; 2) establishing separate local unions; 3) developing tacit agreements with employers not to hire Blacks; 4) establishing seniority rules that impeded promoting Blacks; 5) establishing racially-exclusive licensing boards; 6) refusing to accept Blacks to apprenticeship programs; 7) denying union benefits to Blacks; 8) denying them access to union halls, where hiring took place; 9) and shutting Blacks out of collective bargaining benefits.

These exclusionary tactics were used in cities, rural areas and on agricultural farms. The bottom line was that unions allied with businesses

---

[67] Quarles, Benjamin. *The Negro in the Making of America*, Touchstone Books, New York, 1996, p. 39.

to impede Black socioeconomic advancement and this alliance was a major reason for the high unemployment rates, structural poverty, low technical skill base and the inability of Blacks to provide for stable families and communities.

Question 71. What criteria should Black entrepreneurs use to identify their best business opportunities?

One of the most common questions asked by aspiring Black entrepreneurs is, "What business to go into?" The answer is a simple. Willie-the-Actor-Sutton, an infamous national bank robber, supplied the answer when, in the 1950s, he was asked why he robbed banks. Sutton answered, "Because that is where the money is!" Like Willie Sutton, Blacks should go into business where the most accessible money is and where they have a distinct competitive advantage. Black Americans have an annual disposable income of over $1 trillion, which as a nation within a nation, makes them one of the richest nations on earth. Ironically, because they do not aggregate those dollars to build group strength, approximately 98 percent of their total income is spent in non-Black-owned businesses. The biggest and most accessible pot of money that a Black business owner should have a good chance to capture, is the money held in the hands of Black consumers. Blacks could dramatically increase the group benefit of their consumer dollars if Black merchants and Black consumers practiced group-based economics using the advantages of home court leverage and the cultural buying patterns of their own people. If Black Americans practiced economic nationalism and protected their aggregated resources, it wouldn't be so easy for non-Black businesses to capture Black consumer dollars and weaken the group socially and economically.

To provide a protective environment for Black businesses, the group should model the historical patterns of ethnic immigrants and build business enclaves. Immigrants historically built business enclaves inside of their residential communities, primarily because they felt safer doing business with their own people, wanted to circulate their money through the hands of their own people and it was a form of protection. Institutional racism, by design, will establish Black neighborhoods and establish captive Black consumer markets. Without Black-owned businesses in those neighborhoods, the annual disposable Black consumer dollars are up for grabs for whomever wants them.

Blacks as a group must support Black entrepreneurship by building Black business districts in which they can physically aggregate and practice group-based economics. The reality is that because Blacks do not have communities, it is not always easy to support Black businesses. Most Black shoppers are unwilling to criss-cross all over town in search of a Black business. However, when they aggregate into a Black business district or enclave, Blacks who may live in scattered locations can demonstrate their broad sense of community by supporting the Black businesses in those districts or enclaves. The businesses that are the most important to locate in the district are the ones that meet general consumer needs and are based on cultural characteristics.

The criteria that Black entrepreneurs should use to identify their best business opportunities ought to be structured on two key PowerNomics® elements: 1) build businesses based upon the group's competitive advantages; and 2) dominate in business wherever your group dominates in population and consumer spending patterns.

Building Businesses Based upon Competitive Advantages

A group competitive advantage comes out of whatever the group owns and controls. Blacks have a decisive competitive advantage when they are the majority population and choose to act like the majority and produce and consume in their own best interest. Majority status establishes a potential baseline of income for the community and its businesses. Blacks have unique hair. That should be a competitive advantage that they own and control. It is something the group owns and should control and it should be a competitive advantage. Blacks therefore should own and control the hair salons, wigs, hair products and every aspect of Black hair. Competitive advantages also come from what a group produces. Blacks generate music, dance, clothing and other distinctive cultural products. For aspiring Black entrepreneurs to practice group-based economics, they must first identify the competitive advantages of their race and communities, then capture those disposable consumer dollars. Black dollars should revolve around the community at least 8 to 12 times before leaving. Revolving disposable dollars would enrich the community and businesses by a factor of the number of times that it revolves.

Build Around Black Consumers' Needs and Spending Patterns

Blacks should build business around the basic needs of their people, especially in the essential areas of water, food, medicine, health care and energy. These consumer essentials ought to be readily available in every Black community in normal times but especially during hard times or civil disasters. Further, Black businesses ought to produce and sell consumer items that Blacks spend a disproportionate amount of their disposable income in purchasing. Numerous marketing firms identify the product categories in which Blacks dominate as consumers, for instance, music, cosmetics, fad clothing, hair products and certain foods. When the society provides you with only lemons, go into the lemonade business. In other words, convert negative group characteristics or conditions into positive business opportunities.

Here are two examples of business opportunities based on Black domination. Although Black Americans are only 12.5 percent of the national population, they dominate the national prison population and today are 51 percent, just as they were 150 years ago. Various levels of government spend billions of dollars annually to purchase materials, food, equipment, and supplies for prisons, such as sheets, blankets, beddings, shoes and uniforms. The average construction cost for each jail cell is over $8,000, plus over $24,000 a year in administration costs per prisoner. Prison systems spend more than $3 billion annually procuring shaving lotion, soap, and other toiletries for Black prisoners. Additional billions are spent on contracts to private corporations to manage prisons and provide health care. Prison work and recreation equipment also represent major business opportunities. Business opportunities built around prisons demonstrate a key principle and criteria for Black business development: dominate in business wherever the group dominates in population and consumer spending patterns. Another example is presented by marijuana. Blacks are more likely than other groups to be arrested for use and sale of marijuana. Raising marijuana for recreational and medical purposes will become a major revenue-producing industry. Blacks should be preparing to build vertical business opportunities in this field where they dominate as consumers.

Potential Black entrepreneurs must be careful in selecting business opportunities, but should first apply the PowerNomics® principles of identifying group competitive advantages, consumer patterns, and where possible, build the business where there is a physical Black business district.

PART XI

Forgotten Champions and Defenders

Question 72. Despite the myth, can Blacks compete successfully in cold weather sports?

The inability of Blacks to compete with Whites in cold weather sports is a long-standing myth that ignores both racial reality and the access of Blacks to cold weather sports equipment, facilities and trainers. Judging by the success of the few Black athletes who chose to engage in cold weather sports, there is no basis for believing they would not excel. Granted, most Blacks engage in sports played in warm weather conditions. Throughout this nation's history, however, Blacks have excelled in every sport in which they chose to participate. In the early 1800s, they entered horseracing as jockeys and trainers, and became the best jockeys in the nation for over a century. Later, they entered and dominated professional boxing, basketball, baseball, track and field, tennis and golf. Black domination of sports is so common and accepted today that it is easy to forget that Black athletics were once confined to the front yard of the plantation. Only on rare occasions will anyone speak in public about the superior athletic abilities of Blacks. This is a racially explosive topic in a nation in which Whiteness is supposed to be superior in all things. As our knowledge of genetics, physiology and physical anthropology continues to increase, it is exceedingly difficult for anyone to claim that the participation or domination of Blacks in a given sport depends strictly on air temperature or other environmental factors.

As far as cold weather sports, if Blacks do not participate in cold weather sports, it is not due to intellectual or physiological inabilities. If anything, it is because Blacks simply do not have much interest in those particular sports or they do not have access to the training and environment. However, there is ample evidence that with motivation, proper training and opportunity, a new generation of Black athletes will participate in and dominate in any sport, even cold weather sports. There are numerous examples of Blacks competing and winning in cold weather sports. In 2002, Vonetta Flowers, a Black bobsledder from the warm state of Alabama, made history by becoming the first Black athlete to win a gold medal at the 2002 Winter Olympics in Salt Lake City, Utah, and Shani Davis[68], a Black man, qualified for the U.S. Olympic speed skating team. Four years later, in 2006, Davis went into Olympic history and this nation's record books by becoming the first Black man ever to win a gold medal in speed skating. He holds the world speed skating record in the 1000 meter event. So, it appears that the belief that Black athletes excel only in warm weather sports is a myth that has now been discredited. Clearly, Black athletes can excel in any sport to which they gain access and are properly prepared to compete.

Question 73. The historical preference for professional golf was that it was exclusively White, but did Blacks make contributions to the sport?

Until the late 1900s, Whites semi-limited the role and scope that Blacks were allowed to play in professional golf. But, as in most sports, Blacks had long been engaged in golfing in a variety of ways. As players, they set high standards and achievements within the last century. Charlie Sifford was one of the early golfers and the first Black PGA member. Sifford broke the PGA Tour's color barrier in 1960 and worked hard to build the United Golf Association Tour. He paved the way for Lee Elder, an outstanding Black golfer. Lee Elder broke the color line at the Masters

---

[68]"Davis is the First Black to Win Individual Gold," *The Washington Post*, Sports Section, February 19, 2006.

in 1975 and inspired Tiger Woods, who popularized and dominated professional golf for nearly 15 years.

Blacks were not only great golfers, but they played a significant role in the historical development of professional golf in this country and around the world. Who invented the game of golf is unknown, but there is some documented evidence that golfing was associated with English royalty as far back as the 16th century. In America, Black involvement can be traced back to slavery when Blacks were regularly used as caddies all across the South up until and after the Black Civil Rights Movement of the 1960s. However, in America, Blacks were more than just caddies or middle-class Black golfers who prided themselves on being able to enter and hit golf balls on White golf courses. Some Blacks were more structurally involved in the game of golf. For more than a century, every golfer in America and around the world enjoyed the fruit of a Black man's invention.

In 1899, Dr. George Franklin Grant[69] invented the wooden golf tee that today's golfers like Tiger Woods use in practice and professional competition. Dr. Grant was born in Oswego, New York in 1847 and was the son of a former slave. After graduating from Harvard Dental School, Dr. Grant spent his free time playing golf, but formed a dislike for the tiresome method of *teeing up* a ball by pinching damp sand into a launching pad. He envisioned a small tool, which would make it easier for a golfer to set up the ball and drive it onto a fairway. Dr. Grant carved a piece of wood into a tapered tee golf pin. The U.S. Patent Office gave Dr. Grant patent No. 638,920 on December 12, 1899 and golfers continue to use the wooden golf pin he invented to the present time. It took almost a century for him to receive recognition for his invention.

Another Black man who played a significant role in the development of professional golf was Joe Bartholomew, who established his reputation as a golf course architect. Bartholomew grew up in New Orleans. At the

---

[69]Stewart, Jeffery C. *1001 Things Everyone Should Know about African American History*, Doubleday Dell Publishing Group, Inc., New York, 1996, pgs. 374-375.

age of seven, in 1887, he began caddying for White golfers. As an adult, he attended a New York college and studied golf course architecture. In his off time, he honed his golf course architectural skills by landscaping and maintaining golf course greens. His knowledge of golf courses resulted in his being hired to design and build a number of popular golf courses, such as the Metairie Golf Course and the Pontchartrain Park Golf Course in New Orleans, his old hometown. Bartholomew's success with building golf courses made him a wealthy man, but the realities of Jim Crow segregation in the South prevented him from both playing on the golf courses that he had built and his successes from becoming publicly known.

Question 74. Were any attempts made to save John Brown from the hangman's noose?

In the year before the Civil War began, the majority of White Americans opposed the ending of slavery and viewed John Brown as a fanatic and insane abolitionist who was attacking the nation's oldest, strongest and most beloved institution, Black enslavement. John Brown aggressively confronted slavery wherever he found it. In August 1859, John Brown attacked the Marine armory in Harpers Ferry, West Virginia, in his belief that he was striking a death blow against slavery. He was willing to die based upon his convictions. However, once his attack failed and he was tried and sentenced to hang, few came to his aid or to save him from the gallows. His family petitioned the U.S. government for leniency. The family, along with John Brown's attorney, counseled him to plead insanity. They knew that in America's legal system, a mentally disordered person is rarely tried and convicted. To buttress the claim, Brown's family confessed to a long history of insanity. They claimed that a large number of Brown's relatives were declared insane. For added measure, they informed the government that Brown's wife died insane.

With that much family insanity, the court felt no mental examination was necessary. They had already concluded that any White person willing to fight and die for Black people had to be insane. Although our culture considers it a bad omen to kill a mentally unsound person, the Virginia courts deviated from prevailing practices and made John Brown an exception. Brown had scared the nation and they wanted to make an example out of his act and sympathies for Black slaves. In the eyes of the nation, the government hanged a fanatical lunatic who was a traitor to the White race. In the eyes of nearly five million Blacks, they hanged a hero, a martyr in a just cause. Across the nation, Brown's death was mourned by both Black and White abolitionists. They all felt John Brown's death prophecy of a brewing and unavoidable national conflict would soon occur. A Civil War between the North and South did begin shortly thereafter and lasted for four years.

It is sad that John Brown, who without a doubt was the best White friend that Black Americans have ever had, has received such little recognition and respect. As every student of history knows, or should know, no White American ever cared about or fought harder for Black people than the fighting abolitionist, John Brown. From Bloody Kansas to Harpers Ferry, John Brown and several of his children gave their lives fighting to end slavery and avenge the wrongful deaths of Black slaves. John Brown and other members of his family are buried on the 244-acre farm in North Elba, New York, which he purchased in 1849, barely 10 years before he was executed by the U.S. government for attempting to free Black slaves.

Today, John Brown's peaceful farm and burial ground are tourist attractions that make a mockery of his life and mission. The offense is on a bronze plaque that was erected in 1916 on John Brown's headstone that summarizes his fight against slavery across America. Beneath Brown's portrait, the plaque has three paragraphs that begin with the words, "Here lies buried John Brown" and ends with the words, "buried with him are 12 of his followers." Of the 12, the plaque lists the actual names of the 10 White men who were killed at Harpers Ferry with Brown, but it does not list the names of the two Blacks who were caught and hanged. The plaque also does not identify the four other Blacks who were later captured and hanged. Instead, the plaque simply identifies them as *Negroes* and places them last. If John Brown could comment from the grave about the last commemoration to him, he would not like the lack of recognition and respect accorded the people for whom he and his family lived, fought and died. Where is the justice?

Question 75. Did Blacks ever form organizations to protect themselves from extra-legal and other terrorist groups?

During slavery times, there was a secret Black organization called the Knights of Liberty, founded by Moses Dickson, who was born free in Cincinnati, Ohio in 1824. Dickson didn't see the horrors of slavery until he was an adult working on a steamboat that traveled into the South. After exposure to those terrors, he formed a protective organization that met regularly and privately in St. Louis, Missouri. His organization's plan was to destroy the institution of slavery quickly and by any means. The members were willing to initiate military action, if necessary. Over a 10-year period, the Knights helped hundreds of Blacks escape slavery and find quasi-freedom in the North. The Knights of Liberty was dissolved shortly before the Civil War started. It was remembered, however, by several names, including the Knights of Tabor or the Black Knights. The word *Tabor* had special meaning, referring to a place in the Bible where the Israelite army beat the Canaanite army.

After the Civil War, the South blamed Blacks for its loss and intensified their abusiveness toward Blacks. In response, Blacks created some protection organizations. The most effective were the Glory Brigade and the Buffalo Soldiers that formed after the Civil War. They deserve high praise for the protection provided to Black people. While over 200,000 Blacks fought the South along side of Northern Union soldiers, the Glory Brigade was also associated with the Union, but their highest priority was protecting their own enslaved people. In the belly of the Confederate South, the Glory Brigade was a Black regiment that fought to hold land for Blacks in Florida's Amelia Island. In South Carolina, they fought to hold Hilton Head Island, Jones Island and other offshore land for Blacks throughout the South. Although Confederate rebel forces attacked the islands repeatedly, the Black troops fiercely fought and held those lands for the Union and Black ownership well after the Civil War. General Tecumseh Sherman rewarded ex-slave soldiers by granting them land rights on all of the offshore islands from South Carolina to Florida. However, after the 1960s civil rights movement, Blacks lost most of the land on the various islands to White land developers who took the land through various means such as taxation and gentrification, then built expensive all-White resorts that excluded Blacks.

"Black Rough Riders and Ex-Buffalo Soldiers Who Stood Up for and Defended Blacks." Source: Library of Congress.

During the Black Civil Rights Movement of the 1950s and 1960s, while Blacks were declaring themselves nonviolent, violence against them, especially in the South, was rampant. One group of World War II and Korean War veterans did not accept the nonviolent, turn-the-other-cheek philosophy and organized into a protective group called the Deacons for Defense and Justice. First organized in Jonesboro, Louisiana on July 10, 1964, their primary goal was to combat Ku Klux Klan violence against the Congress for Racial Equality (CORE) volunteers who were entering Southern states and conducting voter registration drives. In various locations in the South, the Deacons patrolled Black neighborhoods. They protected mass meetings, community headquarters, voter registrants and civil rights marchers. The Deacons purposely inflated their membership numbers to appear more menacing to White extremists. The image of thousands of armed and angry Black men in special defensive organizations spreading throughout the country shocked many people and led to speculation that the U.S. was headed for a race war.

In the late 1960s, the Black Power Movement eclipsed the Deacons and the nonviolent civil rights movement. Many Black Americans, especially the young, grew tired of the compromising and passive attitudes of the civil rights leaders and were more inclined to identify with Malcolm X, Stokely Carmichael, Rap Brown and Black Power advocates. The Deacons earned a special place of honor in Black history for the initiatives they took to protect members of their community. The number and kind of Black protective and secret organizations in the 21st century remains a secret.

Question 76. Where and when did the most significant slave revolts occur?

The most significant slave revolts, based upon the sheer number of slaves who participated, occurred during the three Seminole Wars, when Union troops were seeking and depriving Black settlers of their citizenship rights in Florida. In 1835, over 1,000 Black settlers left their home sites to fight and defeat General Thomas Jesup and his Union troops. Even though historians often label that battle a Seminole War, at that time, Blacks made up a large percentage of the Indian forces and the leadership of the Seminoles. General Jesup attempted to set the record straight by reporting that it was not an Indian war, but a *Negro War*. There were a number of other major slave revolts that did not have as many participants. The Stono River Rebellion[70] in the state of South Carolina in 1739 was the first mass slave revolt in America. According to Lerone Bennett, the revolt was led by a Black slave named Jemmy. Encouraged by the Spanish Crown and missionaries' promises of freedom and land, a group of 20 slaves attacked a storehouse in St. Paul's Parish, a community about 20 miles from Charleston, South Carolina, and killed two storekeepers. Armed with guns and powder, they set off for St. Augustine, Florida, which was owned by Spain. As they marched through the country, they captured more weapons, set fire to plantations and screamed, "Liberty!" Gathering recruits along their trek, Jemmy and his band eventually consisted of more than a hundred slaves. During the 10-mile march, they killed more than 30 Whites before an armed militia caught up with them in an open field.

Nearly half of the rebellious slaves died in the intense fighting. The heads of the dead slaves were cut off and set on poles along a stretch of road, about one head per mile. The practice of posting a rebellious slave's head on a pole or hanging his body from a tree was a popular means of warning and terrorizing other slaves. However, some Black slaves did not get the message or did not care about the head-on-a-pole warnings. In the very same year, the Stono River Rebellion was followed by two more slave uprisings in South Carolina. With each successive revolt, the White ruling class instituted new and harsher laws to intimidate and control slaves. Southern Whites were terrified of slave revolts. Since their wealth and quality of life depended upon slaves, they were determined to maintain slavery at all costs. In 1831, Alexis de Tocqueville, a European writer who was touring America and writing his book, *Democracy in America*, said that if freedom was refused to the Negroes in the South, in the end they will seize it themselves.

Another large slave revolt took place at the Andry Plantation, about 35 miles from New Orleans, Louisiana. Hundreds of Black slaves, led

---

[70]Bennett Jr., Lerone. *Before the Mayflower: A History of Black America*. Penguin Books, New York, 1988, pgs. 116-117.

by Charles Deslondes, participated in the slave uprising. They killed a number of Whites and marched down the road to New Orleans, burning, pillaging and killing as they went. At every plantation on the way, more slaves joined in until the group numbered nearly 500. White men and women, who had been warned by a few Sambo slaves and slave drivers, fled on carts and wagons ahead of the revolting slaves into New Orleans. The revolting slaves had only pitchforks and other farm implements to use as weapons, so they were easily attacked and halted the next day by armed White militia. On the second day, January 10, 1811, U.S. military troops arrived with muskets and cannons. Outnumbered and outgunned by a White militia and U.S. military troops, the poorly armed freedom seekers were defeated, then massacred. Local Whites beheaded the dead slaves and placed their heads on spikes at equal distances along the Mississippi River to serve as a public warning to those who might still harbor thoughts of rebellion.

In 1800, Gabriel Prosser, a 24-year-old slave in Richmond, Virginia, carefully planned and inspired the largest potential slave insurrection. Prosser had managed to recruit more than 2,000 slaves who were willing to kill any and all who attempted to stop them. The revolt was postponed for a week due to a terrible rainstorm. Before the weather had cleared up, two house slaves revealed Prosser's planned revolt to their White masters, who then arrested and hung Prosser and a large number of the participating slaves. The goal of the two house slaves was to earn Meritorious Manumission at the expense of members of their own race. Blacks in the 21st century must also be wary of the same self-serving behavior of Sambo Blacks.

Question 77. Was Harriet Tubman a pistol-packing-mama who practiced medicine?

Harriet Tubman, who had been enslaved in the state of Maryland, certainly did carry a pistol when she ventured into slave territory to lead Blacks to freedom. Nicknamed the *Black Moses*, she heads the list of heroines in Black history. After escaping her owner, she committed herself to fighting for other Blacks still in bondage. She was the best-known conductor of the Underground Railroad. She once proudly stated, "On my underground railroad, I never ran my train off the track and never lost a passenger." At the risk of being captured and hung, she made 20 missions into the South, bringing back more than 300 runaway slaves to freedom. In a remarkable coup, she even brought both her parents out of bondage in 1857 and settled them into a home, which she owned in Auburn, New York. Southern slave owners wanted to capture her so badly that they offered a huge reward of over $40,000. She knew the large bounty that had been placed on her head made her a target, so she carried a pistol.

Harriet Tubman took pride in being known as a pistol-packing-mama. With a bounty on her head, she carried a pistol in her dress pocket to enforce her authority. A friend commented to her about the value of the six-shot pistol in deterring slave hunters. She responded, "The pistol is not for slave hunters. It's for the weak Black slaves." While leading a group of Black runaways to freedom, she made it clear she would use the pistol. On one occasion, a slave became frightened and refused to go any further. She pointed her gun at his head and said, "Move or die.[71]" The frightened slave continued North with the rest of the group. Within a week, he was a free man in Canada.

When she wasn't rescuing Blacks from slavery, Harriet Tubman provided invaluable medical assistance to Union troops during the Civil War. In addition to leading Black runaways to freedom and the Union Army into military strikes, she was a root doctor skilled in curing diseases contracted by Union soldiers. Three out of five soldiers who died during the war were killed by diseases unrelated to combat wounds. Unlike military doctors who depended on military-approved-and-dispensed medicines, she used Black remedies and local plants to concoct her medicines. Thousands of Blacks worked as medical and personal

---

[71]Franklin, John Hope. *From Slavery to Freedom: A History of Negro Americans*, Alfred A. Knopf Publisher, New York, 1980, p. 194.

attendants to Union troops, but only she was respected and appreciated as if she were a medical doctor.

In one instance, Ms. Tubman was summoned to a military outpost on Amelia Island, several miles south of the Georgia border in Florida. The Union officer in charge expressed grave concern that his troops were dying off like sheep from dysentery, dehydration, smallpox, and malignant fevers. Miraculous healing powers were ascribed to her when she pulled most of the men through this medical crisis without falling sick herself. Her psychological and medical healing became legendary among her Union comrades.

Harriet Tubman died in 1913. She was buried with military honors in Fort Hill Cemetery in Auburn, New York. With the actions of many Black conservatives and civil rights liberals taking Black people backward to the old master's plantation, one must ask, "Where are today's Harriet Tubmans who will challenge Black America to either move forward or die?" After 20 dangerous missions into the South to save Black slaves, she learned that before you can save Black people, one must be a fearless leader willing to hold them accountable for cowardice and inappropriate behavior.

Question 78. Who was the most heavily-decorated Black soldier in World War I?

Throughout this nation's military history, from the Revolutionary War to present-day military conflicts around the world, Blacks have consistently proven that they are this nation's most patriotic and willing military fighters. As a throwback to slavery, conservative White males promoted the racist myth that Black Americans would be terrible soldiers because they were afraid to fight. There are, however, numerous examples of recognition given to Black soldiers for their myth-busting bravery and heroism in battle. One Black man, Sergeant Henry Johnson, became a World War I military hero and the first American soldier of any race to be awarded the Croix de Guerre, France's highest award for heroism.

Johnson was born in Winston-Salem, North Carolina in 1891. As a teenager, he moved to Albany, New York and later joined the Army's National Guard and became a member of the Harlem Hell Fighters, a self-named group of Black soldiers. Even though the United States Army was segregated, he and other members of the Harlem Hell Fighters were called into active duty with the 369th, the first Black American unit to see combat[72]. He received combat training in Spartanburg, South Carolina and then was transported into combat with French military units. Like all Black soldiers, they were used as common laborers, cooks, stevedores, housekeepers and guards.

"Henry Johnson and a New York Ticker Tap Parade in His Honor."
Source: U.S. Library of Congress; "Henry Johnson" headshot. Source: U.S. Army

While on night guard duty on the front, Johnson was confronted by a late-night German scouting squad. He engaged in single-handed combat, killing four German soldiers and seriously wounding several others. Johnson's bravery not only saved his life, it allowed him to rescue

---

[72]Christian, Charles M. *Black Saga: The African American Experience*, Houghton Mifflin Company, Boston, 1995, pgs. 312-313.

Needham Roberts, a Black wounded comrade and carry him to safety. Johnson and the 369th ended the war with an outstanding combat record. Johnson returned to Albany where he enjoyed a brief moment of fame, but only earned a railroad porter's income. When Sergeant Henry Johnson died years later of alcoholism and poverty, he was laid to rest without ceremony, in Arlington National Cemetery, in Arlington, Virginia. It was ironic, but sad that France, a foreign country, gave Henry Johnson, a Black man, its highest recognition for bravery and military heroism, while his own country barely recognized him as an American or as a man.

Question 79. How did the 1960's civil rights movement benefit or injure Blacks?

The civil rights movement brought attention to the unfair treatment of Blacks, reduced overt terrorism and violence, gave Blacks greater access to the ballot box, removed the legal stigma of mixed marriages and provided educational, career benefits and limited upward mobility to that particular generation. One of the most important and enduring benefits was the demise of the slavery-based mythological belief that Whites were superior, smarter and necessary in all things. However, changes in the perceptions that Whites and Blacks had of each other did little to reverse the economic foundations or the overall socioeconomic conditions of Black America. The wealth gap continues to grow between Whites and Blacks as they move deeper into hostile and unequal classes. For all intent and purpose, the Black Civil Rights Movement's focus on social integration took Blacks down the wrong road; its leaders permitted other interest groups to subvert efforts to make life better for Blacks. That political approach has proven to be a tragic failure. It did not make Blacks a more competitive or socioeconomically self-sufficient group.

Social integration and the Black Civil Rights Movement, in general, failed for a number of reasons. From the very beginning, the goals and purpose of the Black civil rights leaders were not precise. Therefore, they did not fashion measures to correct structural disparities created by slavery and Jim Crow semi-slavery that mal-distributed the resources and rights to White society. Instead they framed their movement as a moral issue and misapplied the promise in the Constitution that *all* men are created equal. Those words did not apply to Blacks. They protested against oppression and indignities rather than the socioeconomic damages inflicted on Black Americans from the beginning of the country when slavery and Jim Crow segregation doled out nearly 100 percent of the nation's wealth, power and advantages into the hands of White society. Blacks have managed to only acquire less than one percent of the assets of value in the richest nation on this earth. More than 50 years after the 1960s Black Civil Rights Movement, it is remarkable that they, as a group, in proportional and comparative terms, have not advanced.

Blacks are still stuck at the bottom of the nation's ranking order of social acceptability. They are buried beneath a continuous inflow of immigrants and newly-dreamed up minorities who rank higher in the scale of acceptability. Black leaders failed to push back when immigrants and women began to usurp the efforts of the Black movement. Black leaders permitted groups with no legal standing to ride on the coattails of the Black Civil Rights Movement and to displace Blacks from it. The leaders failed because they did have not fully understand the core nature of the problem; did not structure or articulate a clear purpose in the self-interest of Blacks and consequently continuously offered social integration and civil rights as the panacea. Relying on civil rights laws to cure what ails Black America is like not getting a correct diagnosis of cancer and hoping iodine will cure it. Whites, in general, and conservative Whites, in particular, do not hesitate to express their unwillingness to give up any portion of their inherited socioeconomic advantages or privileges to Black Americans.

More specifically, the Black Civil Rights Movement failed because: 1) the U.S. Supreme Court rulings forced Black leaders to address Black issues only within the framework of a color-blind society; 2) Black leaders offered patriotic support in exchange for White approval and acceptance; 3) the movement lacked a comprehensive national plan to correct the racial disparities caused by centuries of slavery and Jim Crow semi-slavery; 4) the primary focus of civil rights was gaining social acceptance and access to what Whites and others owned and controlled; 5) the Black over-class believed Blacks could never succeed without the benefit of alliances with competing ethnic and gender groups; and 6) the civil rights movement was always dependent on the support of majority society and its corporate benevolent entities.

Efforts of the Black Civil Rights Movement were laudable in many ways, but future efforts to make Black America more self-sufficient and competitive must not make the same mistakes.

PART XII
Blacks and Religion

Question 80. What was the role of Christianity and the Bible in enslaving and controlling Black people?

Most religions supported enslavement or included negative teachings about Black people and those concepts became elements of many religious practices. The Bible is the sacred book that provided important guidance to Christians, but is also the spiritual book that most influenced slavery and slaves in America.

King James of England was a supporter of Black enslavement. He had the Bible rewritten in 1611, a period of time when slavery was having far-reaching political, economic and social effects in the world—Britain, Europe, America, Africa and all the other interconnected countries. King James' rewrite of the Bible reflected his view that slavery was not just an economic venture, but also a moral and Christian responsibility. The noted writers that King James commissioned to rewrite the Bible in English inserted numerous references to slavery, most likely to soothe the consciences of the British population about slavery and those of the slaveholders in the British colonies. All of the major religious denominations in Europe participated in institutionalizing slavery and taught White superiority over enslaved Blacks. King James' Bible was an important tool to legitimize and cement those concepts.

The Africans brought into the colonies were not Christians and for a long time it was against the law to convert slaves to Christianity. However, in the 1700s the law allowed a person to be both a slave and Christian. Slaveholders used the new Bible to their advantage and usually provided religious training for their slaves, places for them to worship and even allowed them to attend religious services with them, although seating was segregated. Plantation owners let Blacks have their own services as long as their minister was approved, used the King James Bible and at least one White person was present. Slave owners found many advantages to allowing these religious gatherings. The slaves worked out frustrations and the Bible taught them how to be good obedient slaves.

"Whites Monitoring a Black Minister and His Church Service During Slavery," Source: U.S. Library of Congress.

The Bible and Christianity taught Blacks that to accept enslavement was to be Christ-like. The central message White Christian ministers conveyed to Black slaves was to look upon their daily tasks as burdens decreed by the will of God. Thus, offending their earthly master was actually sinning against God. White ministers taught slaves that Blacks did not deserve freedom, that it was God's will that they be eternally enslaved and that it was the devil that created the desires in their breast to run away or to be disobedient and rebellious. Whites usually taught religion to slaves orally because they could not read, but some special materials were prepared especially for teaching slaves. In 1859, a special catechism was prepared just for slaves and published in the *Southern Episcopalian*. Although this catechism was published just before the Civil War, the lessons referred to specific Bible verses and included prepared questions and answers that give insight into the way the Bible and religion were used to indoctrinate the slaves and support slavery. *The American Directory of Certified Uncle Toms, 1st Millennium Edition*[73] offers the following sample of the prepared questions and answers taught to slaves:

Question: Who keeps the snakes and all bad things from hurting you?

Answer: God does!

Question: Who gave you a master and a mistress?

Answer: God gave them to me!

Question: Who says you must obey them?

Answer: God says that I must!

Question: What book tells you these things?

Answer: The Bible!

Question: How does God do all of His work?

Answer: He always does it right!

Question: Does God love to work?

Answer: Yes, God is always at work!

The slave's beatitudes, taught as part of religious training for a slave, normally followed: blessed are the patient; blessed are the faithful; blessed are the cheerful; blessed are the submissive; blessed are the hardworking; and above all, blessed are the obedient.

Religious training and services were welcomed respite from the relentless labor the slaves endured. They desperately wanted some earthly

---

[73]The Council on Black Internal Affair. *The American Directory of Certified Uncle Toms, 1st Millennium Edition*, CBIA & DFS Publishing, USA, 2002, p. 184.

comfort, protection from pain and some level of acceptance. The slaves, therefore, accepted some of the religious untruths taught to them by the slaveholders. Those lies helped control the slaves, made them compliant and taught them to look for rewards, not on earth but in the next life. Black ministers were only approved if they taught the Bible in the same way. Today, while remnants of those old ways persist in some quarters, as the nation moves further into the 21st century, an increasing number of Black ministers are envisioning ways to use their religion to empower their Black congregations, and to lead them to build group wealth, power and self sufficiency.

Question 81. Did Blacks participate in the popular association of Ronald Reagan with the number 666 and the anti-Christ?

In the book of Revelations, the number 666 is highly significant, because it is the identifying mark of the Beast, which many Christians interpret as the worldwide political system. Revelations, Chapter 13, verse 18 says, "This calls for wisdom. Let the person who has insight calculate the number of the beast, for it is the number of a man. That number is 666." The year 1666 was much feared throughout Western Europe and America, because it contained triple sixes—666—the number of the beast. The world did not end in 1666 however, London was nearly destroyed by a great fire. It is worth noting that 1666 is the year the British colonies enacted the slave laws which locked Black people into centuries of enslavement, pain, humiliation and degradation. Revelations makes it clear that the unidentified beast would be an evil and destructive deceiver.

Centuries later, some Americans applied the prophecy in Revelations about the beast, the Great Deceiver, to Ronald Reagan. The number 6 was all around the name Ronald Wilson Reagan. He was born on the 6th day of February; won his first primary victory in the California governor's race in the 6th month of 1966; was elected to the highest office at the age of 69 (a six and an inverted six); each word in his name had 6 letters, which, when put together produced the number 666. He won the presidential election on November 6, and on that same day the winning lottery number in Washington, D.C., a predominantly Black city, was 666. Both Ronald and Nancy Reagan consulted astrologers in scheduling appointments and making other presidential decisions. After completing eight years as President of the United States, Reagan returned to California and moved into a house with the address of 666 St. Cloud Road. Nancy Reagan had the address changed to 668. Lastly, the California Assembly voted 66 to 6 to allow the state to produce a personalized license tag for Ronald Wilson Reagan. Were these things mere coincidences or fulfillment of Bible prophecy? Blacks and countless others still wonder about the association of 666 with Ronald Reagan.

Question 82. Was Kwanzaa the first alternative to Christmas for Black Americans?

Kwanzaa, what many call the Black version of Christmas, has Swahili and Arabic links, and is celebrated by many Blacks in America. It was not, however, the first alternative Christmas-like celebration that Blacks devised. The Christmas season brought a suspension of field work and a period for slaves to make merry and enjoy themselves.[74]

Slaves observed that Christmas season was a joyous occasion for most Americans, but enslavement laws of 1665 imposed Christmas humbug on Black people in the American colonies. Christmas, largely a White Victorian invention of European society, excluded slaves, but they still had an emotional need to participate in the festivities, so they created

---

[74]Franklin, John Hope. *From Slavery to Freedom: A History of Negro Americans*, Alfred A. Knoff Publishers, New York, 1980, pgs. 143-144.

their own Christmas traditions and Santa Claus. Pulling from their African heritage, they organized a version of Christmas that was called *Johnkannaus*. The celebration centered around a troupe of gaily costumed slaves who on Christmas day would get slave owners' permission to travel to several different plantations, singing and playing on homemade musical instruments. The second tradition they created was *Christmas gif*. Slaves carried around small pieces of fruit or candy in their pockets, like Halloween trick or treats. Whoever said Christmas gif first received a present.

In 1966, Maulana Karenga, Ph.D., an author and professor of Africana studies, created Kwanzaa, which injected African traditions into the Christmas season. Since Kwanzaa has become popular among Blacks, mainstream businesses and advertising agencies have followed the money and begun to recognize Kwanzaa as the Black Christmas. Even though there are still different philosophies among Blacks about how best to celebrate the holiday season, Kwanzaa is an opportunity for spiritual upliftment, a chance to assemble in a celebratory gathering and an opportunity to consciously direct commercial dollars into Black hands and business coffers.

PART XIII

Black Reparations and Affirmative Action

Question 83. Did the 1866 Indian Treaties mandate benefits for Black Freedmen and Black Indians?

The Native Indians had a relationship with slavery from the beginning of the country. The relationship of Indians and Blacks came to a critical point after the Civil War and was the reason for the 1866 Treaties.

The White European colonists who established the first settlements were fearful that Native Indians could form an alliance with African slaves and revolt. The colonists decided it was better to convince the Native Indians to identify with the emerging institution of Black enslavement, and to that end the two parties consummated the Treaty of New York in 1516. The Treaty contained provisions that appeared in all subsequent treaties. The colonists promised Native Indians food, clothing, money and weapons. In return, they required the Native Indians to cease being hunters, to build farms, own Black slaves and support slavery. If the Native Indians accepted those terms, the colonists promised to call them *civilized* instead of savages and pay them $25 for each runaway slave they captured and returned to the slaveholder. For more than 300 years, the tribes owned, traded, captured and profited from the enslavement of Blacks. When the Civil War broke out between the North and the South, all five of the Civilized Tribes — the Choctaw, Chickasaw, Creek, Cherokee and the Seminoles — sought to protect their slave investments and signed agreements with the Southern Confederacy to fight with the South against the North to maintain Black slavery.

The 1866 Indian Treaties between the U.S. government and the Five Civilized Tribes, required the tribes to release their slaves after the Civil War and described the legal obligations of the tribes to the Black Freedmen and Black Indians and the benefits that were due them. Initially after the Civil War, the Native Indians who had been slaveholders and had fought on the side of the South to maintain slavery, refused to release their slaves, claiming independent sovereignty. By fighting on the side of the Southern Confederacy, the Indian tribes had broken all previous treaties with the U.S. government, because each treaty required loyalty to the U.S. The 1866 Treaties were drafted by representatives of the U.S. and were signed by Indian chiefs of each of the five tribes. The Treaties required the Native Indians to release their slaves, to give each Black Freedman and Black Indian $150, 160 acres of land and most importantly, they were all to be treated as members of the tribes.

The language of the 1866 Treaties tracked the language of the 14th Amendment that granted citizenship rights to former slaves. The Treaties mandated that Black Freedmen and Black Indians be treated similarly in all manners and equal to members of the Five Civilized Tribes. Today, being treated similarly would mean Black Freedmen and Black Indians should be tax-exempt, exempt from college tuition, have priority rights to reservation resources, have rights to electronic broadcasting airways and have federal recognition of land for gaming licenses. Implicit in the Treaties was a direct relationship with the government through the Bureau of Indian Affairs in the U.S. Department of the Interior. On a side note, the Bureau of Indian Affairs and the Freedmen's Bureau were established at the same time, placing Black Freedmen and Indians into protected classes. But, the Freedmen's Bureau was intentionally corrupted, the funds plundered by Whites, and prematurely terminated because the South again had a need for Black labor. The Bureau of Indian Affairs still stands and is the government entity through which Black Freedmen and Black Indians also should have a direct relationship. Instead, both groups have had to resort to litigation to resolve disputes relating to government financial management of allotment accounts for land and material resources.

Treaties represent the highest form of law, especially in the U.S., which presents itself as a nation of laws. Since the federal government has a fiduciary responsibility to carry out the Treaty mandates, it ought not be necessary for Blacks to file lawsuits against federal agencies for failure to carry out their obligations to Black Freedmen and Black Indians. The Federal government's failure to fully enforce the Treaties represents economic justice denied. The historical significance of these Treaties cannot be minimized because they detail tangible benefits directed to a specific segment of Black Americans and their descendants. The economic benefits should have been enjoyed by the Black Freedmen and Black Indians and passed on to their descendants. Over the course of the last 150 years, these Treaties have served as the basis for Native Indians to demand accountability from the U. S. government for mismanaging Indian assets. Black Freedmen and Black Indians have asked for the same accountability and the same legal questions, but they have not received answers. Blacks cannot let the economic benefits of these Treaties to Blacks be ignored. How is it that legitimate benefits assigned to Blacks are *always* forgotten in history?

In 2006, the Black Indian United Legal Defense and Education Fund, Inc. joined with The Harvest Institute to form the Harvest Institute Freedmen Federation to seek an accounting by the U.S. Department of the Interior for management of the assets of specific Black Freedmen and Black Indian families. It has been a lengthy and expensive legal proceeding. Based on the 1866 Treaties, Native Indians had filed more than 100 similar suits that were at various stages of the legal process. When Barack Obama became President, at the beginning of his first term in office, he promised to help Native Indians and he did during the entire eight years of his administration. His administration cleared the deck and settled nearly all of their pending lawsuits, awarding them approximately $3.5 billions of dollars most years, for a total of approximately $20 billion. The last batch of 17 pending lawsuits were settled by Obama in September 2016 for $492 million. This occurred near the end of his second term and Native Indians were effusive in their thanks to him. The

Harvest Institute Freedmen Federation and Black Freedmen and Black Indians lawsuits, based on the same 1866 Treaties, with nearly identical questions of law, have not been touched or discussed are still stuck in the federal courts.

The Harvest Institute Freedmen Federation encountered only opposition from the Obama administration, an experience very different from that of Native Indians. To date, families that are descendants of the Black Freedmen and Black Indians who are plaintiffs in the lawsuit, have not received an accounting of the assets the government was to have managed for them. This litigation battle to correct the racially-prejudiced behavior of the U.S. government was fought in the 21st century during the period that a Black man was sitting in the President's chair in the White House. The U.S. Department of Justice was headed first by a Black man and finally by a Black woman and a Black man sits as jurist on the bench of the U.S. Supreme Court, yet none of them acknowledged the lawsuits nor sought to intervene on behalf of Black Americans as was done for Native Indians.

The majority of Americans are unaware of the pivotal role Native Indian tribes played in the installation and maintenance of slavery in the United Sates and the way the 1866 Treaties materialized. Once informed, the logical questions ought to be, "Why are the descendants of slaveholding Native Indians getting benefits from Treaties enacted to free slaves, while the descendants of the enslaved Blacks have been denied their mandated benefits and rights for centuries? If slaveholding Indian ancestors are dead and their ancestors are receiving corrective benefits from the 1866 Treaties, what is the logic of denying benefits from those same Treaties to the descendants of the injured Black slaves?"

While the lawsuit filed by the Harvest Institute Freedmen Federation worked its way through the legal steps of Federal Small Claims Court, the Federal Appeals Court and the Sixth Circuit Court, the Obama Administration annually invited approximately 564 Native Indians to White House receptions and awarded them billions of dollars each year of his two terms. Neither the Black Indians nor the Black Freedmen were invited to attend the White House receptions nor did they share in the monetary proceeds. When the Obama administration announced settlement of the last 17 lawsuits for $492 million, the headline of an article in the *Washington Monthly* by Nancy LeTourneau on September 28, 2016 said, "President Obama kept his promises to Native Americans."

The 1866 Treaties had two parts, the Black Freedmen/Black Indian side and the *White* Indian side. What does it mean, if only half of the Treaty mandates were enforced? The land, money, gas and oil resources on Indian lands made other people wealthy and were passed on to *their* descendants. The assets designated for Black Freedman and Black Indians should have been available to pass on to succeeding generations, perhaps making Black descendants wealthy today.

It is up to Black people to express their indignation and demand reparations for the economic losses and mount the political campaign necessary to bring attention to this historic travesty. Why is it that Black people are so reluctant to demand justice and the benefits that are due to them, especially once the legal case has been made? Fatigue is most likely a factor. Lack of leadership could be another factor. To support the case of the Harvest Institute Freedmen Federation's Indian lawsuit, Black political action should demand a government accounting to the families and resolution of the issue at the highest levels of government. Enforcement of the 1866 Indian Treaties is more a political issue than a legal one.

Question 84. Who were the historical and acknowledged terrorists in America prior to 9/11?

The nation had two kinds of terrorists before the 9/11 attacks. The nation, as a whole, enslaved and terrorized Blacks before the country was even a country. After encountering the first Blacks in the colonies, Whites wrote the Maryland edict in 1638, which made it illegal for Blacks to receive any benefits from the infant country. Again, in 1663, the Maryland Legislature declared, "All Negroes shall serve as slaves for life[75]." The provisions of the Maryland edict, denying Blacks any benefits and classifying them as slaves, were accepted by all of the colonies and incorporated into the Articles of Confederation, the U.S. Constitution and subsequent laws, and were used to terrorize Blacks for more than 400 years. Protected by laws, Whites often worked Blacks to death without pay, kept them ignorant, destroyed their families, raped, castrated, lynched, exploited and inflicted other horrific violence upon them.

"White Nationalist Terrorizing a Black Woman and Her Child."
Source: U.S. Library of Congress

The terrorist nation split in two in 1861, when the Southern states seceded from the Union, formed the Confederate States of America with its own flag and fired on American troops at Fort Sumter, South Carolina. Confederate troops killed American soldiers, dishonored *Old Glory*, the flag of the United States of America, and became the first terrorists to

---

[75]Jordan, Winthrop D. *White Over Black: American Attitudes Toward the Negro, 1550-1812*, W.W. Norton & Company, New York, 1968, pgs. 90, 91, 143, 477.

attack the country. This attack ignited a Civil War against the nation and the Confederate flag became the symbol of that terrorism. Many Whites in the North and South still wave the Confederate flag that once stood for anti-Americanism and symbolized traitorous behavior against the U.S. Some believe they are demonstrating patriotism and love for a country they once sought to destroy through a four-year Civil War, and continue to yearn for a return to the genteel Southern life that Whites enjoyed before slavery ended.

The Civil War lasted four years and destroyed an untold number of lives and property worth millions of dollars. The Southern states eventually lost the war and surrendered. Union generals, Northern politicians and abolitionists wanted all Confederate soldiers indicted for treason. Southern politicians acknowledged their war crimes and sought amnesty for their terrorism. President Andrew Johnson, who replaced the assassinated Abraham Lincoln and was a Southerner, granted amnesty to members of the Southern Confederacy who swore a loyalty oath to the Union, returned their property to them and restored the rights of almost all Southern leaders to hold public office again. According to the laws of war, all those who fought against the U.S. should have been punished for treason by hanging, but their sins were forgiven.

After the Civil War, the North and the South reunited, became a solid bloc again, instituted Jim Crow segregation and collectively terrorized Blacks, although it was much harsher in the South. Today's red states, the Southern voting bloc, are an outgrowth of the terroristic Southern Confederacy, the first and oldest organized terrorists in the nation. With the largest Black population living in the Southern and mid-western states and having practically no socioeconomic power and resources, they are just as vulnerable to terrorism as ever. The dark shadows of terrorism of the past still haunt Black America as well as this nation that has been both a practitioner of terrorism and a recipient. There were terrorists in America, therefore, well before the attack by Arab immigrants on 9/11.

Terrorism against Blacks continues as a constant threat even today. In an article in *The Washington Post* on May 26, 2017, Colbert King opinion writer, wrote about the topic. King cited the new report by the Anti-Defamation League (ADL), *A Dark & Constant Rage: 25 Years of Right-Wing Terrorism in the United States.* For this report, the ADL analyzed 150 terrorist acts in the country that were committed, attempted or plotted by right-wing extremists. In analyzing those violent acts, the ADL found that while some targets were Jews and Muslims, Blacks were the most common racial targets. The report found that more than 800 people were killed or injured in the attacks they analyzed and that the number of attacks surged during Barack Obama's presidency. From 2007 to 2016, domestic terrorists killed at least 372 people in the country. Seventy-four percent of those murders were committed by right-wing extremists such as White supremacists, sovereign citizens and militia adherents.

Regardless of where in the country Black people live, because they have practically no socioeconomic power and few resources, they are just as vulnerable to terrorism as ever. The dark shadows of terrorism from the past still casts a shadow on Black America and this nation that has been both a practitioner of terrorism and a recipient. There were terrorists in America well before the attack by Arab immigrants on 9/11 and domestic right wing terrorists are still operative today.

Question 85. Why did the federal government elevate Indian blood and make it sacred?

Many European colonists felt a bloodline closeness with Native Indians, even though the two groups had a long history of pitched battles against each other[76]. In a discussion on importing more Blacks, Benjamin Franklin made the point about a feeling of affinity with Indians when

---

[76]Rivers, Larry Eugene. *Slavery in Florida*, University Press of Florida, Gainsville, FL, 2000, pgs. 12-14.

he said, "Why increase the Sons of Africa, by planting them in America, when we have so fair an opportunity of increasing the lovely White and Red." Thomas Jefferson who used bloodline to agree with Franklin said that the Indian is a degraded yet basically noble brand of White man who is a distant cousin of ours." It is not well known that in the late 1800s, government policies classified American Indians as White and approved public policies that revered having Indian blood. In at least one major instance, government and White social scientists employed a race-based blood tactic to separate and elevate Native Indians over Blacks. Beginning in the 1920s, a person was categorized as Black if he had any Blacks in his lineage. Blacks were depreciated by the *one-drop-of-Black-blood rule* while American Indians were elevated by the *Blood Quantum Rule,* which declared Indian blood to be *sacred.*

In effect, the U.S. government recognizes and provides material benefits to descendants of slave-holding Indians while ignoring and refusing restitution to descendants of the Black slaves owned by Indians. Such public policies and practices are discriminatory and immoral. Moreover, they are illegal and are contrary to the mandates of the 1866 Treaties that this nation consummated with the Five Civilized Indian Tribes, following the Civil War. Southern confederates, the Five Civilized and other Indian tribes were slaveholders and fought on the side of the South during the Civil War to preserve slavery. When the South lost the war, so did the Indians, who declared that their tribes as sovereign entities would not release their slaves. However, all previous treaties required loyalty from the Native Indians to the United States government. The government sent military troops to tell the Indians releasing their slaves was not their choice and that new treaties would be necessary. The Five Civilized Tribes entered into the 1866 Treaties with the government, mandating that Indians release their slaves, pay the Black Freedmen and the Black Indians money, give them land and treat them and their descendants in all ways equal to Native Indians, including tribal membership, land allotments, money and sharing in whatever benefits accrued to the tribes.

Many Whites recognized an opportunity to get in on potential benefits. They paid five dollars to the Dawes Commission in the 1890s to have their names added to the official Census rolls as *Indians*. They were referred to as five-dollar-Indians. At the same time the tribes were allowing Whites to fabricate their lineage to get benefits to which they were not entitled, the tribes were ignoring their Treaty-mandated responsibilities to Black Indians and Black Freedmen. As Native Indians gained a growing sense of respectability, various Indian tribes felt little need to honor their mandated obligations to Blacks and began to distance themselves totally.

In 1938, a number of tribal chiefs contacted the Bureau of Indian Affairs and various Indian commissioners and inquired how they could circumvent their obligations to treat Black Freedmen, Black Indians and their descendants as equal members of the tribes. On August 11, 1938, a commissioner from the Office of Indian Affairs sent a letter to the U.S. Department of the Interior (see www.harvestinstitute.org), posing the question asked by the tribe. In 1943, the Secretary of Interior responded, suggesting that the tribes could initiate a *Blood Quantum* policy, which would redefine *Indian* as a person who could prove they had one-quarter Indian blood. That would make most Black former slaves ineligible for Treaty benefits, although the policy change appears not to have applied to the five-dollar-Indians. The Blood Quantum became policy and has remained in effect ever since, even though the Treaties were not based upon quantities of Indian blood. Non-Black Indians have successfully used the Blood Quantum policy to avoid their fiduciary responsibilities to Black Freedmen/Black Indians and their descendants. The 1866 Treaties placed Native Indians, Black Freedmen and Black Indians in a special protected category. The Bureau of Indian Affairs continues to exist and maintains a protected status for Indians. Blacks were in a protected class when the Freedmen's Bureau was established, but the Federal Freedmen's Bureau no longer exists and the responsibility to protect the status of Blacks was never passed on to a successor federal entity. How different life would have been if the 1866 Treaties had been followed and Blacks had been treated *in all manners similar to how Indians have been treated* and had received the same material and financial benefits over the last 150 years.

The Harvest Institute Freedmen Federation, a collaboration of the Harvest Institute and the Indian United Legal Defense and Education Fund, Inc., filed a number of still-pending lawsuits in federal courts beginning in 2007. The suits constitute a demand for an accounting of the assets the government had the responsibility to manage for the benefit of the Black families who are the descendants of Indian Freedmen. As trustee for the Treaties, the government should have provided an accounting to those families. To date the questions, asked of the government continuously throughout the Obama administration, have not been addressed and the families have not received an accounting.

"Dr. Claud Anderson Meeting with the Chiefs of the Mikasukee and Seminole Indians in Florida. Circa 1970."
Source: Author's Personal Collection.

Question 86. What happened to the Black Seminoles and Black settlers after the Trail of Tears march?

General Andrew Jackson was well-known for conducting government-sanctioned military campaigns against Southeastern Indian tribes, but Jackson was less well-known for conducting non-sanctioned military incursions into Spanish Florida against Blacks who had escaped enslavement, traveled to Spanish Florida and become Black settlers. These Black runaways joined Seminole tribes and other Black settlers who had lived in Spanish Florida for centuries. In his desire to acquire new land and to capture escaped Blacks, General Jackson sent troops into Spanish Florida, which eventually led to three Seminole Wars and the Trail of Tears. General Jackson wanted Spanish Florida to be a safe place for Whites. The United States government proceeded to buy Spanish Florida through the Adams-Onis Treaty and to march nearly all of the Indians and Blacks out the of Florida territory. Florida was a vast territory, with boundaries that included what we know today as Florida, but at that time also included the lower Gulf coast portions of Alabama, Mississippi, Louisiana and parts of Texas[77].

"Black Indian Woman."
Source: Dr. Angela Finley Molette

Initially, the removal process targeted the northeastern part of Florida, where Indians and Blacks lived and owned large tracts of land under Spanish law. Later, White plantation owners laid claims to land in western and mid-Florida seeking to grab land not only for agricultural purposes, but also for the mineral and other resources associated with the

---

[77]Porter, Kenneth W. *The Black Seminoles: History of a Freedom Seeking People*, University Press of Florida, 1996, pgs. 125-200.

land. General Jackson's Indian removal program that began in the early 1830s was a forced march of free Blacks and Indians from Florida across the Mississippi River to Oklahoma.

Black Seminoles and Black Freemen made up approximately 38 percent of those persons who were marched out of Florida on the *Trail of Tears*. When they arrived in Oklahoma, the largest Indian Tribe, the Cherokees, tried to enslave both the Black Seminoles and the Black freemen. Chief John Horse, a Black Seminole, refused to be enslaved, armed his people and split off from other Indian tribes. Chief John Horse and his people were fierce fighters and engaged in numerous battles with the Cherokee Indians, who placed a great deal of importance on owning and trading Blacks as slaves.

The quest of Chief John Horse and his Black Seminole Indians for freedom, acceptance and a secure homeland began in Florida in the late 1790s. Horse was originally a slave who escaped from a plantation in South Carolina and made his way to Florida to become a Black settler, after hearing Spain's offers of freedom, land and citizenship. Like thousands of other Blacks who escaped from enslavement, traveled to Florida and also became Black settlers, Horse lived with the Seminoles and quickly rose up the ranks because he had leadership skills, was bright, knew English and the ways of White culture. He became second to Osceola, top chief of the Seminoles. Eventually Chief Osceola was captured and died. Horse replaced Osceola. For nearly 50 years he fought the three Seminole Wars, endured the *Trail of Tears* march across America and fought in numerous gun battles with slave chasers in the West. Chief John Horse and his Black Seminole Indians finally settled down in the dusty little town of Brackettville, Texas. Horse and his Black Seminoles were hired to track, scout and fight various Indian tribes who were warring with the U.S. government in the West. As compensation for their fighting and scouting services, the U.S. government entered into a treaty with Black Seminoles that promised salaries, moving expenses, material provisions and land in the state of Texas.

When the Indian Wars in the West ended and the services of the Black Seminoles were no longer needed, the United States government developed amnesia. It lost the copies of the treaty it had signed with the tribe and all memory of the promises made in the treaty. Government officials told Chief Horse that no land was available in Texas or elsewhere in the country for his Indians to homestead. The U.S. Army ordered the Black Seminoles off the Fort Clark military base near Brackettville, Texas. The government broke the treaty and neither the Black Seminoles nor their descendants had enough money or political capital to hold the government accountable, unlike other Native Indian tribes that have been supported by government and a sympathetic nation.

Today, outside Brackettville, Texas, there is a graveyard marker that gives testament to honors won by the Black Seminole Indian scouts and the dreams lost by the Black Seminole Indian Nation. Modern-day descendants of Black Seminoles celebrate their Heritage Day each year on the third Saturday in September. They always remember the horrors of the forced march of the *Trail of Tears* by their ancestors.

Question 87. Should Congress repay the $50 million that federal officials stole from the Freedman's Bank?

Congress should definitely investigate and repay the theft of private monies that former Black freed slaves had saved and deposited into Freedman's Bank soon after they were emancipated. An investigation 150 years after the crime was committed would be late, but better late than never. Radical Republican members of Congress (liberals of the day) felt an obligation to aid former slaves to gain land ownership, build homes and businesses and develop financial responsibility. In 1865, after the end of the Civil War, the U.S. Congress chartered Freedman's Bank as a depository for money saved by the newly-freed Black slaves and Black ex-Union soldiers. Congress appointed Whites to operate the banks for Blacks. The temptation proved too great and within 10 years, the Freedman's Bank closed. White administrators had stolen all the deposits of the Black freedmen, misused bank funds and rendered the banks insolvent. Approximately 70,000 Blacks deposited $57 million (adjusted for inflation) from wages, military cashing-out pay, bounty and freedom monies into Freedman's Bank. There were 37 branches of Freedman's Bank located in a number of major American cities, like Washington, D.C, New York City, Philadelphia, Atlanta, Nashville, Memphis, Charleston and Savannah. All of the Black depositors were defrauded of their money. Freedman's Banks were under the control of White boards of trustees and White officers. The bank charters allowed the White trustees and officers to borrow Black deposits and to speculate with those funds that they invested into White businesses instead of Black businesses or Black communities.

The White administrators of the Freedman's Bank not only mismanaged the deposits of Blacks, but also invested the entire $57 million in various kinds of fraudulent deals, theft, skullduggery, nepotism and other conflicts of interests, which left all of the Black depositors broke and without redress. Although Freedman's Bank managed to survive for only nine years, from 1865 to 1874, they died a quiet death. There was no public outcry against the corruption and out-right theft or a demand for restitution or justice for the Black depositors. The federal government did not prosecute the thieves or even attempt to make restitution for the losses. The changing of the U.S. Congress from Republican to Democrat and the growth of the nation's Jim Crow anti-Black attitude made closing the banks acceptable. Until the present time, the descendants of the Black depositors have not demanded restitution for the value of their ancestors' losses nor has the Congressional Black Caucus, other elected officials, civil rights organizations, religious leaders or other prominent Black organizations taken up the fight. Those stolen funds represent wealth that should have become generational wealth, the loss of which was catastrophic for the Black race and for individual families. The compounded interest alone would have amounted to billions of dollars. Black Americans should demand an accounting, public hearings, restitution of the lost funds and identification of those who stole the money.

Question 88. Our government has paid reparations to numerous groups. Why won't it pay reparations to native Blacks for slavery?

Our national government's operational policy on reparations is to pay it to nearly every nation with which it has engaged in a war or military conflict. In reality, institutionalized slavery was a declaration of war, but the U.S. has yet to pay reparations to Blacks. Perhaps there is a link. The U.S. government has for centuries provided reparations to Native Indians and presently provides annual financial support and reparations to countries throughout the Pacific Islands, the Middle East and Latin America. The U.S. paid $12 billion through the Marshall Plan to Germany in post-World War II reparations, which included rebuilding the country and relocating 300,000 Jewish Holocaust victims to the U.S. It also paid reparations to Japan through the Four Point Program to rebuild its country after World War II and to Japanese Americans who were interred in the U.S. The U.S. paid Mexico reparations after the Mexican American War. In the fall of 2016, the U.S. even paid reparations to German Jews who had migrated to America after the Holocaust to relieve their current poverty, even though the poverty of those Jews had nothing to do with the U.S. that had provided them refuge.

Clearly, it is not that White Americans are opposed to reparations; they are opposed to reparations for Black Americans. Most Whites came to America after slavery and they came to this country expressly to receive the preferences, rights and other economic benefits available to them as Whites. They have little inclination to share the benefits they enjoy that came from slavery and Jim Crow semi-slavery. Those deeply-held attitudes have been consistent from slavery through today. According to *The Exclusive Point Taken–Marist Poll* released in May 2016, 81 percent of White Americans oppose reparations for Black descendants of slaves. Yet, a United Nation's report released on September 27, 2016 asserted that the U.S. owes reparations to Black America for past and continuing harm from racism. The report stated, "The colonial history, the legacy of enslavement, racial subordination and segregation, racial terrorism and racial inequality in the U.S. remains a serious challenge and there has been no real commitment to reparations." There are numerous reasons Whites give to oppose Black reparations:

1. Black reparations would reduce White economic dominance and power advantages.

2. The dollar amount would be so great the nation could not afford it, so Blacks will have to continue going without any financial restitution.

3. The statute of limitations for slavery has passed. Even though slavery officially ended in 1865, the legacies of harmful effects continue unabated until the present time. The benefits to Whites of slavery have also survived and continue to be passed down from one generation to the next. There is no argument, however, that the statute of limitations is still open on Jim Crow segregation and its negative legacy that is still in full effect.

4. There is the argument that since some African chiefs participated and cooperated in enslaving Blacks who became slaves in the U.S., the burden cannot be borne by Whites or foreigners. This argument is not consistent with past reparations. For instance, some Jews cooperated with the Germans in the final solution and participated in extermination of other Jews. However, Jews have consistently received reparations, despite the acts of some members of their religion. Any reparations movement should also hold African nations accountable for their role in supplying

Black African bodies for slavery in America. Native Blacks should seek reparations from African countries, whether in the form of monetary or mineral resources then use those resources to form partnerships between the two groups of Blacks to build vertically integrated industries to elevate people of African descent around the world.

5. Some argue that many of the slave-dependent businesses have changed ownership or no longer exist. True! But, many of the companies, members of the White race, and the financial and economic benefits that slavery produced do still exist and are easily available in archival records.

6. Some Whites oppose reparations because they claim the arguments are not compelling. However, even when a respectable neutral party, such as the United Nations, makes a compelling argument, after the initial splash in the headlines, it too is ignored.

Entities with direct involvement in slavery have issued apologies, but no funds. In 1985, Pope John Paul II, while visiting the Caribbean, apologized for the role of the Catholic Church in the commercial enslavement of Black people. In July 2008, the U.S. House of Representatives passed a resolution apologizing to Black Americans. On a voice vote, the House resolution acknowledged the nation's role in slavery, which was a Black phenomenon, but promised to stop *human rights* violations. These kind of weak apologies are insulting examples of symbolism and the sleight of hand of identifying a Black problem but shifting to a minority solution. Human rights do not equate to Black rights. These apologies without resources are political maneuvers. Why? The government has always acknowledged and recognized its obligation to repair official cruelties. Never have reparations or restitution depended on a public survey. The House apology reflects the deep conviction of Whites not to take any actions that would cause them to give up or share resources with Blacks. In essence, the resolution communicated that Blacks have everything that they need; the House does not want to upset the apple cart; it is sorry for the circumstances of Blacks and it promises to go and sin no more.

The U.S. should pay Black reparations immediately. The greater the time lapse between slavery, Jim Crow and the current times, the more difficult it becomes to link historical events with current suffering. Today's social ills on view among Blacks are directly related to the forced pathologies imposed on them by Whites and the theft of what should have been assets in the Black column. Federal, state and local governments that authorized and actively used their powers to maintain Black slavery are still in existence and are complicit. An apology with no funds does absolutely nothing to help 44 million Blacks who are stuck at the bottom of the barrel.

Question 89. How does General Andrew Jackson fit into the call of Blacks for reparations?

Actions taken by General Andrew Jackson established solid domestic and international legal grounds for Black reparations. Free Blacks had lived in Spanish Florida since the 1500s, even building St. Augustine the oldest city in the continental United States. The Spanish Crown invited Blacks to Spanish Florida and promised them rights of citizenship and land, once they crossed the U.S. border into Florida. Many accepted the invitation, therefore thousands of Black settlers lived in Spanish Florida before it was sold to the United States. They owned and worked major portions of land, especially across North Florida, which at the time included the Southern portions of Georgia, Alabama and much of Louisiana and Texas.

As a military general, Jackson had pursued Black Spanish settlers and their property for decades. In 1814, in response to the urging of slaveholders in Georgia and Alabama, Gen. Jackson made an end run around Congress, violated international boundaries and invaded Florida at least twice (1812 and 1818) for the specific purposes of capturing and or killing Black settlers and Black Seminole Indians, who had been granted Spanish citizenship. White plantation owners saw these free Blacks as a threat to their way of life and the institution of slavery in the Southern states. Gen. Jackson did their bidding. When he invaded Florida with a contingency of U.S. military troops and Creek Indians, he slaughtered hundreds of Spanish Black settlers, captured the survivors and seized the land they lawfully owned. Gen. Jackson's military invasions into Florida had no legal authorization from the highest-levels of the federal government. He angered politicians in the nation's capital, who responded by trying to court martial him. However, the powerful Southern slave owners engaged aggressive legal counsel to defend Jackson and saved him from conviction.

The legal arguments the Southern slaveholders used to defend Gen. Jackson are important today for framing claims for Black reparations. Southern slaveholders' arguments to defend Gen. Jackson were: 1) any Blacks living in Florida belonged to American slaveholders who had inherited ownership rights to Blacks from their White ancestors, who had at one time or another, owned slaves; and 2) they asserted that ownership rights of slaves automatically passes down from one slaveholding generation to the next generation of slaveholders. In short, they argued that all Black adults and their children belonged to the descendants of White slaveholders forever and they wanted all slaves returned. Gen. Jackson and his followers accepted the inheritance claims of the slaveholders and used them as the basis for invasion, for his defense and as justification for seizing lands owned by Spanish Black settlers.

Despite all his unlawful activities, Andrew Jackson became President of the United States and continued his assault against Native Indians and Black settlers. He presided over the Indian Removal Act of the early 1830s and the resultant *Trail of Tears*, a grueling cross country march in which Native Indians and *incorrigible* Spanish Black settlers, who constituted approximately 40 percent of those forced to march from Florida to the Oklahoma territory. Southern slaveholders took ownership of and enslaved all of the weak and compliant Blacks who remained. The *Trail of Tears* effectively cleared the land of both undesirable populations and left a clear path for the Southern plantation owners to own, control and develop Florida land into what became the great wealth-generating cotton belt. When Blacks mount a fight for reparations today, the issues presented by the actions of General Jackson should form the foundation for their demand for restitution. The major issues for reparations are:

1. In 1815, General Jackson captured, killed and imported Black settlers from Spanish territory as slaves into the United States. In doing so, he violated the prohibition in the U.S. Constitution as ratified in 1789, that stipulated it was illegal to import slaves into the country after 1808[78], international law, various treaties and U.S. law. He piled legal violation upon legal violation. In his roundup of Blacks, he comingled settlers who were international citizens with no previous experience with slavery with those who had fled the U.S. to escape slavery and had become Spanish citizens. Jackson transported all to the United States to be made slaves.

2. Jackson's misuse of government military and other resources to invade another country multiple times made the U.S. government liable for the results of his unauthorized actions. Jackson's actions violated the law and the legal justification used by the slaveholders was unsound: that slave ownership passed from one White generation to the next and was perpetual. If that is true, then the corollary is also true. The responsibility for restitution for illegal and immoral acts committed against the Spanish Black settlers also pass from one slaveholding generation to the next generation that enjoyed the benefits of Black enslavement. It will continue to pass down through White families until reparations are made

---

[78]Black, Eric. *Our Constitution: The Myths that Bind Us*, Westview Press, Boulder, Colorado, 1978, p. 42.

for physical, psychological and financial damages inflicted on the descendants of 10 generations of Blacks.

Jackson captured and killed Spanish Black settlers, stripped them of their freedom, citizenship rights and worldly possessions. Though his actions were illegal on several levels, the government has never paid restitution to the injured parties or their descendants. The government has a clear moral and legal obligation to cross generational lines in reverse and use public resources to compensate the descendants of Spanish Black settlers in Florida for the land and lives that were stolen and the economic, emotional, educational and social damage done to their ancestors. It would be a violation of the 14th Amendment's Equal Protection provision for the government to refuse to use its power and resources to right the wrongs inflicted by Jackson. It is also the moral responsibility of Blacks to use the foundation presented here to organize a public effort to seek restitution and reparations to restore what was stolen from Black Spanish citizens.

Question 90. Does Black humor provide psychological release from the stress of being Black?

Humor flows from the life experiences of an individual or a group. Black humor is a distinctive part of Black culture that tracks back to slavery. It is a distinctive expression of Black cultural heritage that expresses joy and the harsh realities of life as a Black person in a society in which Blacks will always be on the bottom. During slavery and Jim Crow segregation, Black humor was a way to safely denounce and jab White society and to vent frustration and rage. White entertainers have always mimicked Black mannerisms and expressions, but without understanding the rebelliousness expressed in Black humor. A White lifestyle cannot possibly provide even a glimpse of what daily life is like to be Black. What is funny to Blacks is not necessarily funny to Whites and the reverse is equally true. Below are three different examples of Black humor during different time periods. (The author maintained the dialect, but updated the language to make the stories more readable.)

1. Black Outwitting a White:

    "Pompey, how do I look?" the master asked.
    "O, master, mighty. You look mighty."
    "What do you mean 'mighty,' Pompey?"
    "Why, master, you look noble."
    "What do you mean by 'noble'?"
    "Why, sir, you look just like a lion."
    "Why, Pompey, where have you ever seen a lion?"
    "I saw one down in yonder field the other day, master."
    "Pompey, you foolish fellow, that was a jackass."
    "Was it, master? Well, sir, you look just like him.[79]"

2. A Satisfying Prayer

    Back in the days of steamship liners, like the *Titanic*, only rich White folk could enjoy sailing oceans and seas from one country to another. The *Titanic* was supposed to be an unsinkable vessel, but on its maiden voyage it struck an iceberg and started to sink. Knowing there were not enough lifeboats, terrified *Titanic* passengers did not know what to do. Then someone suggested they do what Negroes always do . . . *pray* and call on the Lord. Unfortunately, no one knew exactly what to say in the prayer. So, they called Sam, the ship's Black cook, and asked him to come up on deck and lead the group in a prayer.

---

[79]Watkins, Mel. *African American Humor*, Lawrence Hill Books, Chicago, Ilinois, 2002, p. 67.

Sam agreed to go topside. When he arrived on the top deck, he removed his cook's hat and began to pray like this, "Lord, one day I was hungry, I went to a restaurant to get something to eat and the sign said, 'FOR WHITE FOLKS ONLY.' Then, I went to the water fountain to get some water and the sign said, 'FOR WHITE FOLKS ONLY.' Then I went to the toilet room and the sign said, 'FOR WHITE FOLKS ONLY.' So, Lord Almighty . . . when You decide to let the big old boat sink . . . let it be 'FOR WHITE FOLKS ONLY.' In Your name I pray . . . AMEN!" (Source unknown)

3. Telling it like it is

When you're Black, you're Black
When I was born, I was BLACK
When I grew up, I was BLACK
When I went in the sun, I stayed BLACK
When I got cold, I was BLACK
When I was scared, I was BLACK
When I was sick, I was BLACK
And when I die, I'll still be BLACK
NOW, you White folks
When you're born, you're PINK
When you grow up, you're WHITE
When you go in the sun, you get RED
When you're cold, you turn BLUE
When you're scared, you're YELLOW
When you get sick, you're GREEN
When you bruise, you turn PURPLE
And when you die, you look GREY
So why are you calling us COLORED folks?
—*Anonymous*

Whites have always been attracted to and mimicked Black humor. Blacks have always used humor as an acceptable vehicle to criticize and to make fun of Whites. It allows Blacks to vent their anxieties, fears and frustration and to build self esteem.

PART XIV

Science and Medical Experiments

Question 91. What is the single most impactful and enduring medical contribution unknowingly made by a Black person to modern science?

Without a doubt, one of the greatest medical contributions made unknowingly was that of Henrietta Lacks, a poor Black tobacco farmer born in Southern Virginia and treated for cervical cancer at Johns Hopkins Hospital in Baltimore, Maryland in 1951. The doctors and scientists who treated her found that her cells had unique characteristics, ones that they had been trying unsuccessfully to formulate in the laboratory for many years. The cancer cells from Henrietta Lacks seemed to be immortal; they never died. Unlike other human cells, Lacks' cells regenerated continuously and at an extraordinary rate. To this day, scientists do not know why her cells are immortal, but they transformed medical science and created an entire advanced medical industry that made some researchers and others who had a part in monetizing her cells, enormously wealthy.

Henrietta Lacks died a few months after her cancer diagnosis, but her cells, designated as HeLa by researchers, lived on. She never knew the major impact the cells taken from her cervix, used without her permission or knowledge, would have on medicine or the wealth her cells would create for scientific researchers and their friends, while her family remained in poverty. Her cells were grown and sold to researchers around the world. New businesses were created to produce the HeLa cells and the culture medium in which to grow them. Specialty businesses were also developed to package the cells and to ship them to laboratories across the world. HeLa cells enabled Jonas Salk to create the Salk vaccine and to respond quickly to the polio epidemic that was exploding in the 1950s. HeLa cells were used to grow viruses, conduct experiments, to test medicines, map DNA and other scientific research. They were in the first space missions to see what would happen to cells in zero gravity. Gene mapping, cloning and invitro fertilization are scientific landmarks that were achieved because of the cells from the cervix of a poor Black woman with cancer.

The story of Henrietta Lacks was told by investigative journalist Rebecca Skloot in her book, *The Immortal Cells of Henrietta Lacks*[80]. In telling the story, Ms. Skloot describes the many ways profit was made from Ms. Lacks' cells and the story has raised numerous moral, legal, political and financial issues. The medical industry has addressed the issue of permission by requiring more thorough patient medical disclosure and permission forms. What does not seem to have been addressed, however, are the financial and ethical issues about the wealth and industry creation that bypassed her family—her children, her grandchildren, her great grandchildren.

There are many lessons for all in the story of Henrietta Lacks. Her story demonstrates that economic racism continues to be practiced in modern society; that the practice of so easily stealing Black assets and shifting the financial benefit to the White side of the ledger is so engrained culturally that it generates no sense of wrongdoing, no outrage and no corrective action is expected.. Those who benefited financially from her unusual cells most likely are viewed, and most likely view themselves, as enterprising, respected wealthy individuals. Henrietta Lacks indeed made a contribution that was important to medical science in many ways.

Question 92. How do some researchers connect race to the AIDS virus, and view its possible fabrication and African origin?

AIDS, the deadly disease that seems to have appeared from nowhere, generates many questions, but few concrete answers. In the vacuum created

---

[80]Skloot, Rebecca. *The Immortal Life of Henrietta Lacks*, Broadway Books, New York, 2010.

because of so few satisfying answers, curious people have generated their own research and theories. Some of them are summarized here.

The U.S. Center for Disease Control and Prevention[81] reported that deaths due to HIV/AIDS are highest among Africans and Blacks. This fact is supported by a great deal of science, but does it defy the odds that everything bad happens to Blacks whether here in the U.S. or in Africa? Is it a believable coincidence that AIDS would first appear in Black Africa among the oldest population on earth? How did it just pop up in the 1970s and 1980s? If, as generally accepted, it was found decades earlier in monkeys, by what mechanism did it spread to humans? Did it really originate with monkeys? There are many examples of nefarious medical experiments and procedures performed on Black people. The U.S. Public Health Service conducted a 40-year experiment of syphilis in Black men without informing or treating them. During the Cold War, a radiologist at the University of Cincinnati conducted experiments in intense radiation to determine how much radiation soldiers could withstand[82]. Most of the patients were poor and Black. Eugenics and unwanted sterilizations on Black women were programs advocated by academics and became popular social movements in and around the 1930s. LSD experiments were performed on Black prisoners by the CIA and psychological experiments were conducted in Louisiana State Prison in which electrodes were surgically implanted in the brains of Black prisoners[83]. Questionable medical practices have been inflicted on Blacks often enough that it is not beyond belief that some might consider race a factor as people seek to explain a complicated enigma like AIDS.

Dr. Alan Cantwell, a retired dermatologist, and Dr. Robert Strecker, an internist and gastroenterologist, investigated the origin of AIDS

---

[81]"HIV Among African Americans," Center for Disease Control and Prevention, May 16, 2017. www.CDC.gov

[82]Schneider, Keith. "Cold War Radiation Test on Humans to Undergo a Congressional Review," *The New York Times*, April 11, 1994.

[83]Winbush, Ph.D., Raymond A. *Should America Pay? Slavery and Raging Debate on Reparations,* HaperCollins, New York, 2003, pg. 262.

and concluded that it was a genetically-engineered virus created in a laboratory to remove Blacks and homosexuals from society. Cantwell, in his book *Queer Blood*, says that HIV came out of experiments with Hepatitis B vaccine trials and that homosexuals were injected with the virus. He discounts the theory frequently offered that AIDS was first discovered in a green monkey in Africa by observing that it was not possible for a disease supposedly confined at the time to Africa to be transported to New York City and infect only young White homosexual men. He also noted that the African AIDS epidemic was not uncovered in Africa until 1982, yet the first cases of AIDS were reported in New York in 1979.

Dr. Strecker made several video tapes—some available on YouTube—in which he discusses his theory that AIDS is a man-made virus first concocted at the National Institutes of Health, then passed on to Fort Detrick military base to be used as a political and military tool. Dr. Strecker's claims include that the fabricated AIDS virus was intentionally introduced into Africa by the World Health Organization's smallpox vaccine programs and is a racially-targeted virus. He concludes that Black people and Black Africa are doomed. Statistics from more traditional sources do indicate that there are more people of African descent infected with the AIDS virus than all the other populations on earth added together. Dr. Strecker died unexpectedly from mysterious causes.

Another AIDS researcher out of the main stream was Dr. Boyd Graves, a Black civil rights lawyer infected with AIDS. According to the *Tallahassee Democrat*[84] newspaper in 2003, Graves sued the U.S. government in 1998, charging that it had created AIDS and was infecting Black people of African descent around the world. Graves believed that HIV was a synthetic biological agent particularly attracted to Black people. In his court filing, Graves asserted that AIDS was the product of decades of ultra-classified government research on developing a race-specific virus designed to reduce the Black population in the U.S. and

---

[84]"Activist in Court to prove AIDS is Lab-Created Conspiracy," *Tallahassee Democrat* Newspaper, Tallahassee, Florida, June 27, 2003.

in African countries. Dr. Graves' lawsuit was eventually dismissed as frivolous. He died at the age of 57, still convinced that his theory about the development and spread of AIDS was correct.

On a positive note, on March 3, 2003 *USA Today* reported that nearly two decades after the discovery of AIDS, scientists supposedly discovered an AIDS vaccine, AIDSVAX, which on an ironic note, appears to work best on Blacks. Jose Esparza, Director of AIDS Vaccine Research for the Joint United Nations Program on HIV/AIDS, indicated this medical finding could be the most important accomplishment in vaccine research in over a generation. Esparza said, "This is the first time anyone has shown protection against HIV in humans." Maybe this finding holds some hope for Blacks, since 26 times more Blacks are infected with the disease than Whites. The finding also raises another question about AIDS. How is it that people find it hard to believe it is possible to create a race-specific killer virus, but have no trouble accepting that a life-saving vaccine could have race-specific results?

Question 93. What are the advantages of Black skin?

Dark skin has many inherent advantages, even in a race-based society. Dark skin was the original skin color of the world's Homo sapiens. Dark skin has a high amount of melanin, which provides invaluable protection against sunrays and will be especially helpful if the earth's ozone barrier continues to deteriorate. The word *melanin* is a Greek word that means *black* and *dark*. It is a powerful biological material and regulates body coloration. The primary function of melanin is to protect humans from the sun's harmful ultraviolet rays that destroy essential folic acid. The quantity of melanin in the body determines whether human skin color will appear pale white, pink, black, yellow or brown and also determines the color of hair and eyes.

Although all humans have approximately the same number of melanin-making cells, what differs among individuals is how actively the cells make melanin. The more melanin in the skin, the greater the protection one receives from the damaging effects of the sun. As the ozone layer, the protective barrier between the earth and the sun, continues to be depleted, humans will face more skin health problems. Albinos are the only humans whose bodies do not produce melanin. White blonde-haired people are second to albinos, their bodies producing small amounts of melanin. Dark skin seems to protect the body from damage from tropical sun and ultraviolet rays. Medical research indicates that White Europeans living in tropical and semitropical areas have the world's highest rates of skin cancer. This gives people with melanin another unexpected advantage. People with dark skin or Black people can survive the physical elements of Europe or cold climates, just as easily as people with White skin, however the reverse is not true. It is more difficult for people with white skin to live in and survive in hot, sun intensive environments. Perhaps race mixing or medical science will eventually find ways to enhance melanin production where it is needed or lacking such as in albinos and blonde-haired people. According to several reports, synthetic melanin is in production today, and has varied uses that range from cosmetics to coating the circuits of NASA space vehicles. Additional uses will be found as the quality of the product improves. All colors come from Black, the dominate color in the spectrum. Dark skin is the carrier of natural melanin. For 1,300 years of negativism about dark skin, it would be quite a twist of fate if the melanin it produces becomes the biological property that makes the difference between life and death on earth.

Question 94. Did South Africa prepare chemical and biological weapons to use against African Blacks?

On April 20 and 21, 2003, *The Washington Post*[85] writer Jo Warrick wrote a chilling two-part story about Wouter Basson, former commander

---

[85]Warrick, Jo. "Biotoxins Fall Into Private Hands," *The Washington Post*, April 20-21, 2003.

of South Africa's notorious 7th Medical Battalion. Warrick candidly revealed information about the top-secret biological and chemical weapons program called Project Coast. Basson, known in foreign circles as *Doctor Death*, revealed that two decades earlier, South Africa's ruling White government had paid him to develop a biological and chemical weapons program that could be used on its majority Black population. Basson sought to, "… use science against the country's Black majority population to suppress population growth among Blacks."

Basson explained how he developed pathogens, equipment, and plans for introducing anthrax, cholera, brucellosis and other toxic agents to start epidemics in Black communities. Basson's chemical warfare program included an approved plan for distributing biological and chemical toxins into the Black population using sugar cubes laced with salmonella, poisoned bottles of beer, peppermint candies, cigarettes, letter-sized envelopes sprinkled with anthrax spores and contaminating drinking water with contraceptives.

In Warrick's article, Daan Goosen, a member of Project Coast's biological research division, reported, "He was ordered to develop ways to suppress population growth among African Blacks using a biological 'Black bomb,' which could seek out Black skin color." Goosen further said that, "When apartheid ended, an effort was made to destroy or sell off as much of the assets [biological weapons] as possible. That's because the White leadership didn't relish the prospect of this technology ending up in the hands of the new Black government." So, when the controls of South Africa's government shifted from the hands of the White minority to the Black majority population, Project Coast and its biochemical weapons disappeared. Where they went is an unanswered question. Goosen admitted that numerous foreign governments had sought possession of the agents and that although all evidence of Project Coast was to have been destroyed, that is not what happened. After the project was disbanded, Goosen said many scientists kept bacterial agents and documents in their private laboratories; others most likely sold some of the agents and a great many of the documents, bacterial strains and chemicals were simply never destroyed, but have not been found and cannot be accounted for. One can chide those who believe in conspiracy theories, but that does not mean conspiracies do not exist.

Question 95. Have you heard that laziness is a Black disease?

Negative myths about Black people abound. One of the most interesting and amusing theories of slave misbehavior was put forth by Dr. Samuel W. Cartwright of Louisiana. In 1851, Dr. Cartwright, a prominent Louisiana physician, published an essay in the *New Orleans Surgical Journal* entitled, "Report on the Diseases and Physical Peculiarities of the Negro Race." In the article, Cartwright claimed to have discovered two mental diseases unique to Blacks that he believed justified their enslavement. Cartwright coined his own terms, calling his newly-discovered diseases, *drapetomania*, a disease that causes Black slaves to run away; the other, *dysaesthesia aethiopica*, a disease that causes *rascality* in both free and enslaved Blacks. Dr. Cartwright claimed these *diseases* caused Blacks to have an uncontrollable urge to get away from their slaveholders or to be disobedient, disrespectful and lazy.

Dr. Cartwright did not apply his diagnosis of drapetomania disease to White indentured servants who ran away or dysaesthesia to lazy Whites. Both of these diseases were peculiar only to Black slaves. For a so-called doctor to proclaim that Black slaves had a laziness disease raises at least two important questions. First, why would any slave want to be energetic, hardworking and work for no pay to enrich those who claimed ownership of him? Secondly, why would any reasonably intelligent White person go through the time and expense to fight a four-year Civil War to continue owning *lazy* slaves?

A different perspective might have produced a different outcome. If, perhaps, Dr. Cartwright had viewed the same behavior of running away and not working hard from the perspective of a slave, perhaps he would have reported not a disease but that those Black slaves had finally acquired some *common sense*. These questions did not occur to Dr. Cartwright, and his cure for both diseases was for slave owners to simply, *beat the devil out of the Black slaves.*

In modern times, laziness has been used to explain the distinctive way some Blacks pronounce some English words. Speech counselors have long attributed that pronunciation to Blacks having lazy lips and lazy tongues. You have to wonder why Blacks became lazy in that particular part of their anatomy, while poorly educated Whites are not afflicted with such laziness.

Question 96. Why did grave robbers choose Black corpses?

Whether in the tombs in the Middle East or plantation fields in America, Black bodies, dead or alive, have always had a high value. Modernization of medicine has come about in large measure because of the practice of using living and dead Blacks for research. During the days of slavery and Jim Crow, White medical students were studying medicine to treat White patients, but they opposed cutting up White cadavers. One medical school administrator is said to have suggested using Black bodies, because the Black communities couldn't stop Whites from doing whatever they chose to do with dead Blacks. The medical community began to set rules for acquiring human bodies. The moral and legal clashes that occurred over the ownership status of the human body kept the practice of medical dissections of humans illegal until 1834. Several states even prohibited dissections on executed criminals. Medical schools, however, needed bodies to train physicians. Some schools became so desperate that they turned to grave robbing. By 1878, stealing recently deceased bodies from graveyards and selling those bodies to medical schools had become a lucrative business. Grave robbing became a misdemeanor in most states, but it did not deter most schools or medical students from the practice.

Although robbers sometimes stole the bodies of paupers and lower-level Whites, the gravesites of Blacks, especially those buried in slave graveyards, were particularly vulnerable and popular, simply because few Whites of the day held any respect for living or dead Blacks. Their relatives tended to be powerless to protest effectively. In William Wells Brown's 1853 novel, *Clotel*, he talks about a White doctor, in association with a local college, who ran ads offering to pay cash for sick enslaved Blacks considered incurable by their owners. The ad boasted that Black bodies acquired for medical research were, "Producing great men of science." Often, sick Blacks were put to death for medical experimentation and scientific advancements. In Mississippi, an infamous Dr. J. Marion Sims bought slaves at slave auctions in order to conduct experimental operations with new surgical instruments that he had designed.

In the 20th century, the live bodies of Black prisoners were still being used for medical experiments. A number of those experiments are discussed in the book, *Should America Pay? Slavery and the Raging Debate on Reparations*[86], Edited by Raymond Winbush, Ph.D. In New Orleans, Louisiana, Black prisoners were used for psychosurgical experiments, which involved implanting electrodes into their brains. These experiments were conducted by psychiatrists at Tulane University. Two doctors boasted in later years that the school used Black prisoners in experiments because it was, "Cheaper to use niggers than cats." The book also indicates that the CIA funded experiments on Black prisoners at the Louisiana State Penitentiary to determine if certain drugs could cause loss of speech, loss of sensitivity to pain, loss of memory or loss of willpower.

Black bodies, either alive or dead, entered the 21st century still unable to protect themselves from experiments and other medical violations.

---

[86]Winbush, Raymond A. *Should America Pay? Slavery and Raging Debate On Reparations*, HarperCollins Amistad Publishers, New York, 2003, p. 262.

Question 97. What were the circumstances surrounding the death of Dr. Charles Drew and his invention of liquid blood plasma?

The Red Cross is an international organization that was founded in 1863, at a time when the country was engaged in the Civil War. The Red Cross had minimal contact with Black Americans until its path intersected with that of Dr. Charles Richard Drew, a noted Black physician[87]. While working at New York's Presbyterian Hospital around 1938, he discovered that when whole blood was separated, the liquid part that contains the red cells, the plasma, could be used for transfusions. The liquid plasma could be refrigerated to make it last longer and reduce the likelihood of contamination. Liquid plasma could be stored and shipped more easily than whole blood.

This discovery made it possible to give lifesaving blood transfusions in many more medical situations. When the London Royal College of Surgeons heard about Drew's blood plasma, they requested to use it for their injured soldiers, who were in dire need of blood transfusions. He established what he called his Blood Transfusion Association to ship blood plasma to British blood banks. Shortly thereafter, the American Red Cross took his advice and established a similar blood program in the U.S.

The federal government became concerned that within the American Red Cross blood bank, a White person could accidentally receive a transfusion of Black blood. The Red Cross, aware of the importance of federal funds, directed that all donated Black blood be conspicuously labeled, then segregated from White-donated blood. Military units were racially segregated at the time and the government did not want the blood supplies commingled. Dr. Drew protested the Red Cross decision, arguing there was no physical difference in the blood of Whites and

---

[87]Stewart, Jeffrey C. *1001 Things Everyone Should Know About African American History*, Doubleday Publishers, New York, 1996, pgs. 346-347.

Blacks. However, both the military and the American Red Cross clung to their blood prejudices throughout World War II and Drew resigned in protest over the policy. In 1949, both the United States Army and the American Red Cross reversed their racial policies and stopped segregating blood by the donor's race, allowing all donated blood to flow together.

Ironically, Dr. Drew died in a car accident in 1950. He was driving to a conference with three friends when the accident occurred. He was the only one who died[88]. His death spawned many accounts and rumors, the most enduring of which was that he died at the scene because a Whites-only hospital refused to treat him. Actually, according to Spencie Love, in her book, *One Blood: The Death and Resurrection of Charles Drew*[89], he was treated in the emergency room of a small segregated hospital where two White surgeons worked hard to save his life. He had multiple injuries and died about an hour after admission. Even though the facts do not match the myth, Love recounts the story of Black individuals who actually *did* die because they got caught in the circumstances of the myth. She says that even though the facts of the myth were not completely accurate, they reflect the reality that befell some Blacks and that preservation of oral history has an enduring value.

---

[88]Boyd, Herb. *Down the Glory Road*, Avon Books, New York, 1995, pgs. 66, 67.

[89]Love, Spencie. *One Blood: The Death and Resurrection of Charles Drew*, North Carolina: University of North Carolina Press, November, 1997.

PART XV
Birth of New Classes

Question 98. As political concepts, are gender issues elevated above and in competition with Black issues?

There are some Americans, both White and Black, who understand how women's issues and the sisterhood have been systematically used to divide and impede Black progress in America. One such person was Eric Foner, a White writer who recited how leading White feminists and champions of voting suffrage for women in the 1860s felt about Black people. He quoted several telling statements that were made by leading suffragette, Elizabeth Stanton, in the mid-1860s. According to Foner, Ms. Stanton questioned Blacks having voting rights equal to a White woman, saying, "Just think of Sambo... who [does] not know the differences between a monarchy and a republic, who never read the Declaration of Independence, making laws for [White women] Lydia Marie Child, Lucretia Mott or Fanny Kemble." She further stated, "The Black woman would be better off as the slave of an educated White man than a degraded, ignorant Black one[90]."

When White and Black women stand together on women's issues, like voting and socioeconomic opportunities, it promotes an illusion of gender equality between the races. Women's issues are class issues, which are different from race issues. The feminist movement of the mid-1800s was primarily over voting rights. Contrary to popular myths, White women did have voting rights if they were property owners. The passage of the 19th Amendment in 1919 gave White women full voting and civil

---

[90] Anderson, Claud. *Black Labor, White Wealth*, PowerNomics® Corporation of America, Inc., Maryland, 1994, p. 59.

rights, which White women used to strengthen the electorate power of the White male. The 19th Amendment did not help Black women, who had to wait until the 1960s for the enactment of civil rights voting rights laws.

It is important that Black women who support women's issues do not become confused and divided from their Black male counterpart over gender-related issues. Once divided, they are conquered. White women and White men play as a team. Apparently, Sojourner Truth, a Black feminist, as well as a Black freedom fighter, knew the difference between being a woman and being a Black person. After listening to a White man talk about how White women were in a protected class, she rose to her feet and asked, "Ain't I a woman? I have borne 13 children and have seen them sold off to slavery, and when I cried out with my mother's grief, none but Jesus heard me." She knew no White women were suffering such pain simply because they were women. Today, when Black and White women join together, both groups should understand the difference between being a woman and being Black in our society.

Conservatives and liberals alike have successfully blurred the distinctions between White women and Black Americans. In form, degree and intent, racism against Blacks is vastly different from the class discrimination that women have received from the White male. Unlike Blacks who are an obsolete labor class, White women are essential to the propagation of the White race. She not only lives with and bears the children of the White male, but most importantly, she has co-owned, co-controlled, co-influenced and inherited nearly 100 percent of everything the White male owns since the founding of the country. Blacks have held no power over White women, nor has the Black race benefitted from any gender or class discrimination against women. Equating gender discrimination and racism is like comparing a headache to cancer. It might be a headache being a woman, but throughout history it was cancerous to be Black.

Question 99. Did a Black ex-slave cause Virginia to divide into two different states?

It is a little-known fact that the skin color commitment of an ex-slave, Nat Turner, brought forth a new political state. Born a slave in 1800 in Southampton, Virginia, he was exceptionally intelligent and known as a deeply religious young man. Considered a prophet by many, in 1831, he organized an unsuccessful slave rebellion that he began with four close friends, but the number of his soldiers quickly grew. Eventually captured, he was tried, convicted and executed. His rebellion in 1831 frightened Whites in Virginia so badly the state legislature not only considered abolishing slavery, but also after much debate about slavery they decided to divide the state into Virginia and West Virginia. The old state of Virginia was more conservative and wanted to maintain a slave economy. The new state of West Virginia was less conservative and had second thoughts about continuing to enslave people of African descent.

Nat Turner's slave revolt changed some minds and hearts in Virginia. Inspired by a vision and a solar eclipse, he tried to eradicate the evils of slavery by killing everything White. For nine days, he and his band of revolting slaves wreaked havoc. They killed nearly 55 Whites, using simple farming tools. The killings frightened many Virginians, especially since Blacks were the majority population in that state, as well as most Southern states. White Virginians demanded and received immediate government protection. However, Whites were traumatized by the fact that a Black man had the audacity and wit to plan and carry out a slave revolt.

The following winter of 1831-32, the Virginia General Assembly debated slavery and came within four votes of abolishing it. Virginia Whites were split over how best to protect themselves from slave revolts. Poorer Whites in hilly western Virginia could barely scratch out an existence and were so poor they could not afford slaves. They feared slave revolts and wanted slaves freed then recolonized out of the country. The problem was that those Whites living in the western part of the state were taxed the same as the rich Whites east of the mountains who owned large plantations and needed a large contingent of Blacks to cultivate the land, make it productive and to run the households. Thus the plantation owners were reluctant to give up the hundreds of millions of dollars they had invested in Black enslavement.

The Virginia legislature debated the issue in an attempt to find an acceptable compromise. Assemblyman Thomas Jefferson Randolph, the son-in-law of Thomas Jefferson, who represented most of the poor Whites in the western portion of the state, challenged his fellow legislators saying, "If we are to remain united, we must have some guarantee that the evils under which you labor shall not be extended to us." The state remained united through another 30 years of slavery, during which the debates between the eastern and western parts of Virginia continued.

Finally, the issues that Nat Turner's slave revolt had raised were settled by the Civil War. Virginia and its wealthy eastern plantation owners joined the Confederate States in 1861, while the poor Whites in the western Virginia counties remained loyal to the Union and formed a separate government of West Virginia. In nearly every major presidential election, West Virginia has continued the pattern of supporting the less conservative candidate and issues.

Question 100. What was the scenario that led to the death of the Black Civil Rights Movement?

For everyone, but the caretakers of old Black civil rights organizations, the civil rights movement for Blacks is dead. Civil rights for Blacks had a brief life twice within a 100-year period. It reached a point of diminishing returns and then died a premature death during the late 1960s. Today, all of the rights gained by the Black Civil Rights Movement have been bequeathed to groups that are more acceptable to the larger society:

women, LGBT, Hispanics, Asians, handicapped and poor Whites. The first Black civil rights efforts formally started shortly after the Civil War, as slaves realized they had received paper freedom and rights they couldn't exercise. For nearly a century, they pursued their phantom freedom and rights nationally by way of public forums, courtrooms, schoolhouses, union halls and journalism.

In the 1954 *Brown v. Board of Education* desegregation decision, Blacks won a battle, but the decision had incalculable destructive effects on the Black community. During the subsequent civil rights protest period, Blacks stimulated a rush of new social movements by a mélange of social groups which co-opted the language and historical evidence that Blacks used to justify their own quest for equal rights and freedom. The barrage of liberal social causes offended the larger society, in general, and motivated conservatives to orchestrate a backlash. Since Blacks were the largest, most visible and least acceptable group seeking social change, they became the primary target of conservative angst.

The movement was drowned out by the new groups and out-flanked by the conservatives. In the heat of various civil rights battles for control over jobs, schools, housing, community services, businesses and tax dollars, Black leadership ran out of insight, social tools and strategies for effectively dealing with the more subtle and less direct forms of racism that cropped up.

As the competing social groups began to appropriate the Black civil rights agenda, conservative political forces started using their government and media power to diminish the Black component of the civil rights movement. They successfully destroyed the legitimate base of the Black movement by diluting it beyond recognition. They identified every group that could possibly perceive itself as aggrieved and made it equal to Blacks. Thus, the public perception of Blacks was severely damaged and distorted. The unique problems they faced were made to appear no more important than the problems faced by other, so-called victims of *discrimination*.

The Black Civil Rights Movement, though successful in many respects, did not change the power relationship between Blacks and Whites. The movement had at least four flaws that left unaddressed, critical imperatives for Black America, as described below:

1. The movement's Black leadership placed the entire weight of its resources on achieving social integration and gaining access to White society by making themselves acceptable in all respects. They believed, perhaps naively, that by removing the symbols of Jim Crowism and acquiring access to various segments of White society, Black people would gain equality.

2. Black leaders did not recognize that effective empowerment strategies for Black America had to address the historical mal-distribution of the nation's wealth, power, resources, rights and privileges reserved exclusively for White society. Without acknowledging the economic disparities and seeking correction, it was not possible to neutralize the forces behind Jim Crow. Equality was structurally not possible.

3. Black leadership did not develop a long-term national plan with goals and strategies, spelling out where Blacks ought to be going and how best to get there.

4. The civil rights movement, like any successful social movement, needed three core components to substantially change the circumstances of Blacks: 1) strong grass roots organization; 2) a research-based entity to provide policy structure and guidance; and 3) a wealthy class to financially subsidized the movement.

Unfortunately, the movement only had the first component—the passionate support of the Black masses. The cumulative effect of these flaws left the Black Civil Rights Movement with no place to go, no way to get there and no leadership to take them. Black people were no longer at the top of any agenda. A few visible Black organizations managed to survive by becoming politically correct and expanding their focus to include so-called minorities, immigrants, poor people, LGBT, women and abused children. They could not survive in the powerful conservative climate by continuing to target the problems of Blacks alone. Although Black conditions continued to need attention, most Black organizations could not raise enough money to survive by focusing solely upon their own people. The surviving Black organizations remained visible by continuing to pursue the integration dream. It would not have been necessary for Black organizations to abandon their own community if the Black Civil Rights Movement had established a sense of community cohesiveness founded on group economics and group politics.

The National Urban League and the NAACP are still active, but have lost much of their influence and membership. The Student Nonviolent Coordinating Committee and the Black Panther Party are defunct. The Congress of Racial Equality joined the conservative ranks of a national political party and the Southern Christian Leadership Conference barely survives. This nation's political apparatus disabled many of the civil rights groups by destroying or neutralizing Black leadership: Adam Clayton Powell and Stokely Carmichael were discredited; Rev. Dr. Martin Luther King, Jr., Malcolm X and Medgar Evers were assassinated; Rap Brown, Eldridge Cleaver, Angela Davis and prominent members of the Black Panthers were criminalized.

Many of the others were enticed into mainstream society. Consequently, the large bloc of Black leadership was eradicated, changed or disappeared after just one generation following the great movement. Having failed to address the structural conditions of Black America, the 1960s left little structure upon which Blacks could build. Instead, that colorful era only left faded memories and soul-stirring songs.

The void created by the death of the Black Civil Rights Movement presented the opportunity for a cadre of Black neo-conservatives to join the popular White conservative movement and proclaim themselves and their new organizations the new Black leadership. They were publicly blessed by the highest levels of government and corporate America and they offered Black America political and economic ideologies that were taken right from the conservative right-wing political bible. Their politically correct ideologies advocated for less government and taxes, free market economies, privatization of government services and race-neutral government policies. Black traditional leadership, like the Black masses, is ignored by government and the media, except during times of racial disturbances or movement anniversaries.

PART XVI

A PowerNomics® Agenda: Ethno-aggregation

Question 101. What steps should Blacks immediately take to become a self-sufficient and competitive group in America?

To become self-sufficient and competitive in America, Blacks must first practice *Ethno-aggregation*[91], a PowerNomics principle that is best defined as the voluntary concentration of individuals, resources and votes around a population's common need to improve their economic and political competitiveness. The term Ethno-aggregation may be new, but the concept is not. It describes a behavior pattern used every day by religious, gender, language and ethnic groups. The culture of these groups encourages members to rally around their respective common characteristics or attributes (ethno) in order to pool their collective (aggregation) resources and empower themselves to compete with non-group members.

Ethno-aggregation is important for Blacks to adopt as a part of their culture. It could aid Black Americans in a number of ways. First, Ethno-aggregation could correct the negative effects of failed social integration, which stripped Blacks of the positive benefits of their skin color commonality and historical exceptionality, and misdirected them into integration and political correctness. Unlike all other socio-political out-groups, Blacks scattered themselves in the integration process, instead of unifying to strengthen and protect themselves. Ethno-aggregation can be the basis for group unity, and the coming together of Black individuals into a virtual group and a national team with concentrated resources. Through Ethno-aggregation, Blacks as a group can place their own

---

[91]Anderson, Claud. *PowerNomics®: The National Plan to Empower Black America,* PowerNomics® Corporation of America, Inc., Maryland, 2001, pgs. xvii, 49, 80-81.

self-interest first, before all other groups. The more concentrated their resources, the greater their group impact and competitive advantage will be.

For Black Americans, the Ethno-aggregation paradigm can be a cure or antidote for Meritorious Manumission, the strategy of Black individuals working against group interest in exchange for personal benefits. It is a hard truth that we live in a capitalistic and competitive society in which power and wealth follow the numbers. The individual things people do yield greater power when their achievements are viewed as emanating from the power of a group. An aggregated group has a competitive advantage over one with scattered resources. Likewise, Ethno-aggregation is most effective when the resources are organized and directed toward a common and specific purpose, in this case Black self-sufficiency and competitiveness as a group.

Whites dominate and control the society because they are the population with the greatest ownership of concentrated resources. Group power does not emanate from what a single White person owns and controls, but from what Whites as a group own and control. They control collectively and behave in their group's self-interest first. A Black person can succeed individually, but if that person fails to identify with and connect with his group, then the group does not gain in strength and competitiveness. If there is no group-based connectedness, the group will not miss nor care about what a given individual has or has lost.

Ethno-aggregation encourages Blacks to unite with their own people before seeking to unite with members of other groups. It encourages Blacks to pool their tangible and intangible resources. A fist has greater impact than five separate fingers. For example, Blacks come together when they attend church or when they participate in a civil rights march or demonstration. If the dollars aggregated at church were targeted to build a credit union, or if a demonstration was targeted specifically to demand government funds for starting and growing Black-owned businesses, those Blacks gathering together would become examples of Ethno-aggregation. Ethno-aggregation is a tool for Blacks to use to practice group-based competitive economics targeted specifically to the goals, needs and history of their group.

AFTER THOUGHTS

A Black History Reader is my last book and I hope you enjoyed it. It was written out of my passion for fairness, and justice and out of a deep love for my race. The information is intended to explain answers to questions that have been posed to me and a guide to help Blacks frame more strategic action steps. Writing this book was my moral responsibility and commitment to help resolve the nation's long standing racial problems. Those who read this book have a choice to be moved to action or to be entertained. May you glean something positive from this book and put it to good use.

APPENDIX

Biographical Summary of Dr. Claud Anderson

Dr. Claud Anderson has devoted most of his life to critically analyzing the social economic dilemma of Black America and crafting solutions. His life has been a rare combination of experiences. The PowerNomics® Corporation of America, Inc. includes this brief bio in *A Black History Reader* so that readers, current and future, will have a way to validate his authority to make the recommendations he does in this book to help Black America become self-sufficient and competitive. It is this background and his independent research that is the basis and foundation from which he has written five books and developed the strategies he offers to Black America.

CURRENT:

- Author of four books that have been national bestsellers for more than 20 years; books are ranked best sellers by Amazon; he is president of PowerNomics® Corporation of America, Inc., the company that publishes his books. *A Black History Reader* is his fifth book.

- Established The Harvest Institute, a non-profit public policy research and education organization that works for the self-sufficiency of Black America; is current president.

- Doctorate degrees: earned and honorary.

NATIONAL:

- Campaign Manager for political candidates seeking the office of president (Jimmy Carter), governor (Reubin Askew), state attorney general, state legislators, mayors and the U.S. Congress.

- Identified and guided appointment of three Black federal judges.

- Special Project Director, the 1988 Democratic National Convention in Atlanta.

- Marketing Development Officer, Federal Minority Bank Development Program.

- Turned down ambassadorship appointments to the Bahamas and Ghana.

- Appointed by President Jimmy Carter as Assistant Secretary of Commerce, Federal Chairman of the Coastal Plains Commission; chaired meetings with governors of the Southeastern states and approved funds for economic development projects in the region.

  - Funded and constructed a Jones Island crab storage facility for Blacks in South Carolina.

  - Funded and constructed Hilton Head Island Seafood Co-op for Black fishermen.

  - Awarded millions of dollars of supplies, and equipment to Florida A&M University (FAMU) from the U.S. government surplus program.

  - Secured the installation of a Black Fire Chief Training Program and facility for FAMU.

  - Secured the installation of a Navy ROTC Program for FAMU.

  - Chief of Mission for Governors; organized and headed international trade missions to Europe, Africa and Latin America, and developed profitable trade programs with West African countries and countries in the Middle East and Latin America.

  - Instituted an Underutilized Species Program, which reclaimed seafood species not popular in the U.S., froze them and shipped primarily to African and other poor countries.

FLORIDA:

- Appointed by Florida Governor Reuben Askew as his advisor and Coordinator of Education for the state.

- Authored first state and nationally approved Affirmative Action plan in 1971.

  – Impeded Florida's legislative plan to downsize FAMU to a community college and merge it into Florida State University.

  – Proposed, wrote and collaborated with the Governor's Commission of Education to enact the Statewide Equalization Policy, the first in the nation.

  – Funded and chaired Governor's Task Force on School Integration and directed the Disruptive Student Studies research on the negative impact of school integration on students, teachers and parents.

- Established the State Action Council, an organization of Black activists and other leaders who formed a voting bloc that supported candidates who promised and delivered benefits to the Black community. The State Action Council became powerful and was decisional in numerous elections.

- Appointed to Florida Appointments Committee and instituted a policy requiring Blacks get 20% of all political appointees.

- Executive Director of Miami Capital Development, Inc. and Miami Citywide Development, Inc. Provided funding to approximately 60 businesses in Miami and Dade counties.

- Authored successful $3 million grant from the U.S. Department of Education for the Teacher Corps Program that was awarded to FAMU.

ADDITIONAL ACHIEVEMENTS:

- Designed and constructed radio stations, aquaculture and other businesses.

- Professorships at Wayne County Community College, Highland Park Community College, FAMU and Bowie State University.

- Detroit Public Schools: Elementary and Special Education teacher, Assistant Principal and Principal.

- Held numerous championship titles in wrestling, Judo and Karate; Member of Black Belt Federation during the 1950s through the1960s.

- Certified pilot.

- United States Marine Corps: Aviation, Survival Flight Specialist.

Semper Fi—Always Faithful

BIBLIOGRAPHY

Adams, Francis D. & Sanders, Barry. *Alienable Rights: The Exclusion of African Americans in a White Man's Land*, 1619-2000, HarperCollins Publishers, New York, 2003.

Anderson, Claud. *Black Labor, White Wealth*. Powernomics® Corporation of America, Inc., Bethesda, MD, 1994.

Anderson, Claud. *PowerNomics®: The National Plan to Empower Black America*. Powernomics® Corporation of America, Inc., Bethesda, MD, 2001.

Anderson, Claud. *Dirty Little Secrets About Black History, Its Heroes, and Other Troublemakers*. Powernomics® Corporation of America, Inc., Bethesda, MD, 1997, pgs. 102-103.

Bennett Jr., Lerone. *Before the Mayflower: A History of Black America*. Penguin Books, New York, 1988.

Bergman, Peter M. *The Chronological History of the Negro in America*. Harper and Row Publisher, New York. 1969

Black, Eric. *Our Constitution: The Myth that Binds Us*. Westview Press, Boulder, Colorado, 1988.

Boskin, Joseph. *Sambo: The Rise and Demise of an American Jester*. Oxford University Press, New York, 1986.

Boyd, Herb. *Down the Glory Road*. Avon Books, New York, 1995.

Browder, Anthony T. *From the Browder Files*. The Institute of Karmic Guidance, Washington, D.C., 2000.

Christian, Charles M. *Black Saga: The African American Experience*, Houghton Mifflin Company, New York, 1995.

Conant, Michael. *The Constitution and the Economy*. University of Oklahoma Press, Norman, Oklahoma, 1991.

Cruse, Harold. *Plural But Equal: Blacks and Minorities in America's Plural Society*. Quill-William Morrow, New York, 1987.

Davis, Kenneth. *Don't Know Much About History*. HarperCollins Publishers, New York, 2003.

Fireside, Harvey. *Separate and Unequal*. Carroll & Graf Publishers, New York, 2001.

Foner, Eric. *The Story of American Freedom*. W.W. Norton & Company, New York, 1998.

Franklin, John Hope. *From Slavery to Freedom: A History of Negro Americans*. Alred A. Knopf, New York, 1980.

Fukuyama, Francis. *Trust: The social Virtues and the Creation of Prosperity*. The Free Press, New York, 1995.

Goldstone, Lawrence. *Dark Bargain: Slavery, Profits, and the Struggle for the Constitution*. Walker & Company, New York, 2005.

Greenberg, Kenneth S. *Honor and Slavery*. Princeton University Press, Princeton, New Jersey, 1996.

Hacker, Andrew. *Money: Who Has How Much and Why*. Scribner Publishing, New York, 1997.

Hacker, Andrew. *Two Nations: Black and White, Separate, Hostile, Unequal*. Charles Scribner's Sons, New York, 1992.

Jordan, Winthrop. *White Over Black*. W.W. Norton and Company, New York, 1968.

Katznelson, Ira. *When Affirmative Action Was White*. W.W. Norton & Company, New York, 2005.

Lazare, Daniel. *The Frozen Republic: How the Constitution is Paralyzing Democracy*. Harcourt Brace & Company, New York, 1996.

Lind, Michael. *Up From Conservatism: Why the Right is Wrong for America*. The Free Press, New York, 1996.

Lind, Michael. *The Next American Nation: The New Nationalism and the Fourth American Revolution.* The Free Press, New York, 1995.

Loewen, James W. *Sundown Towns: A Hidden Dimension of American Racism.* The New Press, New York, 2005.

Love, Spencie. *One Blood: The Death and Resurrection of Charles Drew,* North Carolina: University of North Carolina Press, November, 1997.

Millhiser, Ian. *Injustices: The Supreme Court's Histgory of Comforting the Comfortable and Afflicting the Afflicted.* Nation Books, New York, 2015.

Montagu, Ashley. *The Fallacy of Race: Man's Most Dangerous Myth.* The World Publishing Compay, New York, 1964.

Perry, John C. *Myths and Realities of American Slavery.* Burd Street Press, Shippensburg, Pennsylvania, 2002.

Porter, Kenneth W. *The Black Seminoles: History of a Freedom Seeking People,* University Press of Florida, 1996.

Quarles, Benjamin. *The Negro in the Making of America.* Touchstone, New York, 1996.

Rivers, Larry Eugene. *Slavery in Florida,* University Press of Florida, Gainsville, FL, 2000.

Robinson, Randall. *The Debt: What America Owes to Blacks.* A Dutton Book, New York, 2000.

Sears, David O., Sidanius, James and Bobo, Lawrence. *Racialized Politics: The Debate About Racism in America.* The University of Chicago Press, Chicago, Illinois, 2000.

Skloot, Rebecca. *The Immortal Life of Henrietta Lacks.* Broadway Books, New York, 2010.

Smith, Robert C. *We Have No Leaders: African Americans in the Post-Civil Rights Era.* State University of New York Press, New York, 1996.

Steinberg, Stephen. *The Ethnic Myth: Race, Ethnicity, and Class in America.* Beacon Press, Boston, Massachusetts, 1989.

Steinhorn, Leonard and Diggs-Brown, Barbara. *By The Color of Our Skin: The Illusion of Integration and the Reality of Race*. Plume, New York, 1999.

Stewart, Jeffery C. *1001 Things Everyone Should Know About African American History*. Doubleday, New York, 1996.

Stowe, Harriet Beecher. *Uncle Tom's Cabin*. The New American Library, Bibliographic Copyright, 1981.

The Council on Black Internal Affairs. *The American Directory of Certified Uncle Toms, 1st Millennium Edition*, CBIA & DFS Publishing, USA, 2002.

Vaca, Nicolas C. *Presumed Alliance: The Unspoken Conflict Between Hispanics and Black Americans*. HarperCollins Publishers, New York, 2004.

Wicker, Tom. *Tragic Failure of Integration*. William Morrow and Company, Inc., New York, 1996.

Winbush, Raymond A. *Should America Pay? Slavery and Raging Debate on Reparations*. HarperCollins Publishers, New York, 2003.

Woods Jr., Thomas. *33 Questions About American History: You're Not Supposed to Ask*, Crown Forum, New York, 2007.

INDEX